P9-CFK-580

il faut me photographier avec la chaise
août 1999

Malick Sidibe 1999

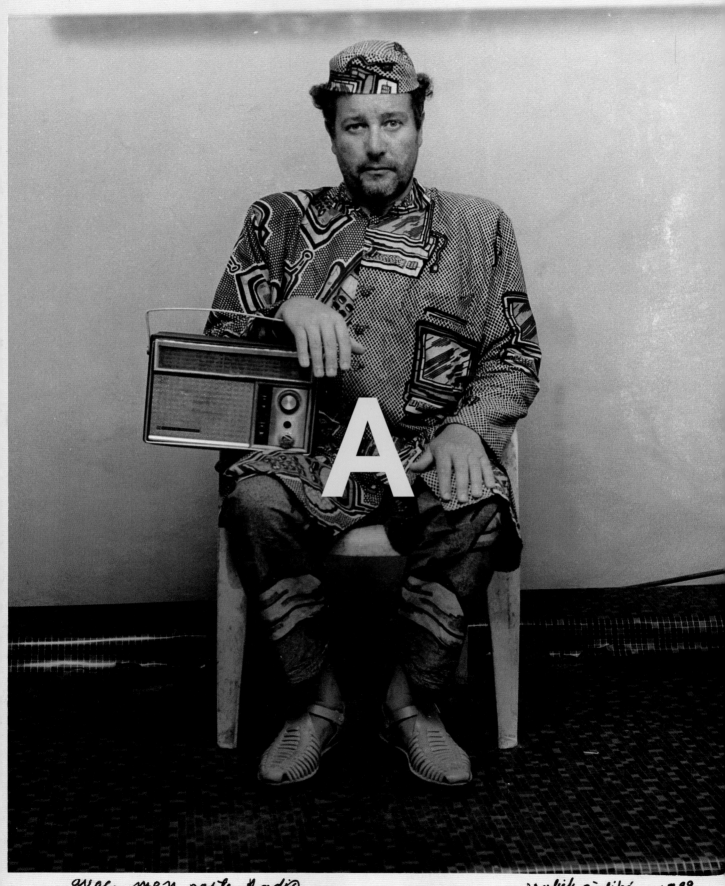

avec mon paste Radio
Août 1999

Malick Sidibé 1999

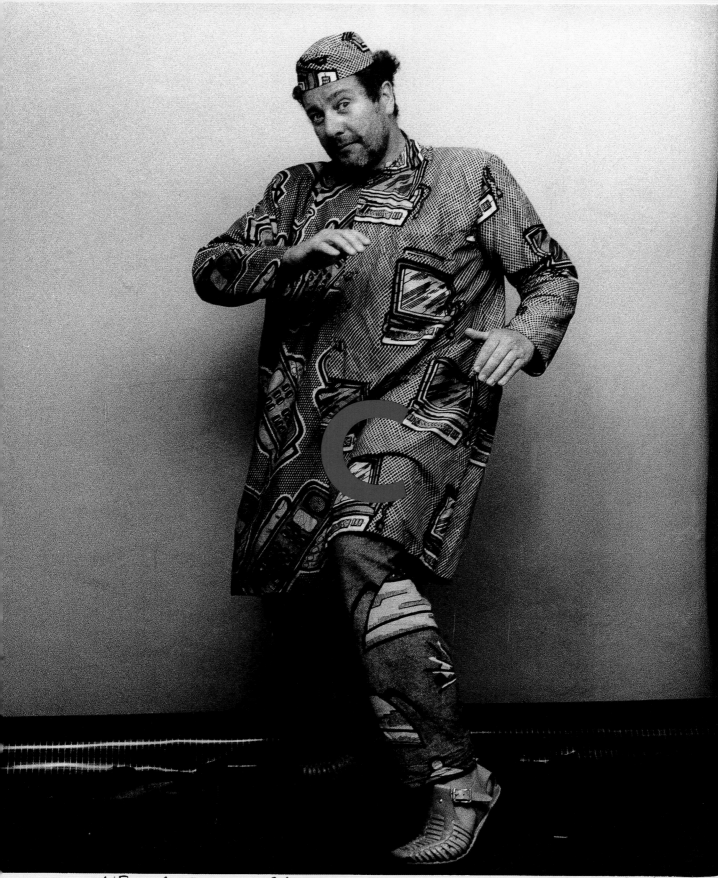

en position de TWIST. août 1999   Malick Sidibé 1999

STARCK
TASCHEN GmbH
ISBN 3–8228–2432–1

© 2003 TASCHEN GmbH
Hohenzollernring 53, D–50672 Köln
www.taschen.com

© 2003 Philippe Starck, Paris
© 2003 for the cover and back cover: Jean-Baptiste Mondino, Paris

Edited by Simone Philippi, Cologne
Designed by Mark Thomson, London, and Catinka Keul, Cologne
Captions and index by Susanne Husemann and Anja Lenze, Cologne
Production by Ute Wachendorf, Cologne
German translation by Stefan Barmann, Cologne
English translation by Chris Miller, Oxford
Printed in Italy
Endpapers: Jean-Baptiste Mondino, Paris

Kominform (1947) et engage contre l'Occident la « guerre froide ». Objet d'un culte, célébré tant en U. R. S. S. que dans les partis communistes des démocraties populaires et des pays occidentaux, il fait procéder à de nouvelles purges (« procès de Prague », « complot des blouses blanches ») avant de mourir en mars 1953. Le XX⁰ Congrès du parti communiste (1956) amorça la « déstalinisation » et en 1961 le corps de Staline fut retiré du mausolée de Lénine dans lequel il avait été placé.

Stalingrad *(bataille de)* [sept. 1942 - févr. 1943], victoire décisive remportée après de durs combats — qui se sont déroulés autour de Stalingrad (auj. Volgograd) — par les Soviétiques sur la VI⁰ armée allemande (Paulus), qui capitula le 2 février 1943. Elle marqua le tournant de la guerre sur le front russe.

STAMBOLIJSKI (Aleksandăr), homme politique bulgare (Slavovica 1879 - *id.* 1923). Chef de l'Union agrarienne depuis 1905, il fut Premier ministre en 1919-20 puis en 1920-1923. Il fut fusillé lors du coup d'État de 1923.

STAMFORD, port des États-Unis (Connecticut) ; 102 000 h.

STAMITZ (Johann Wenzel) ou **STAMIC** (Jan Václav), compositeur tchèque (Německý Brod, Bohême, 1717 - Mannheim 1757), chef de l'école de Mannheim, un des foyers de l'art symphonique en Europe, à l'origine du style galant.

Stampa (la), quotidien italien de tendance libérale progressiste, créé à Turin en 1894.

Stamp Act (1765), loi britannique, qui frappa d'un droit de timbre les actes publics dans les colonies de l'Amérique du Nord. Très impopulaire, elle fut à l'origine de la guerre de l'Indépendance.

Standaard (De), quotidien belge de tendance catholique, créé en 1914 à Anvers.

STANHOPE (James, 1ᵉʳ *comte* **de**), homme politique britannique (Paris 1673 - Londres 1721). L'un des chefs du parti whig, secrétaire d'État (1714-1721), il dirigea la politique étrangère, privilégiant l'alliance avec la France.

STANISLAS *(saint),* martyr polonais (Szczepanow, près de Tarnów, 1030 - Cracovie 1079). Évêque de Cracovie (1072), il fut tué par le roi Boleslas II, qu'il avait excommunié. — Il est le patron de la Pologne.

STANISLAS Iᵉʳ LESZCZYŃSKI (Lwów 1677 - Lunéville 1766), roi de Pologne en titre de 1704 à 1766, en fait de 1704 à 1709 et de

STANLEY POOL → *Malebo Pool.*

STANLEYVILLE → *Kisangani.*

STANOVOÏ *(monts),* chaîne de montagnes d la Sibérie orientale ; 2 412 m.

STANS, comm. de la Suisse, ch.-l. du demi canton de Nidwald (Unterwald) ; 6 000 h.

STARA PLANINA, nom bulgare du **Balkan**

STARA ZAGORA, v. de Bulgarie ; 142 000 h

STARCK (Philippe), designer et architect d'intérieur français (Paris 1949). Créateur d séries de meubles et d'objets d'une structur simple, mais inventive, il est attaché à l'expres sion symbolique des formes comme de l'espace

STARK (Johannes), physicien allemand (Schi ckenhof 1874 - Traunstein 1957). Il a découver le dédoublement des raies spectrales sou l'influence d'un champ électrique. (Prix Nobe 1919.)

STAROBINSKI (Jean), critique suisse de lan gue française (Genève 1920). Une formation d psychiatre et une vision philosophique, fondé sur la « sympathie » pour l'auteur, sous-tenden sa méthode critique *(Jean-Jacques Rousseau, l transparence et l'obstacle).*

STASSFURT, v. de l'Allemagne démocrati que ; 26 000 h. Mines de potasse et de se

STATEN ISLAND, île des États-Unis, consti tuant un borough de New York, au S.-O. d Manhattan.

STAUDINGER (Hermann), chimiste alleman (Worms 1881 - Fribourg-en-Brisgau 1965), pri Nobel en 1953 pour ses recherches sur le macromolécules.

STAUDT (Karl Georg Christian **von**), mathé maticien allemand (Rothenburg ob der Taube 1798 - Erlangen 1867). Il essaya de reconstitue l'ensemble de la géométrie projective, indépen damment de toute relation métrique.

STAUFFENBERG (Claus **Schenk,** *comte* **von**) officier allemand (Jettingen 1907 - Berlin 1944) Il prépara et exécuta l'attentat du 20 juill. 1944 auquel échappa Hitler. Il fut fusillé.

STAVANGER, port de Norvège, sur l'Atlanti que ; 93 000 h. Port de pêche, de commerce de voyageurs et pétrolier. Centre industriel Cathédrale romane et gothique.

STAVELOT, v. de Belgique (Liège) ; 6 000 h Restes d'une ancienne abbaye (musées).

Stavisky *(affaire)* [1933-34], scandale financie au Crédit municipal de Bayonne, dévoilé en déc 1933. Elle contribua à la chute du ministèr

STEINBECK (John), écrivain américain (Salinas, Californie, 1902 - New York 1968). Ses romans peignent les milieux populaires californiens (*Tortilla Flat*, 1935 ; *Des souris et des hommes*, 1937 ; *les Raisins de la colère*, 1939 ; *À l'est d'Éden*, 1952). [Prix Nobel 1962.]

STEINBERG (Saul), dessinateur américain d'origine roumaine (Rîmnicu Sărat, Munténie, 1914). Il a renouvelé l'humour et la satire par son exceptionnelle invention plastique, nourrie aussi bien d'anciennes traditions calligraphiques que de l'influence du cubisme.

STEINER (Jakob), mathématicien suisse (Utzenstorf 1796 - Berne 1863), l'un des plus grands spécialistes de la géométrie.

STEINER (Rudolf), philosophe et pédagogue autrichien (Kraljević, Croatie, 1861 - Dornach, près de Bâle, 1925), auteur d'un système, l'anthroposophie, et d'une pédagogie qui décloisonne les matières traditionnelles et intègre l'activité artisanale.

STEINERT (Otto), photographe allemand (Sarrebruck 1915 - Essen 1978). Ses théories sur la *photographie subjective* (objectivité illusoire, irréalité partout présente et perceptible) sont à l'origine du renouveau de la photographie abstraite.

STEINITZ (Ernst), mathématicien allemand (Laurahütte 1871 - Kiel 1928), fondateur de la théorie algébrique des corps.

STEINKERQUE, auj. Steenkerque, anc. comm. de Belgique, auj. rattachée à Braine-le-Comte. Le maréchal de Luxembourg y vainquit Guillaume III le 3 août 1692.

STEINLEN (Théophile Alexandre), dessinateur, graveur et peintre français d'origine suisse (Lausanne 1859 - Paris 1923). Il a représenté, dans un esprit libertaire, le peuple de Montmartre et la vie ouvrière.

Steinway, manufacture américaine de pianos fondée à New York en 1853 par le facteur allemand Heinrich Engelhard Steinweg (Wolfshagen 1797 - New York 1871).

STEKEL (Wilhelm), médecin et psychanalyste autrichien (Boian, Bucovine, 1868 - Londres 1940). Il se sépara de Freud et préconisa une cure plus courte où le thérapeute intervient plus activement.

STEKENE, comm. de Belgique (Flandre-Orientale) ; 15 000 h.

Stèle du roi serpent (musée du Louvre), monument comportant, sculpté dans le calcaire,

la musique, la peinture et un récit de Rome, *Naples et Florence* (1817-1826) qu'il si nom de « Stendhal ». Il publie ensuite *De* (1822) et un essai sur le romantisme (*R Shakespeare,* 1823-1825). Méconnu, il fait *Armance* (1827), *le Rouge* et le Noir* (1830 il retourne en Italie comme consul à Civ chia, persuadé que son œuvre ne pe immédiatement comprise. Pendant un c Paris, il publie *les Mémoires d'un touriste* (1 *Chartreuse* de Parme* (1839) et les *Ch italiennes* (1839). Son œuvre posthume a c vement consacré sa gloire (*Lamiel,* 1889 *Henry Brulard,* 1890 ; *Lucien Leuwen,* 189 style nerveux fait vivre dans une action des héros lyriques qui dissimulent une sensibilité sous un apparent cynisme.

STENTOR. *Myth. gr.* Héros de la gu Troie, célèbre par la force de sa voix.

STEPHENSON (George), ingénieur b que (Wylam, près de Newcastle, 1781 - House, Chesterfield, 1848). Il est co comme le véritable créateur de la tra vapeur sur voie ferrée (locomotive *Rocker* Son œuvre principale fut l'établissem chemin de fer de Liverpool à Ma (1826-1830).

STERLITAMAK, v. de l'U. R. S. S., d'Oufa ; 240 000 h. Centre industriel.

STERN (Isaac), violoniste russe n américain (Kremenets, Ukraine, 1920 fondé, avec Eugene Istomin et Leonar un trio pour défendre le répertoire rom

STERN (Otto), physicien américain c allemande (Sohrau, auj. Żory, 1888 - 1969). Il a découvert, avec W. Ger propriétés magnétiques des atomes et concept, introduit par de Broglie, d'on ciée à une particule. (Prix Nobel 1943

STERNBERG (Josef von), cinéaste a d'origine autrichienne (Vienne 1894 - geles 1969). Peintre des passions violent atmosphères troubles, magicien de l'im la lumière, il a fait de Marlène l'archétype de la femme fatale : *l'A* (1930), *Cœurs brûlés* (id.), *Shanghai Expres l'Impératrice rouge* (1934), *la Femme et* (1935).

STERNE (Laurence), écrivain bri (Clonmel, Irlande, 1713 - Londres 1768 de *la Vie et les opinions de Tristram Shandy,* (1759-1767) et du *Voyage sentimental* (1

12   Architecture

74   Interiors

190   Furniture

296   Industrial Design

510   Magma

518   Words

542   Overview

574   A–Z

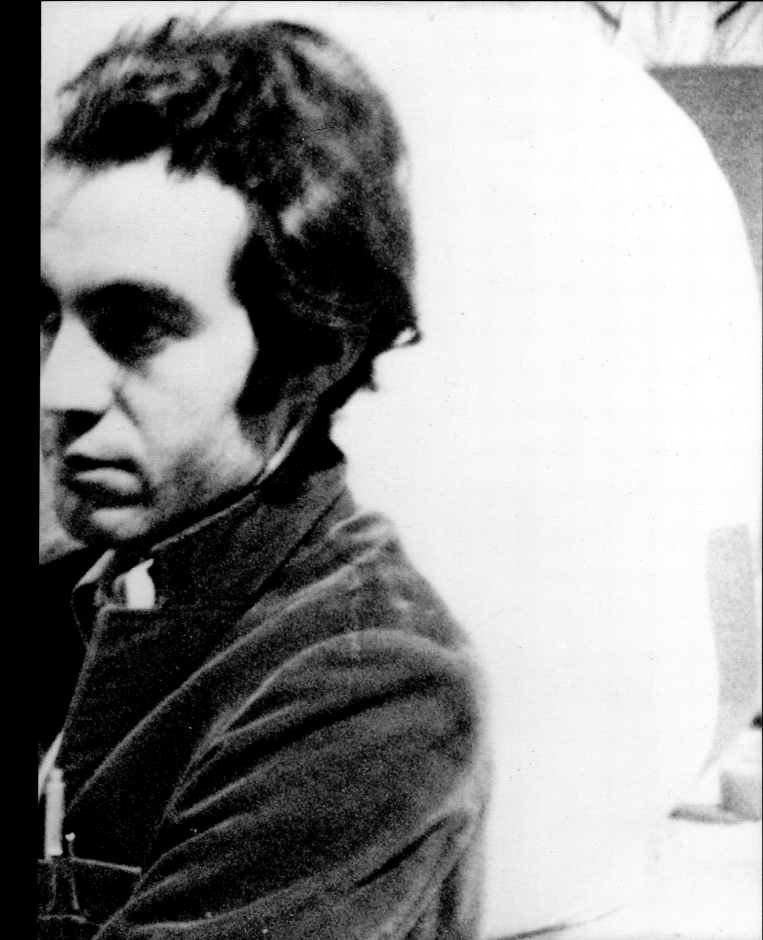

Asahi Beer Hall, Tokyo 1990

Le Baron Vert, Osaka 1992

Nani Nani, Tokyo 1989

Formentera House 1995

Starck House (3 Suisses) 1994

MODE D'EMPLOI A LIRE IMPERATIVEMENT

STARCK

La maison de
STARCK
est chez
3 SUISSES

Du carnet de route de la maison de Starck au vôtre, le coffret
Starck vous raconte les premières pages d'une histoire
à écrire à votre façon.

Le coffret STARCK
4900F

Le Moult House, Paris 1985–1987

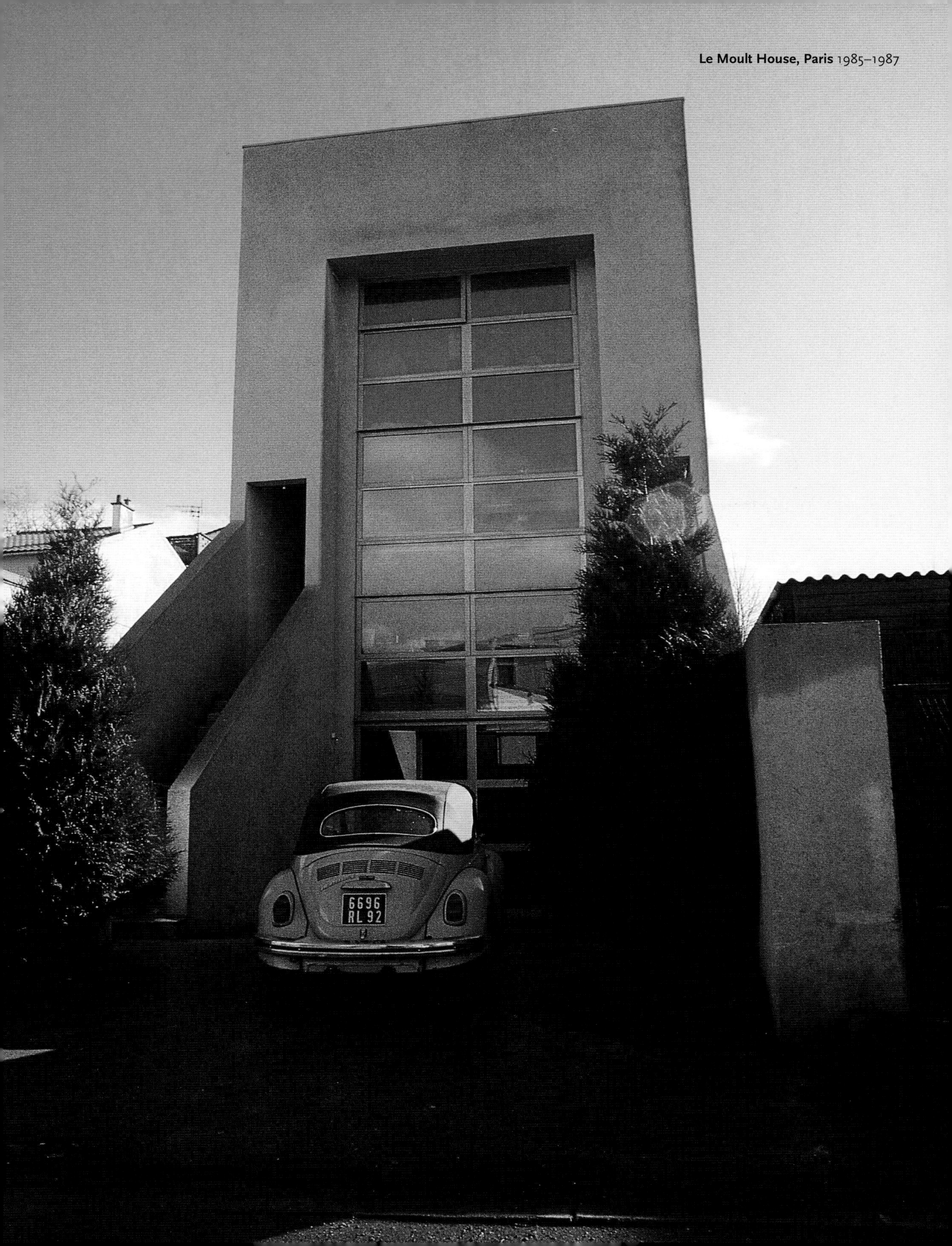

Le Moult House, Paris 1985–1987

Starck House, Issy-les-Moulineaux 1991

Le civisme est d'avant-garde

Groningen Museum 1993
(with Alessandro Mendini)

1982

CITIES WILL DIE
ROADS WILL DISAPEAR
SCHIZOPHRENIA WILL REIGN
ARCHAEC FAMILY TRIBES RETIRED
IN FAR-AWAY FORESTS
WILL PARTICIPATE IN THE BIG RACE
THANKS TO THEIR VIBRATING ANTENAE
THE SATTELITES WILL BE THE
ONLY MEANS OF EXCHANGE
STARCK FUTURE.

Groningen Museum 1993
(with Alessandro Mendini)

Laguiole factory, Laguiole 1987

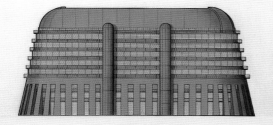

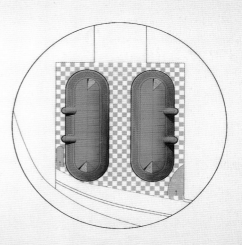

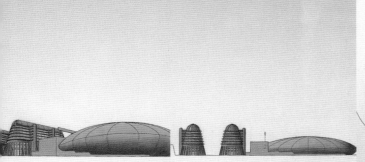

Mutons

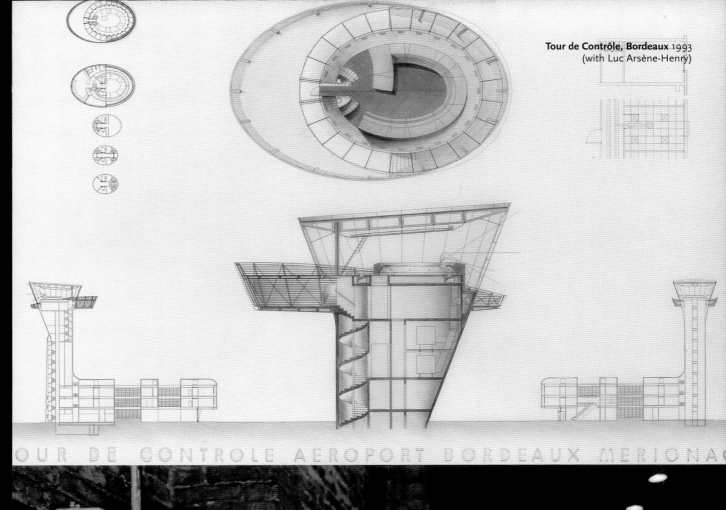

Tour de Contrôle, Bordeaux 1993
(with Luc Arsène-Henry)

TOUR DE CONTROLE AEROPORT BORDEAUX MERIGNAC

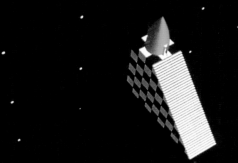

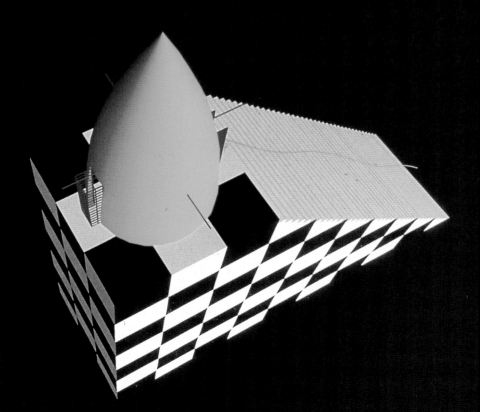

ONAVAITREMPLICETTEBOITEDE
TANTD'ESPRITFRANCAISQU'ALAFIN
ELLES'INCLINAETDEVINTVENITIENNE

Vitry 2001
(with Luc Arsène-Henry)

FAÇADE SUR LE QUAI JULES GUESDE · ECHELLE 1/500e

FAÇADE SUR LA RUE LEON MAUVAIS · ECHELLE 1/500e

Ecole des Beaux-Arts, Paris 1991
(with Luc Arsène-Henry)

PLAN D'ENSEMBLE DES TOITURES

FACADE VERS LE PONT

FACADE VERS LA ROTONDE

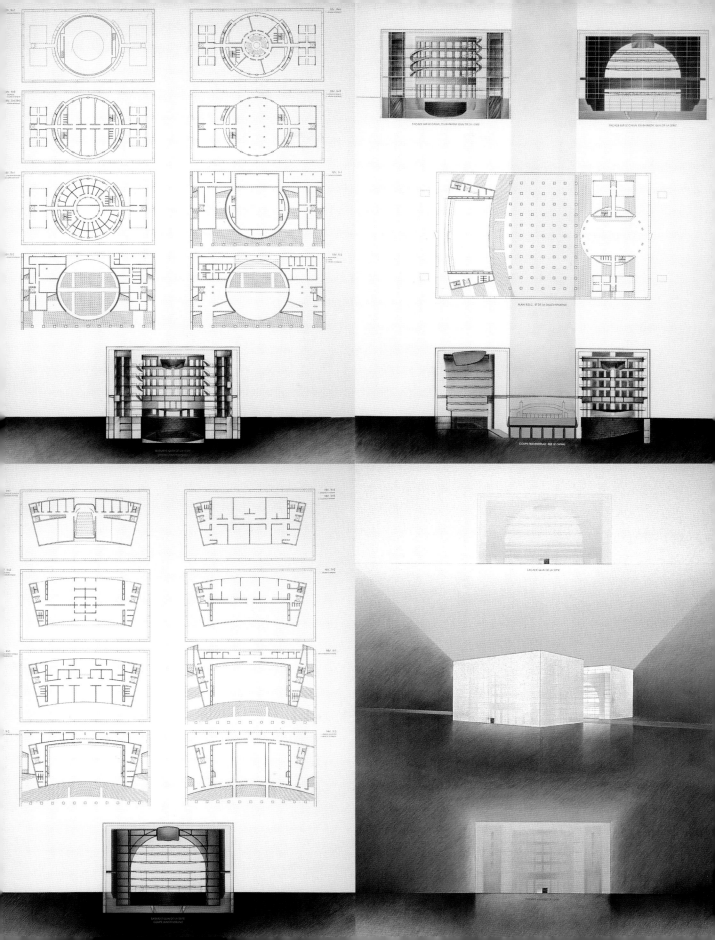

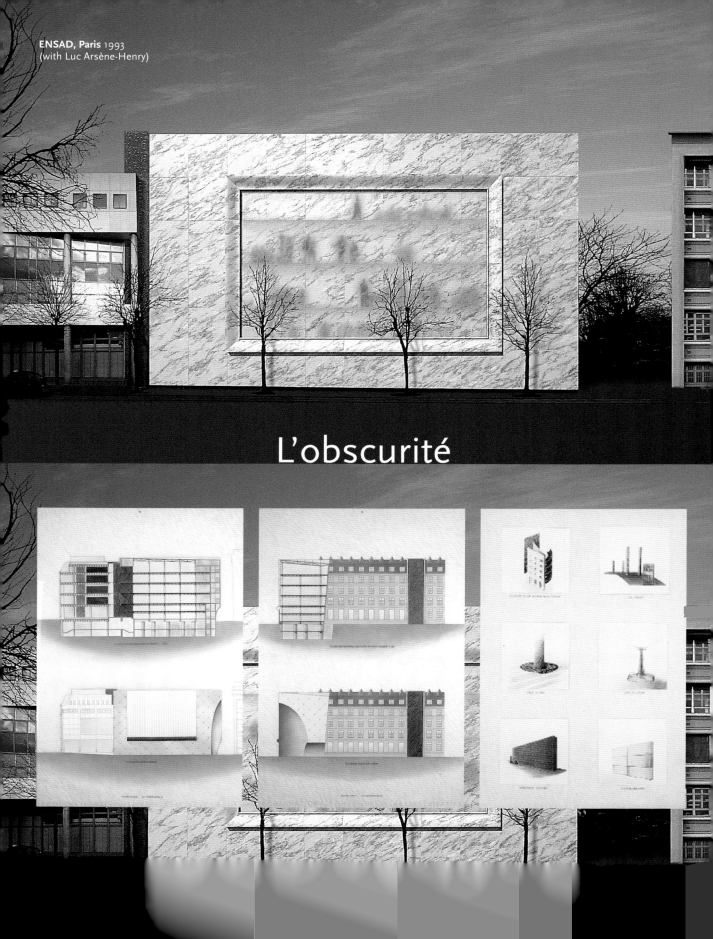

L'obscurité

s'épaissit

ENSAD, Paris 1998
(with Luc Arsène-Henry)

ENSAD, Paris 1998
(with Luc Arsène-Henry)

Starck House (project), Issy-les-Moulineaux 1991

Condominiums (project), Los Angeles 1992

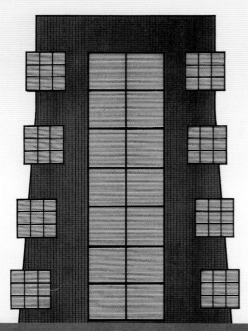

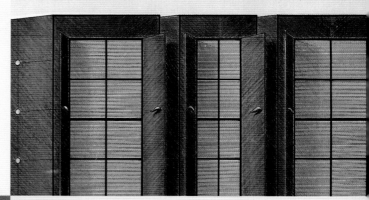

Condominiums (project), Los Angeles 1992

Angle (project), Antwerp 1991

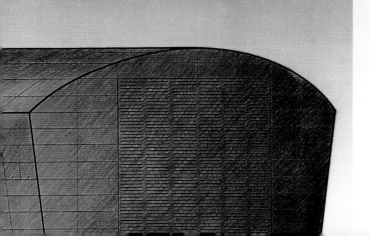

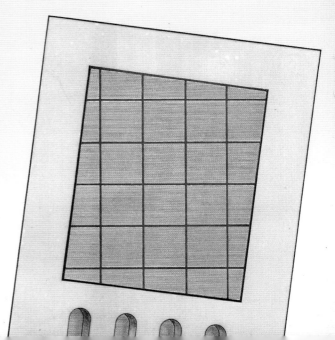

Duravit Headquarters, Hornberg 2002

Bond Street Hotel, New York 2001

Be a Citoyen

12   Architecture

74   Interiors

190   Furniture

296   Industrial Design

510   Magma

518   Words

542   Overview

574   A–Z

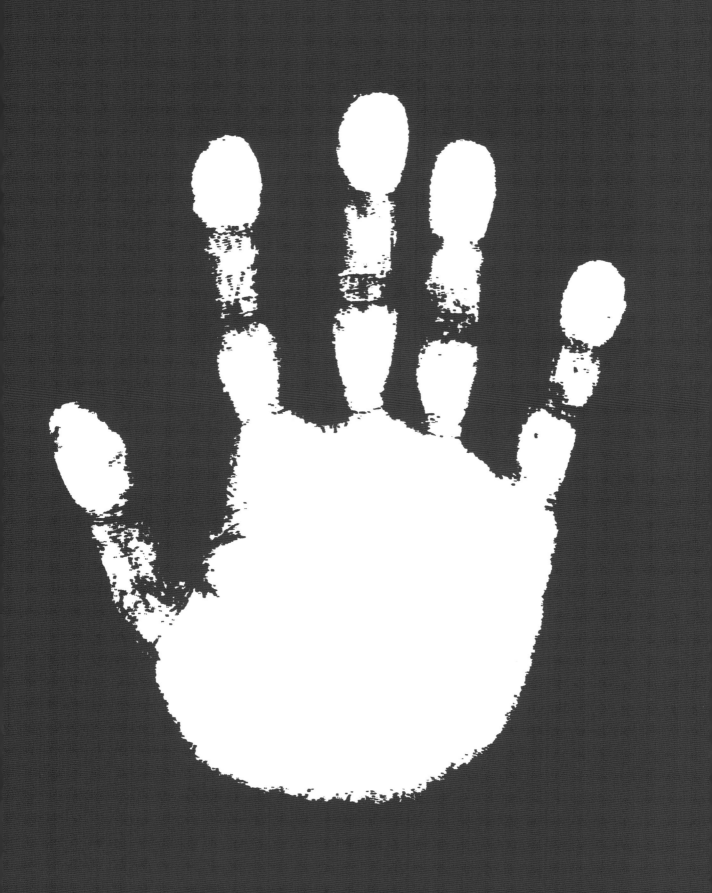

Café Costes, Paris 1984

S

Café Costes, Paris 1984

Royalton Hotel, New York 1988

Paramount Hotel, New York 1990

SUN
RAIN
SNOW
CLOUDS
WARM
COLD

WARM AIR

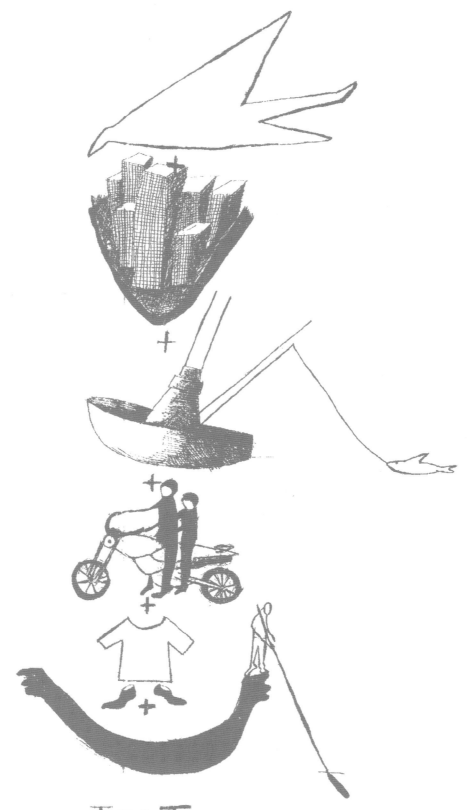

MERCi POUR TOUT PAPA CHERi
JE T'AiME   ARA

MOINS 300 g...

S T A R

RODEO
PARTY

WEDNESDAY
NOVEMBER 20
WITH GUESTS
THE TRUE BELIEVERS

S   T   A   R   C   K

D A L L A S

The Dallas Brewery / 703 McKinney
Dallas, Texas 75202
720-0130

arck Club
Dallas Brewery
Kinney, Suite 107
Texas 75202
0-0130

M. PHILIPPE STARCK
4 RUE DE DION
MONTFORT-L'AMAURY
FRANCE   78490

STARCK CLUB 703 McKINNEY DALLAS TEXAS 75202

L'amour est une espèce en voie de dispariti

Restaurant Manin, Tokyo 1987

Boutique Hugo Boss, Paris 1991

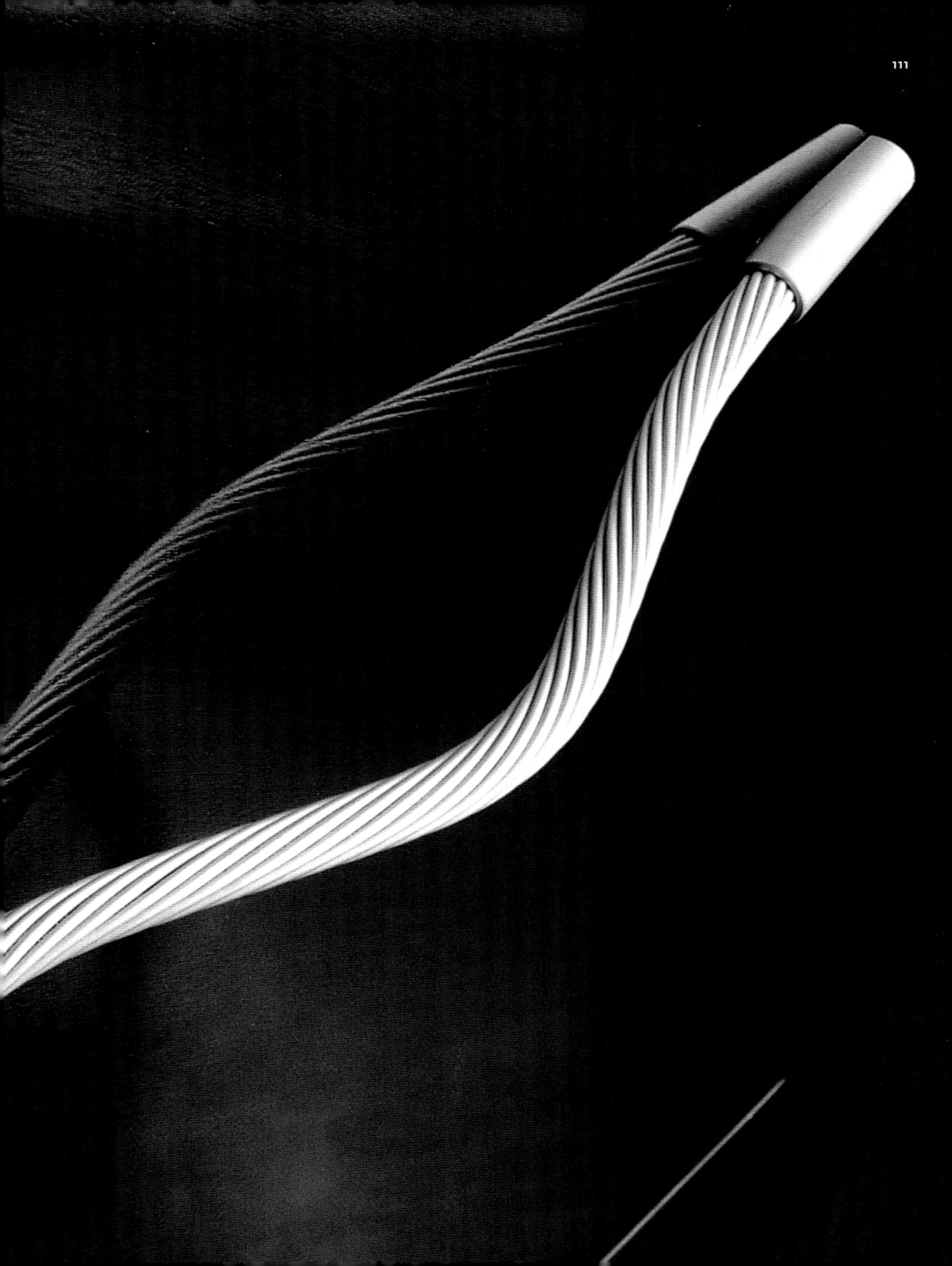

Puzzle, Paris 1987

Salon Coppola, Milan 1992

Restaurant Teatriz, Madrid 1990

Restaurant Teatriz, Madrid 1990

La Cigale, Paris 1988

Restaurant Theatron, Mexico 1985

Restaurant Theatron, Mexico 1985

Delano Hotel, Miami 1995

Delano Hotel, Miami 1995

Delano Hotel, Miami 1995

Oyster Bar in the Peninsula Hotel, Hong Kong 1994

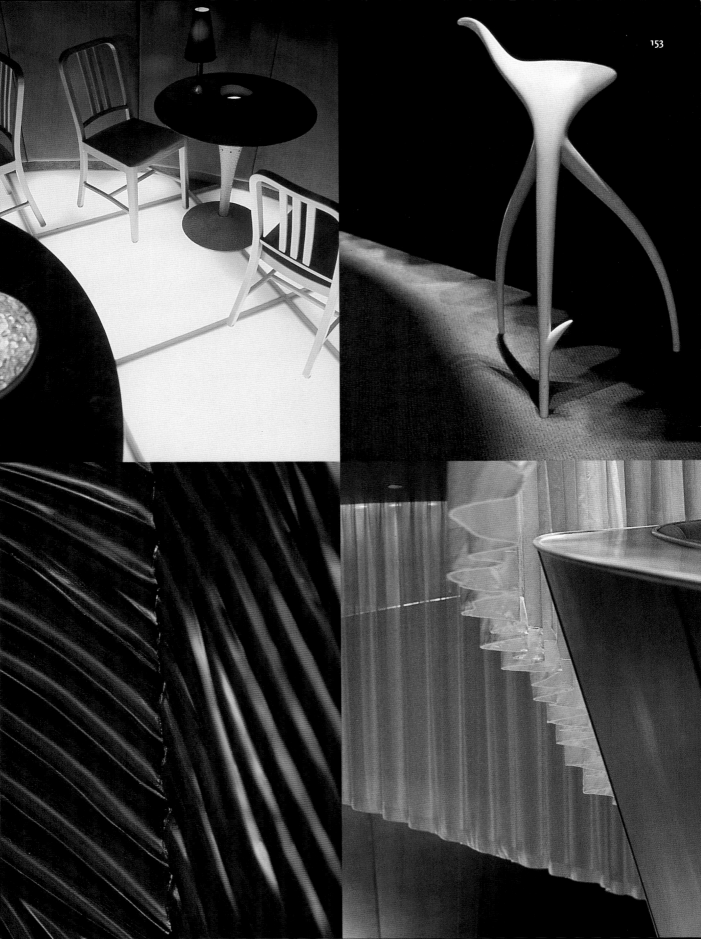

Asia de Cuba Restaurant, New York 1997

STARCK DECOUVRE LE SEX...

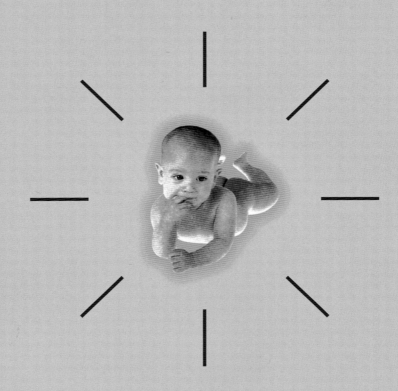

We just need Love

Restaurant Bon 2, Paris 2001

Hudson Hotel, New York 2000

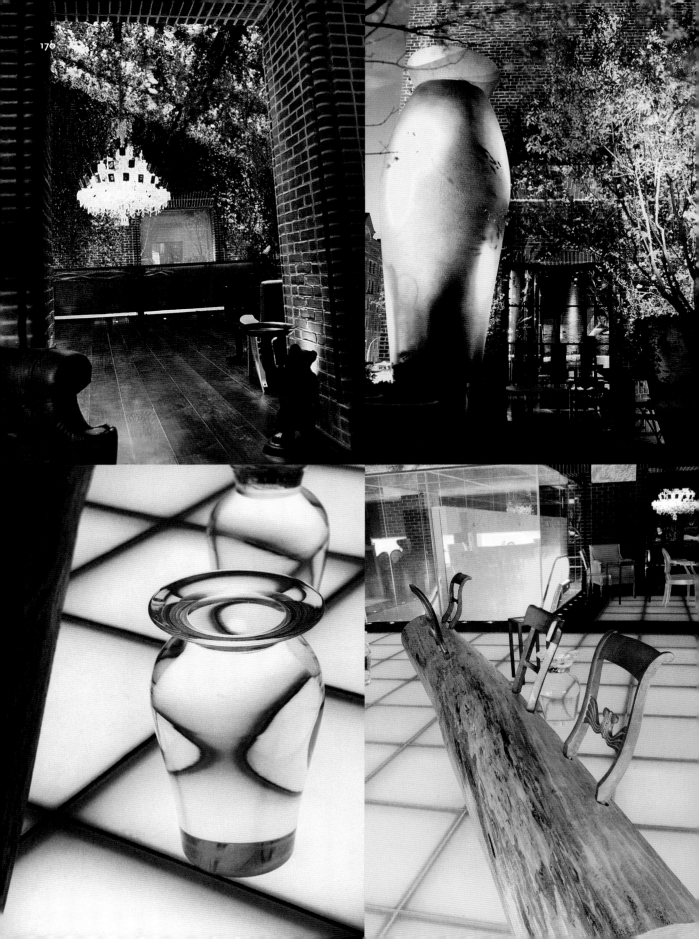

El Porteño Apartments and Hotel, Buenos Aires 1999

Clift Hotel, San Francisco 1999

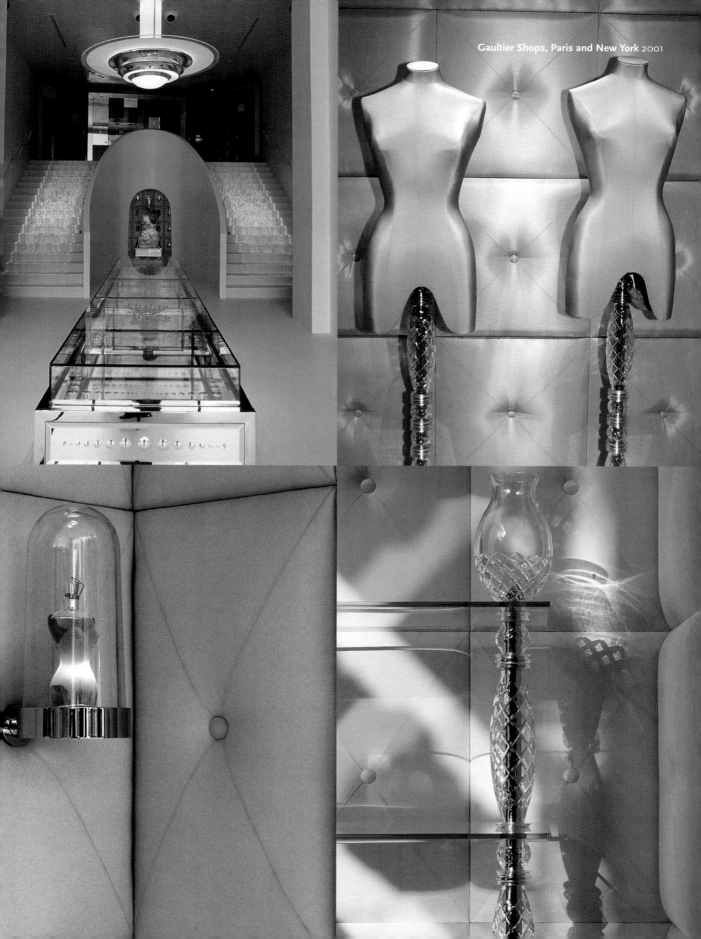

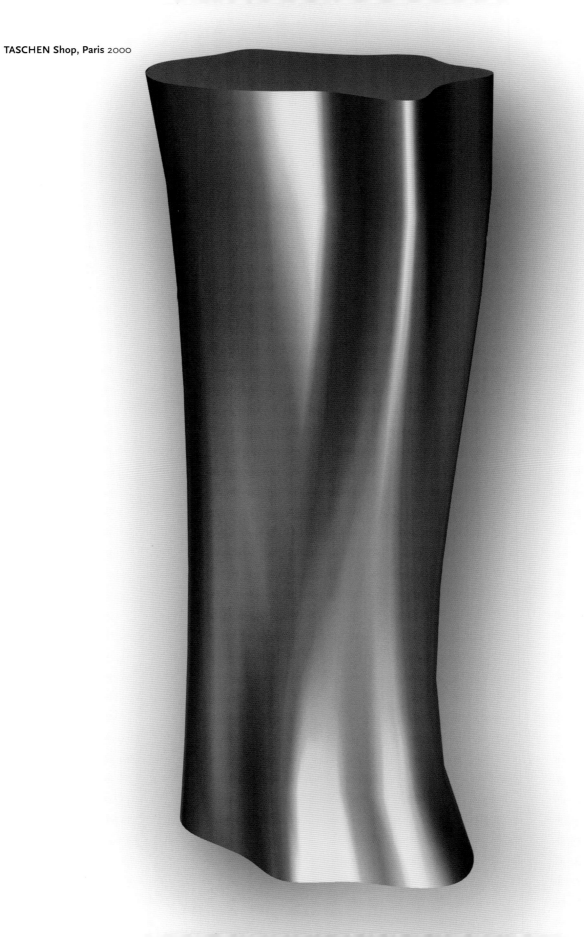

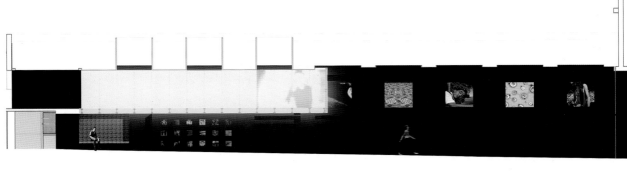

Yoo

Everything has a Birth a Life a Death

12 Architecture

74 Interiors

190 Furniture

296 Industrial Design

510 Magma

518 Words

542 Overview

574 A–Z

Louis XX 1992

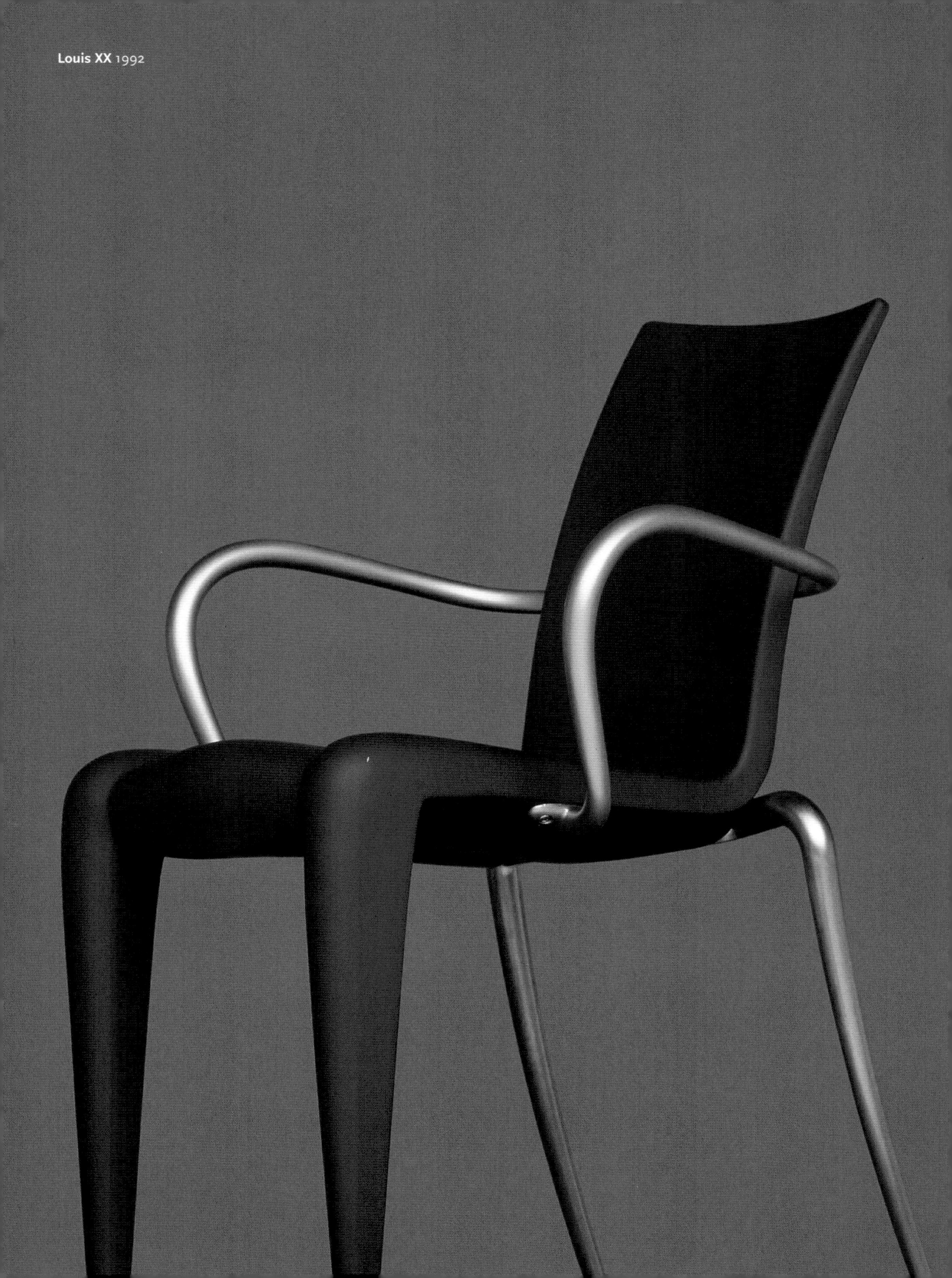

Président M. 1984

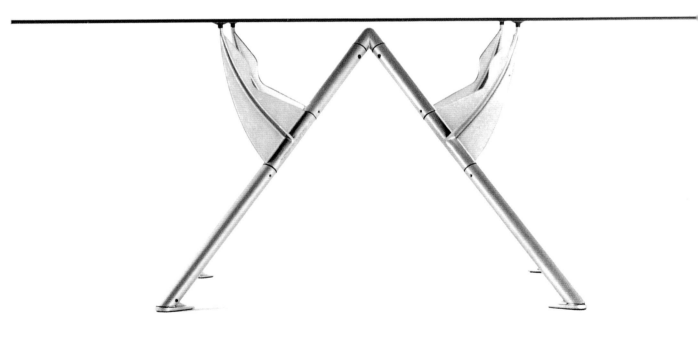

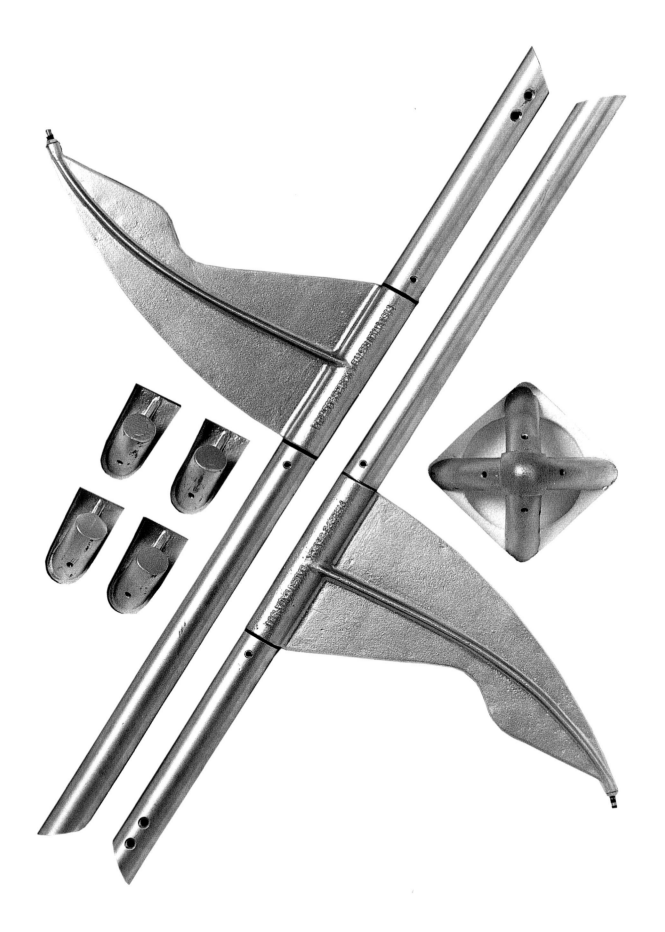

Coque 1999

Partageons

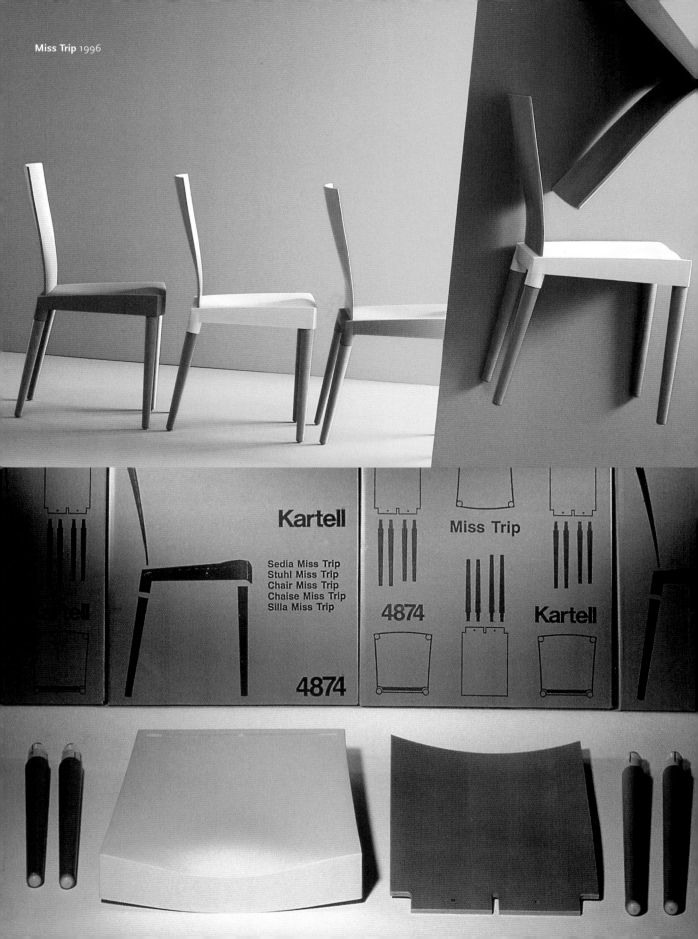

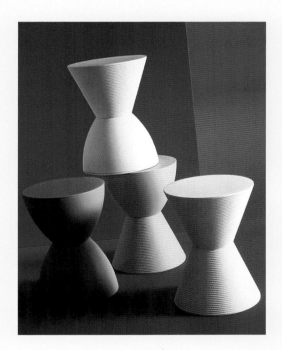

Nous sommes des mutants

Saint Esprit and Napoléon 1999

Attila 1999

Bubble Club 1998

Bubble Club 1998

Ploof 1999

Ploof 1999

Zbork 2000

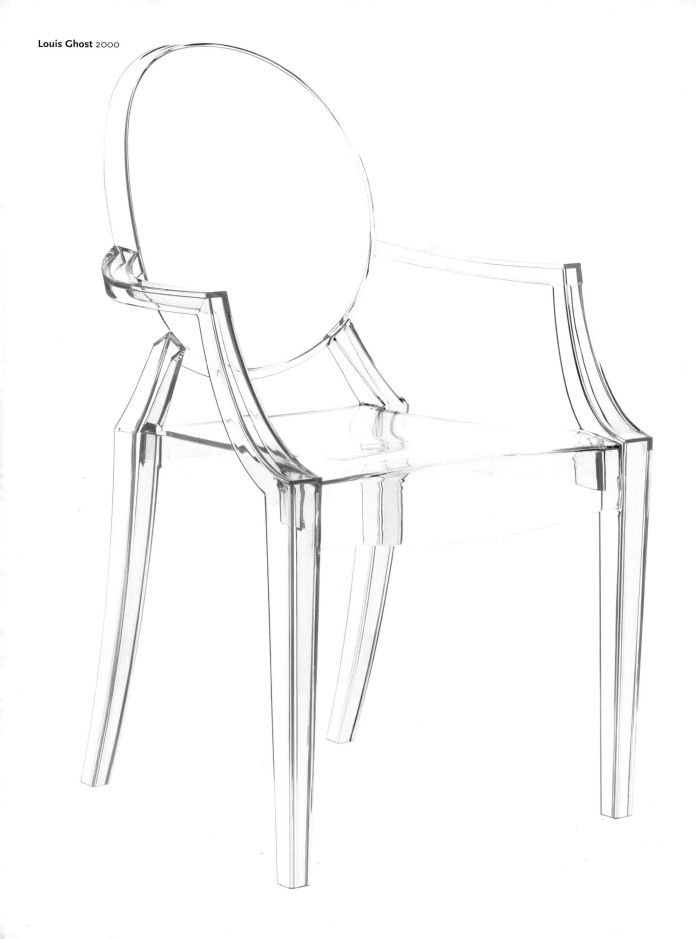

Gérons la décadence de l'Occident

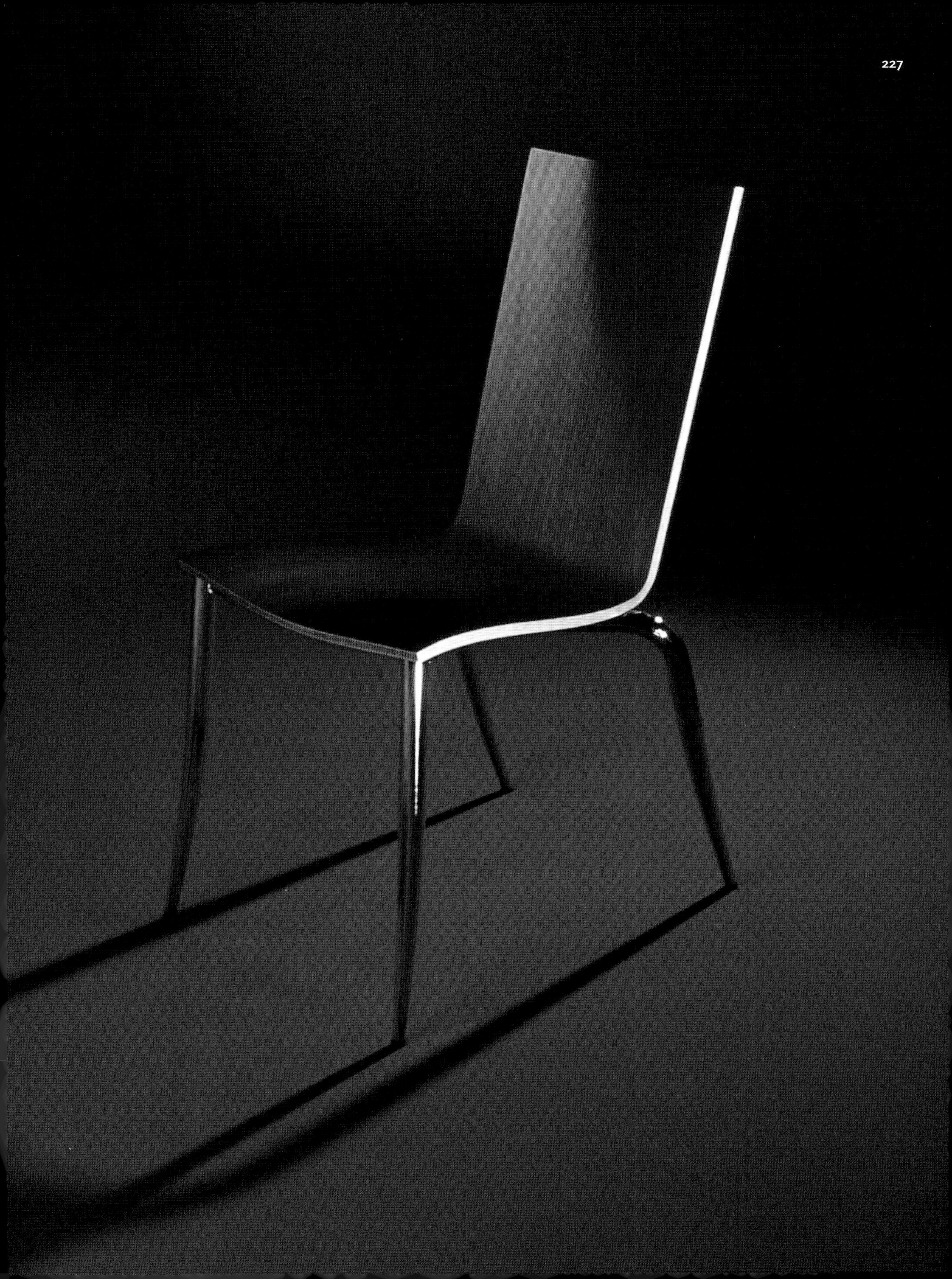

Asahy 1991 and Paramount 1991

Vicieuse 1992 and Boom Rang 1992

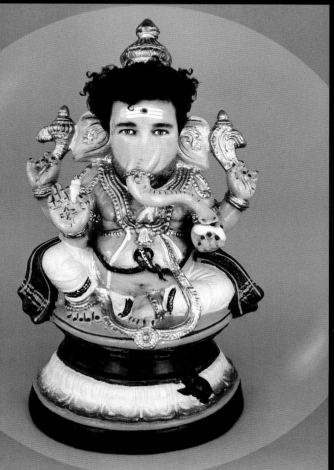

Boom Rang 1992   **Asahy** 1991

Royalton 1991

Lola Mundo 1988 and Titos Apostos 1985   J. (Série Lang) 1987

Costes 1984 and Costes Alluminio 1988   Pratfall 1985

J. (Série Lang) 1991

Colucci 1986 and Tippy Jackson 1985   Sarapis 1986 and Von Vogelsang 1985

Titos Apostos 1985

Romantica 1987   **Dick Deck** 1989

Costes Alluminio 1988

Bob Dubois 1987

Tessa Nature 1989

Cameleon 1992   **Placide of the Wood** 1989

Royalton Long Chair and **Armchair** 1991

Asahy 1991 and **Paramount** 1991

Le paravent de l'autre 1992

Royalton Bed 1992

Royalton 1988

Neoz 1997–1999

GLOIRE
ô
GRAND
MOi
MOi

merci pour ce wonderfull NEW YEAR les MONDINO'S.

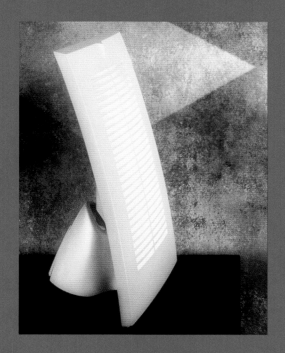

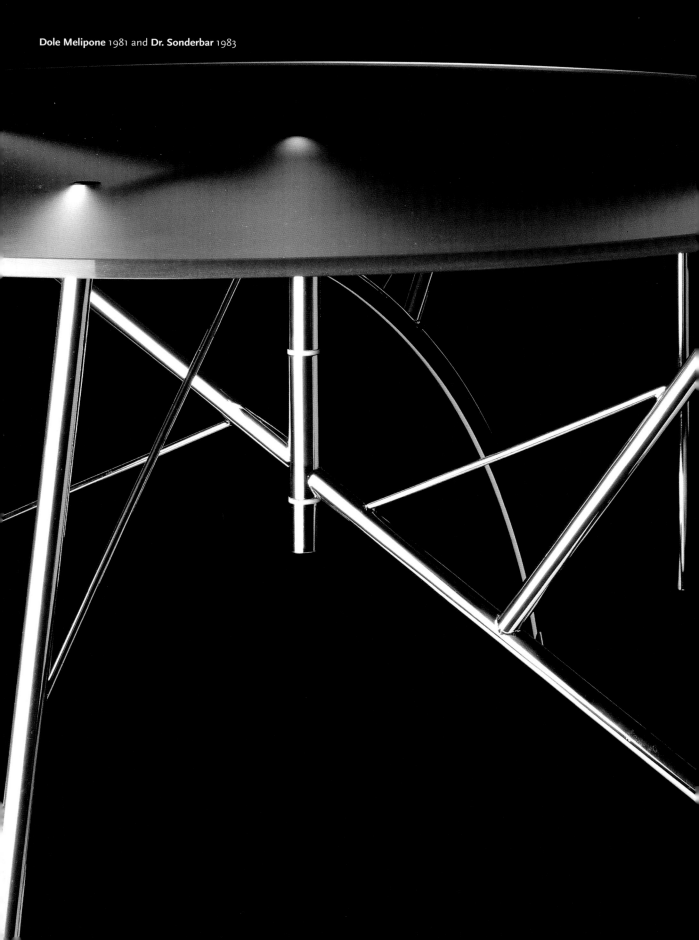

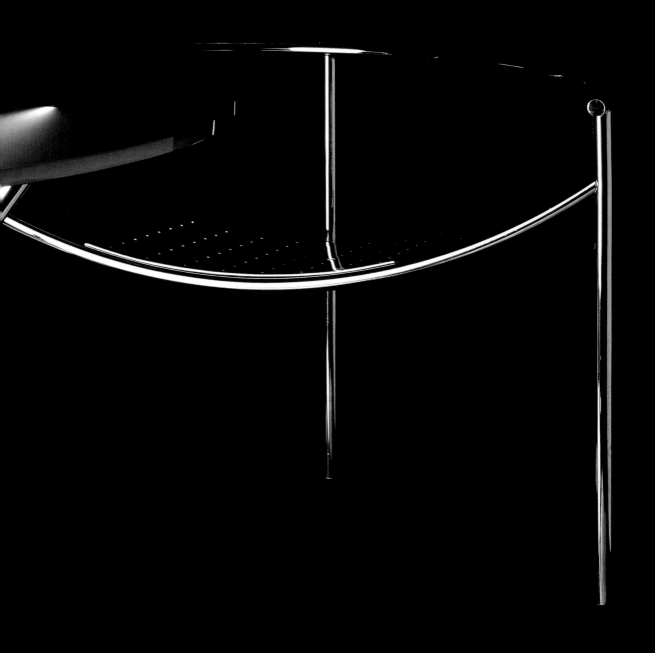

SUMO Table 1999

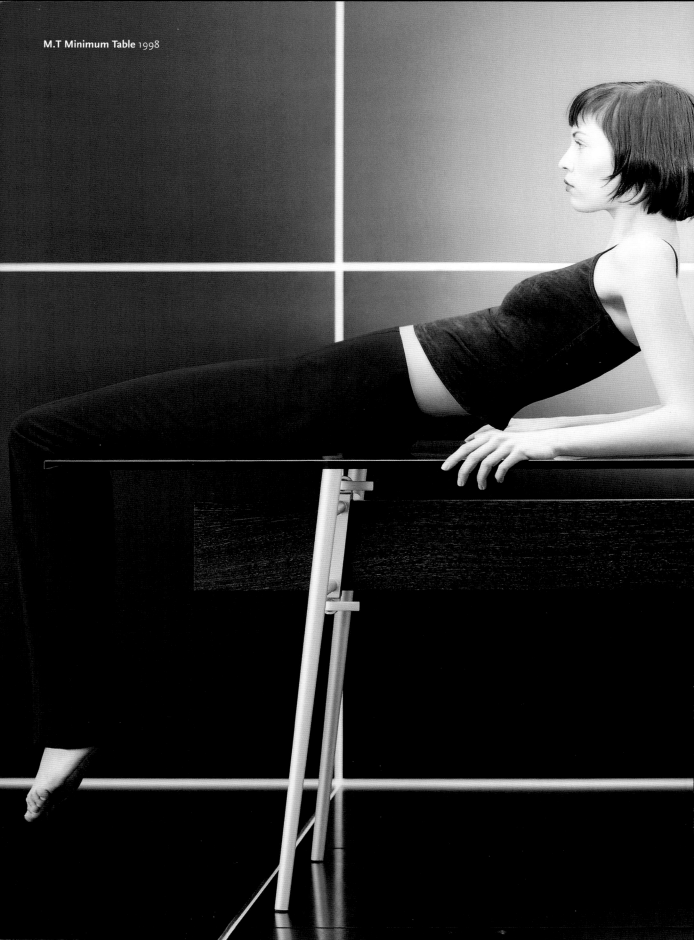

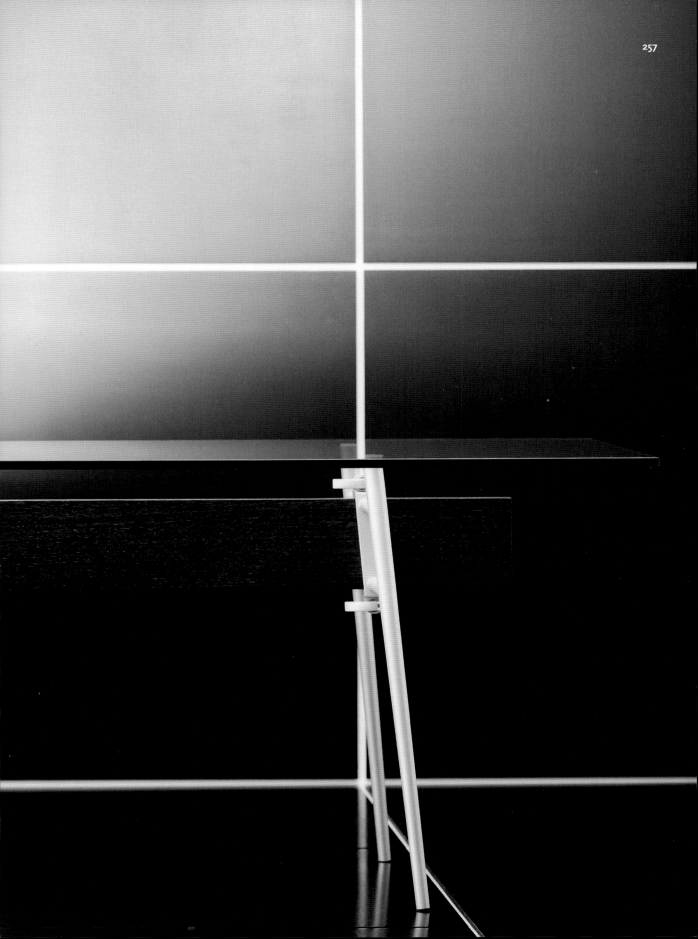

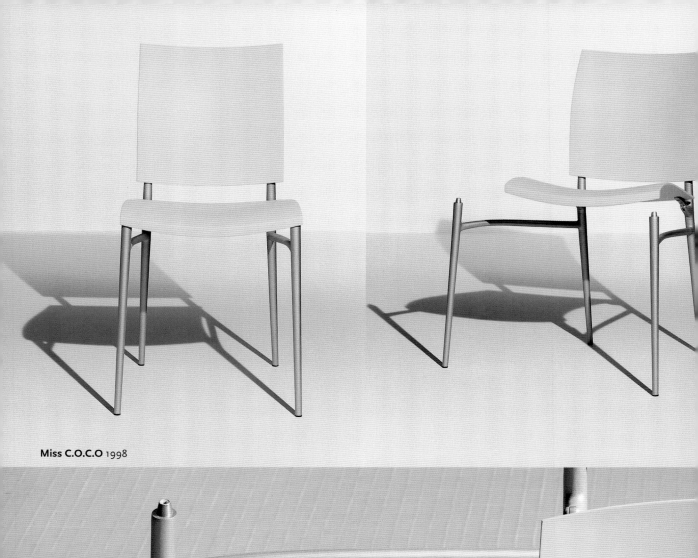

Miss C.O.C.O 1998

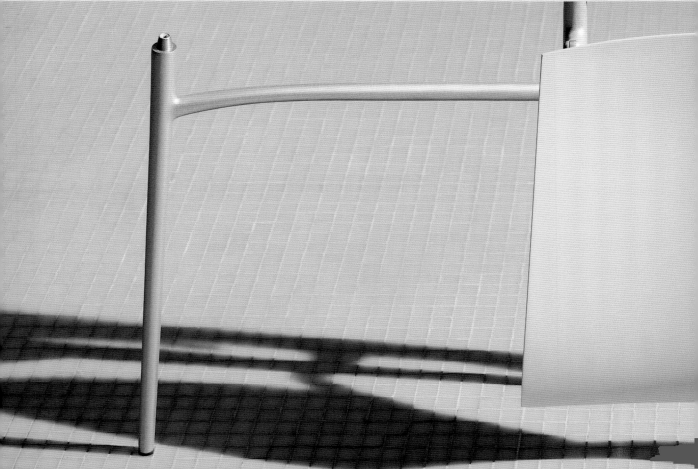

L.W.S Lazy Working Sofa 1998

L.W.S Lazy Working Sofa 1998

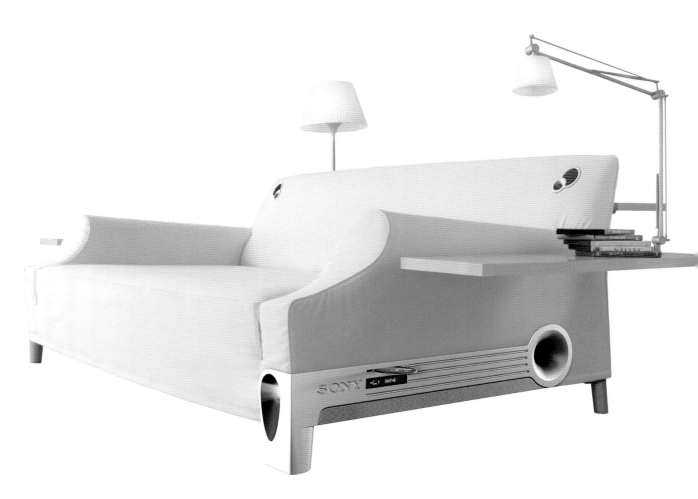

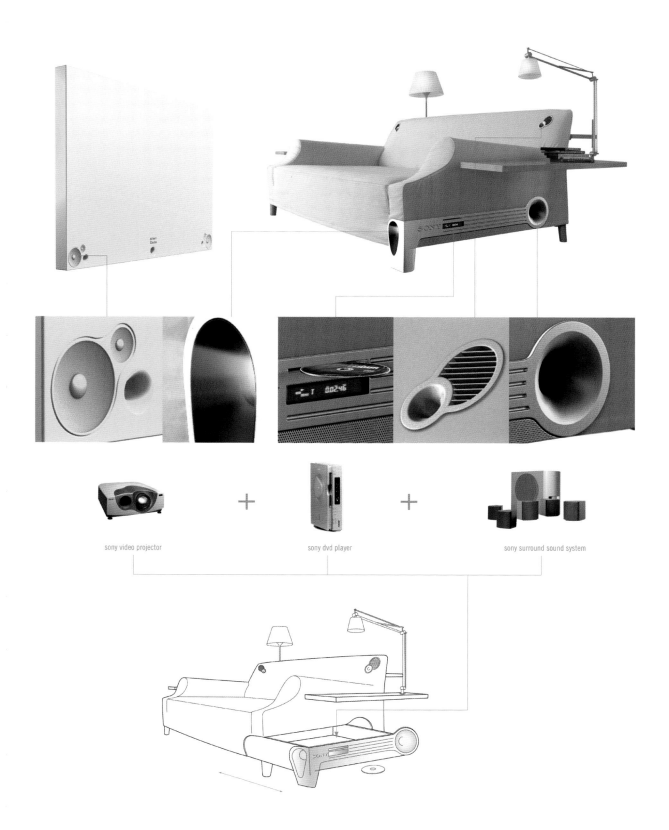

sony video projector + sony dvd player + sony surround sound system

le Garde-forestier • *le Président des 3 Suisses* • *le Designer*

L'ESPRIT DE LA FORÊT
COLLECTION O.N.F.* 3 SUISSES BY STARCK

DEPUIS L'ORDONNANCE DE COLBERT (1669),
LES FORESTIERS SONT LES GARDIENS DE LA FORÊT
POUR LA CONSERVER, L'ENTRETENIR ET LA RENOUVELER.

LA FRANCE EST AUJOURD'HUI LE PAYS
LE PLUS FEUILLU D'EUROPE.

LA NOUVELLE COLLECTION DE PHILIPPE STARCK
VOUS DONNE L'ESPRIT DE LA FORÊT
AFIN QUE VOUS EN DEVENIEZ LES GARDIENS.

Office National des Forêts

Dans le colis du meuble STARCK que vous commandez aux 3 SUISSES, vous trouverez une notice explicative vous permettant de contacter le Forestier de l'Office National des Forêts. Celui-ci vous remettra le rondin de bouleau brut qu'il choisira dans une forêt proche de chez vous (dans un rayon maximum de 150 km), ainsi que la plaque numérotée «Collection ONF/3 SUISSES by STARCK», qu'il scellera, en votre présence, sur la tranche du rondin. Pour contacter le Forestier, vous disposerez d'un numéro vert inscrit sur la notice ●

T A B L E   S T A R C K en hêtre massif teinté et verni polyuréthane avec piétement (livré monté) possédant un système de serrage à l'intérieur de chaque pied pour le réglage du rondin. (le prix comprend le rondin de bouleau distribué par l'O.N.F. - Dimensions du rondin : 1,40 m x 13 à 14 cm de diamètre). RÉFÉRENCE : 791.0440. ● ● ● ● **F**

C O N S O L E   S T A R C K en hêtre massif teinté et verni polyuréthane avec piétement (livré monté) possédant un système de serrage à l'intérieur de chaque pied pour le réglage du rondin. (le prix comprend le rondin de bouleau distribué par l'O.N.F. - Dimensions du rondin : 1,40 m x 13 à 14 cm de diamètre). RÉFÉRENCE : 791.5830. ● ● ● ● **F**

B A N C   S T A R C K en hêtre massif teinté et verni polyuréthane avec piétement (livré monté) possédant un système de serrage à l'intérieur de chaque pied pour le réglage du rondin.(le prix comprend le rondin de bouleau distribué par l'O.N.F. - Dimensions du rondin : 1,40 m x 8 à 10 cm de diamètre) RÉFÉRENCE : 791.0740. ● ● ● **F**

Mister Bliss 1982   Dr. Sonderbar 1983   Pat Conley II 1986

Royalton Bar Stool 1988   Peninsula 1995   Théâtre du Monde 1984

Lundi Ravioli 1995   Lila Hunter 1988   Lio Comun 1991

Slick Slick 1999

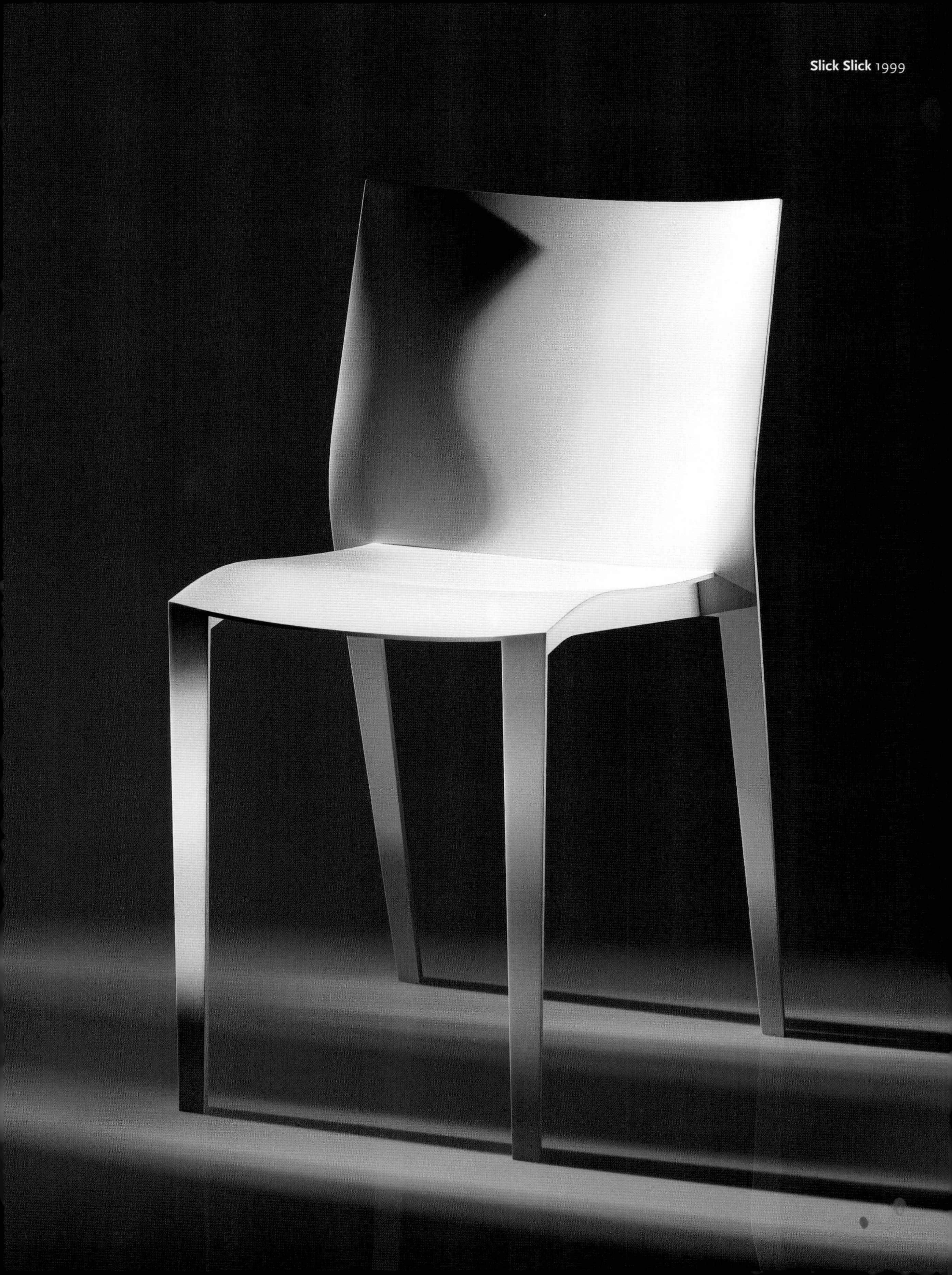

Monsieur X Rocking 1996   **Os Library** 1998

Popopo 1993   **Monsieur X Chaise longue** 1996

Cheap Chic 1997

You are God

Poaa 1999

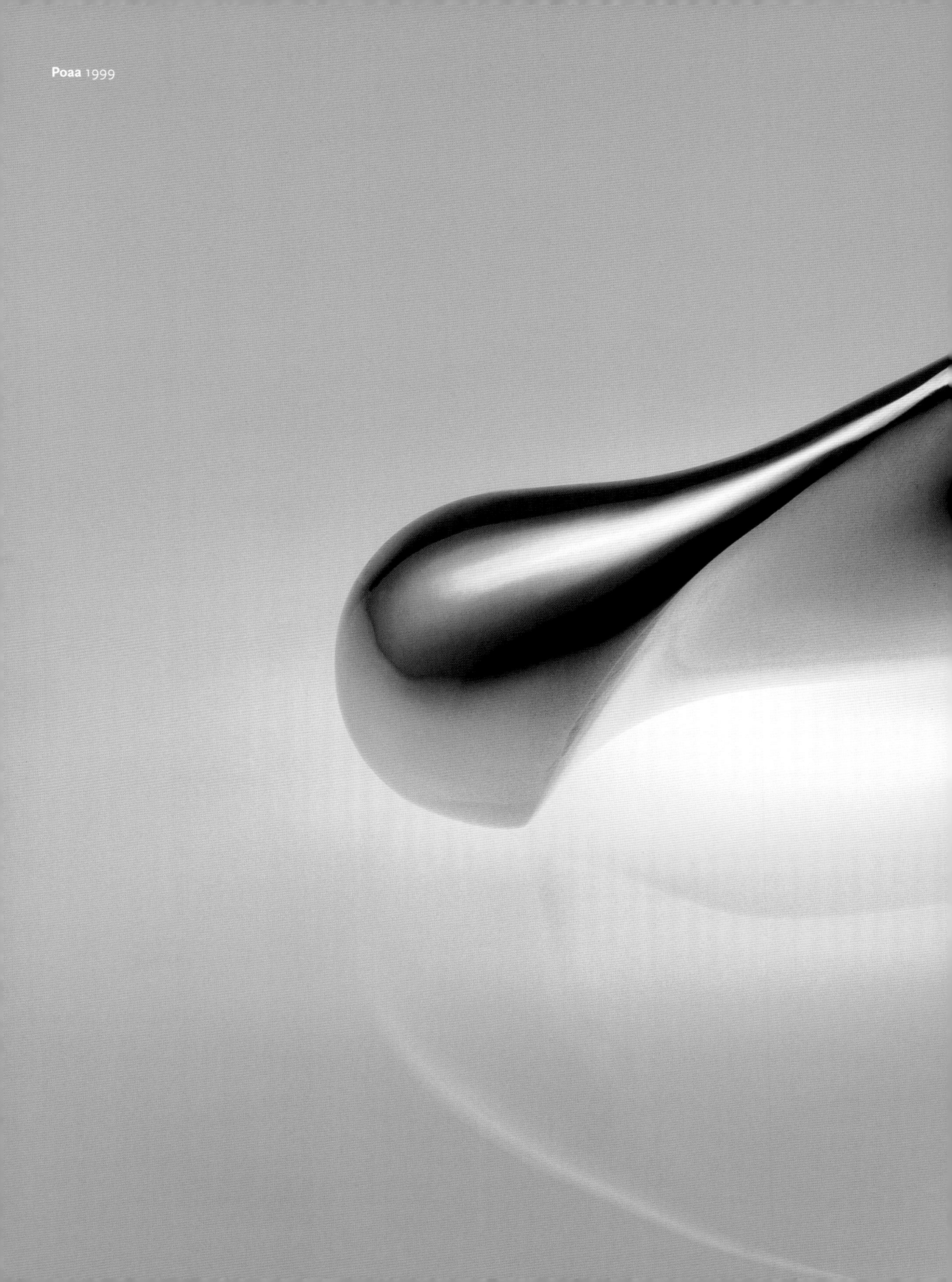

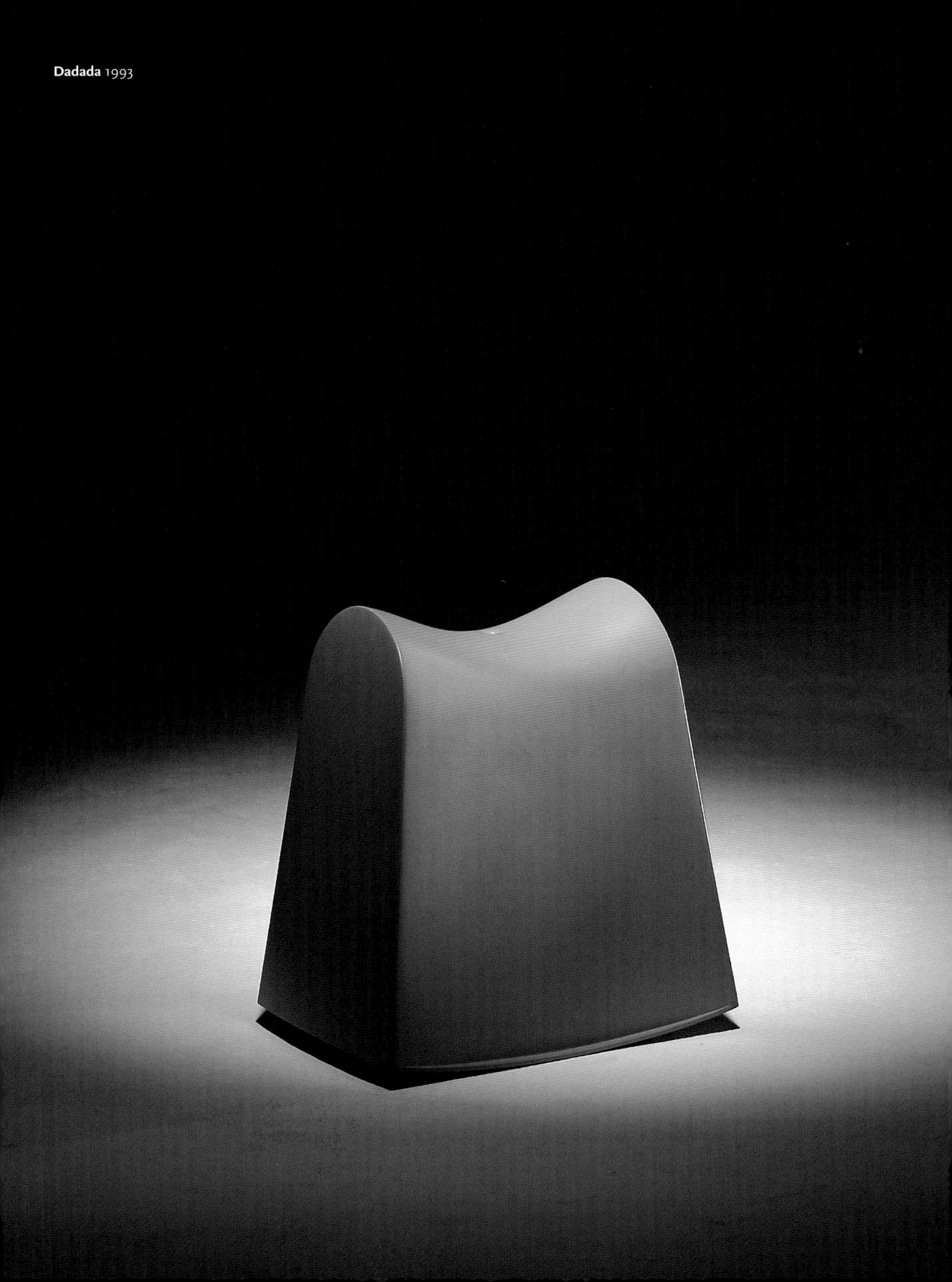

Dadada 1993

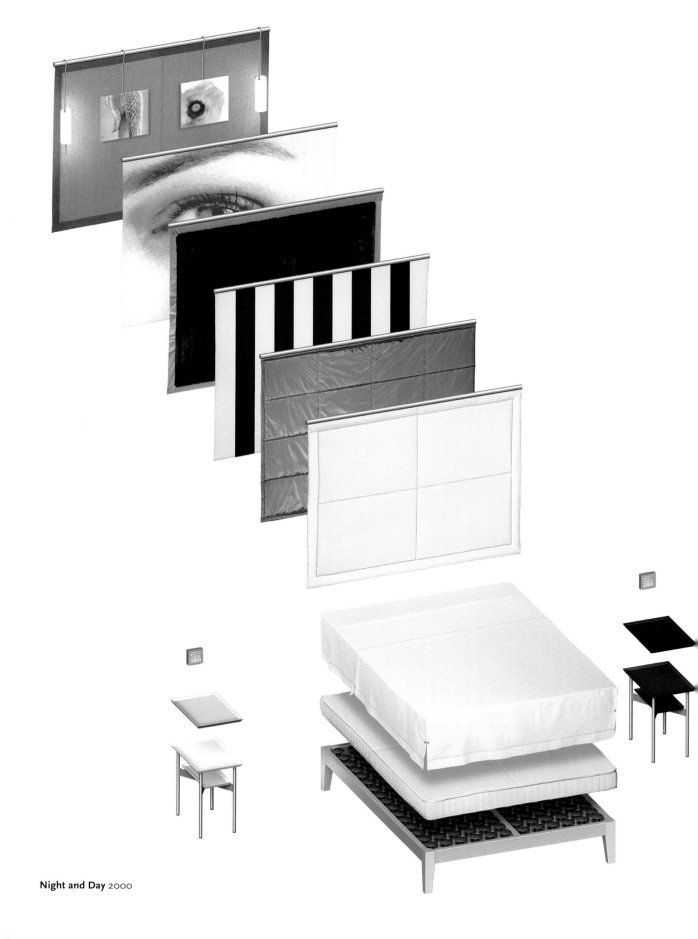

Night and Day 2000

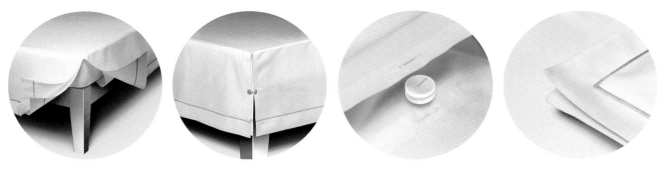

Trimmings

Bathwear

Bedding

Pax Now

12 Architecture

74 Interiors

190 Furniture

296 Industrial Design

510 Magma

518 Words

542 Overview

574 A–Z

Plywood car (project) 1990

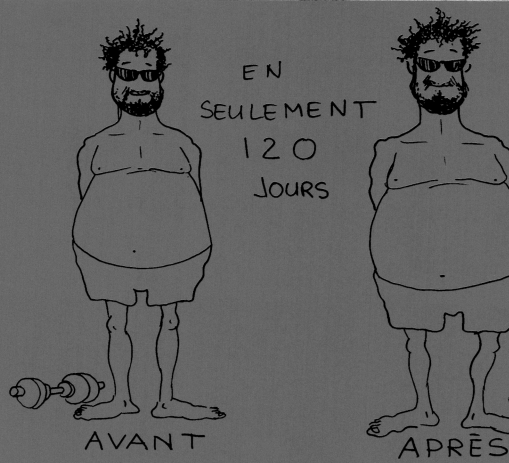

EN
SEULEMENT
120
JOURS

AVANT   APRÈS

TO A TOTO

BY *STARCK*

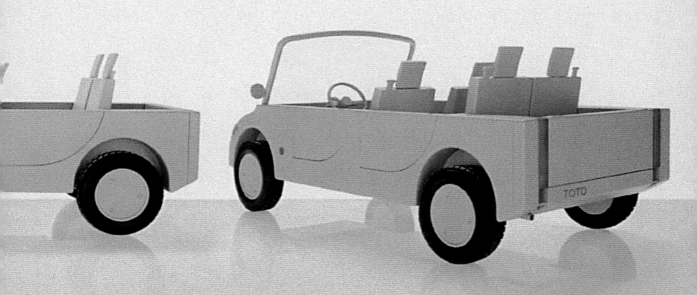

BAD BADS...

Doctor Life 1991   **Rosy Angelis** 1994

Miss Sissi 1990   **Romeo Moon** 1995

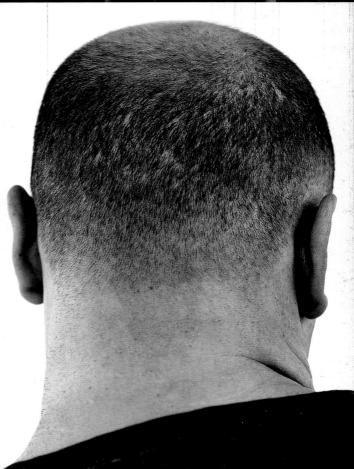

Light Lite 1992   Walla Walla 1994

Ara 1988

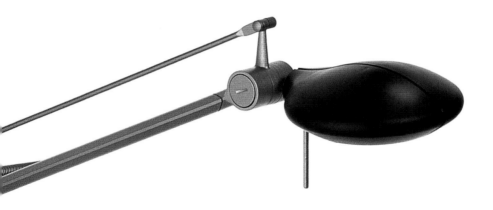

ArchiMoon Tech 1998

ArchiMoon Eco 1998

ArchiMoon Classic 1998

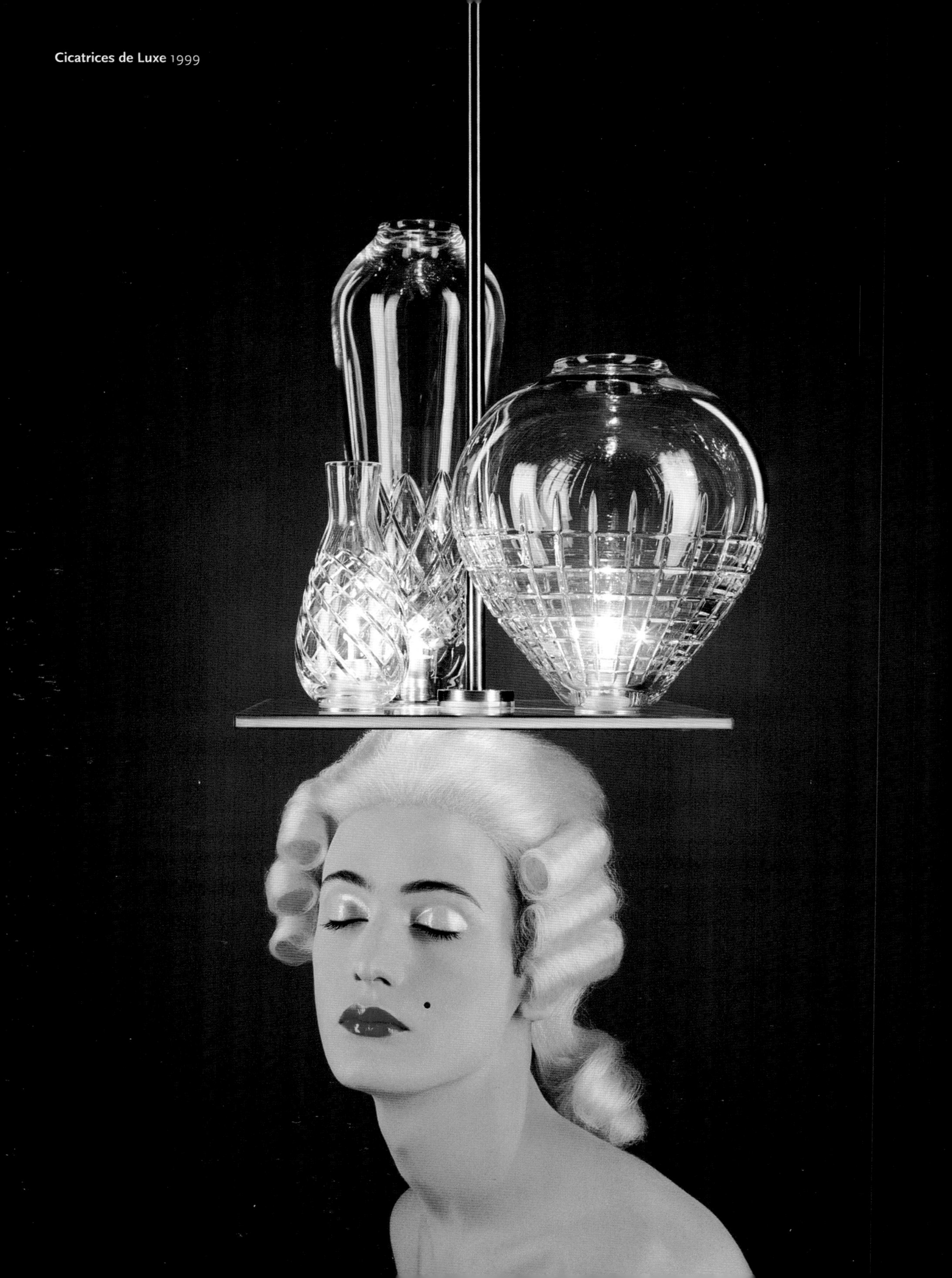

Oa

STARCK®

240
200
150
100
50
10

Baby Fork / Spoon $ 2.99

Toilet Training Set $ 16.99

Scale $ 39.99

Sippy Cup $ 3.49

Toy Car $ 29.99

Short Pop-Up Playhouse $ 24.99

Cozy Chair $ 19.99

Ethno Plastic Stool / Table / Container $ 9.99

Stapler $ 7.99

Tape Dispenser $ 3.99

Magazine Rack $ 14.99

Book Ends $ 7.99

Pencil Cup $ 4.99

Mechanical Pencil $ 6.99

Letter Opener $ 2.99

Scissors $ 5.99

Letter Tray $ 7.99

Letter Sorter $ 7.99

Mail Center / Bulletin Board $ 14.99

Calculator $ 7.99

Wet Tunes $ 24.99

Light Table $ 49.99

Table Lamp $ 14.99

Tissue Box $ 5.99

CD Storage Box $ 7.99

Project File $ 12.99

Wastebasket $ 19.99

Plastic Food Storage $ 2.

p Dish / Nail Brush $ 5.99

Lotion Dispenser $ 6.99

Beard Trimmer $ 19.99

Men's Foils Shaver $ 99.99

Hair Dryer $ 24.99

Curling Iron $ 24.99

Bath Towels $ 7.99

Tumbler $ 5.99

Adult Sonic Pick $ 39.99

Juvenile Sonic Pick $ 19.99

Juvenile Ultrasunex Toothbrush $ 49.99

Toothbrush / Holder $ 4.99

Baby Bowl $ 4.99

Baby Soft Carrier $ 34.99

Tall Pop-Up Playhouse $ 24.99

Pop-Up Playhouse Tunnel $ 19.99

aby Bottle Brush $ 3.99

Bottle Warmer $ 34.99

Diaper Backpack $ 34.99

Diaper Weekend Bag $ 34.99

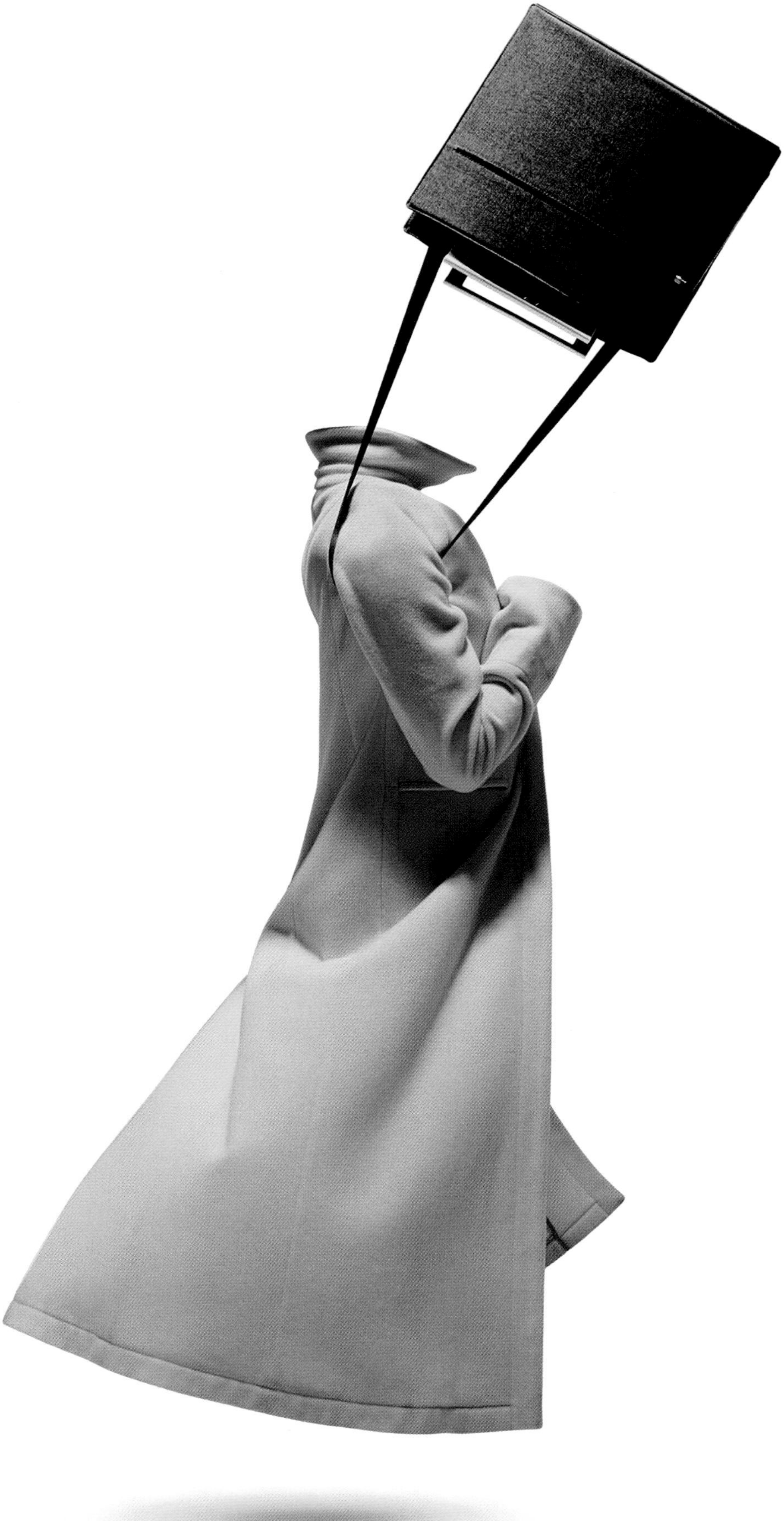

Gaoua 1999

Yeza 1999

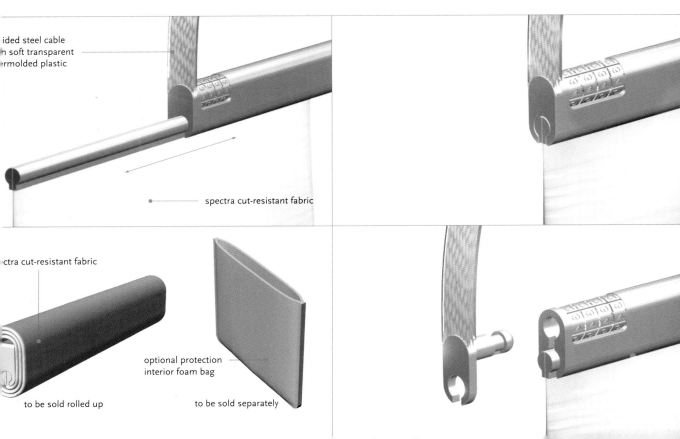

ided steel cable
h soft transparent
rmolded plastic

spectra cut-resistant fabric

ctra cut-resistant fabric

to be sold rolled up

optional protection
interior foam bag

to be sold separately

God is dangerous

We must share

Ti Tang 1992 and **Su Mi Tang** 1992

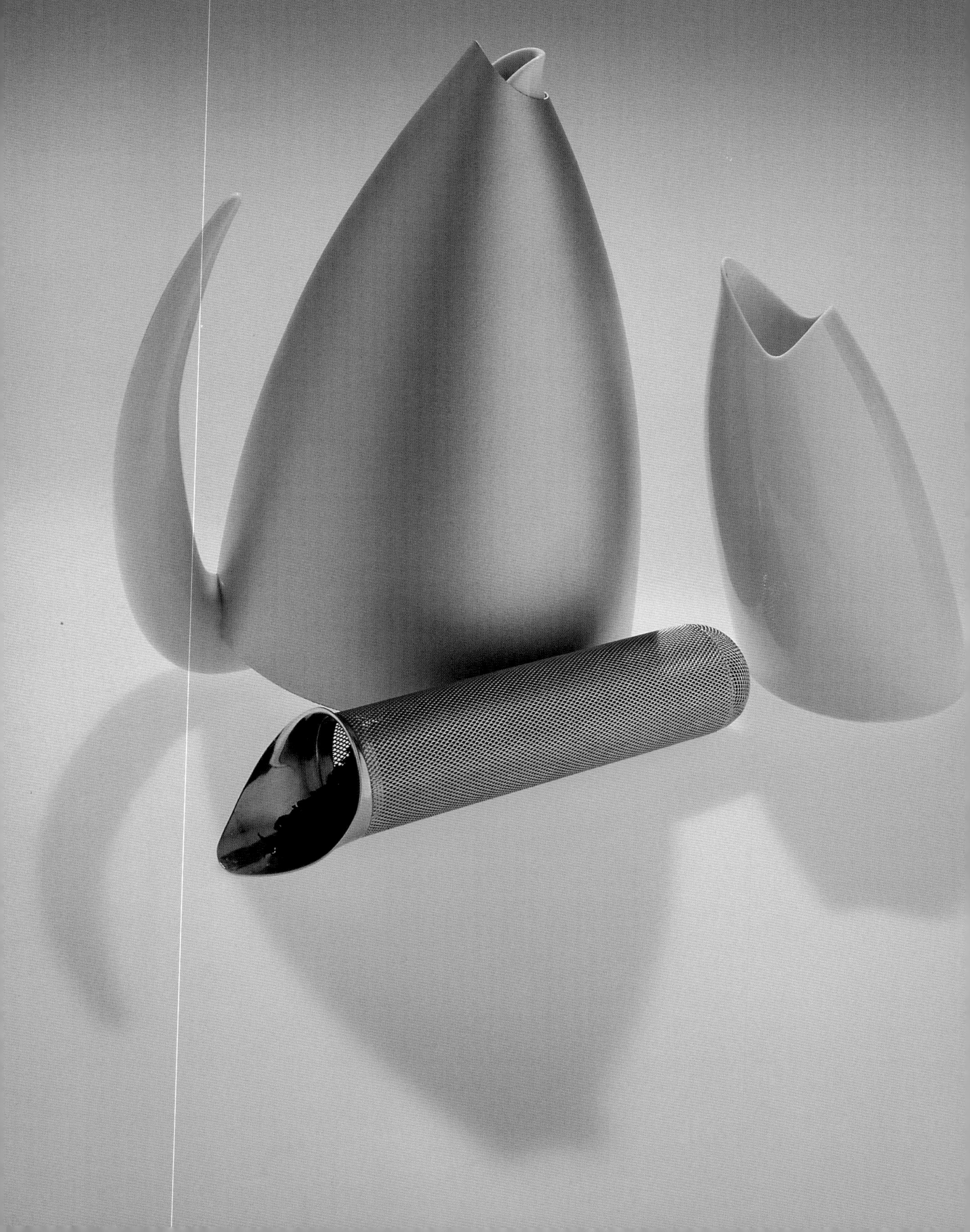

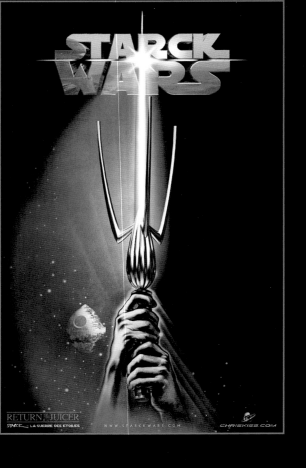

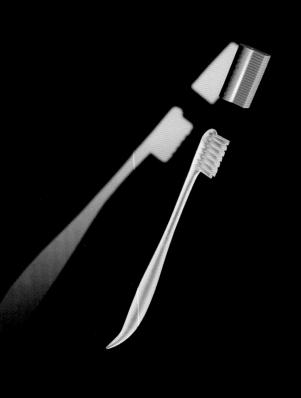

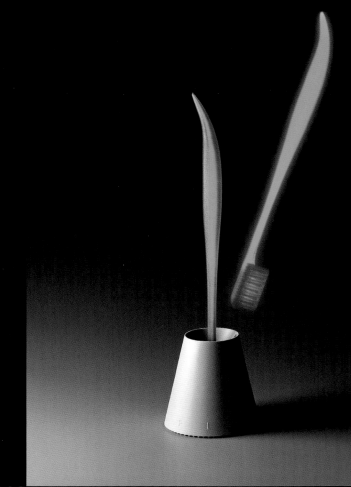

Dr Skud 1998

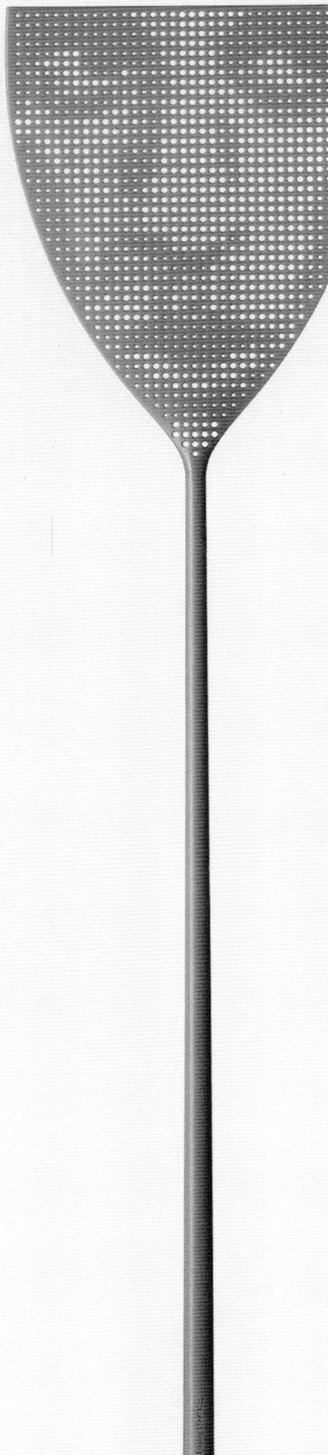

Nous n'avons pas
besoin de tuer pour survivre

Washbasin 1994

Washbasin mixer 1994

Bathtub 1994

Toilet and bidet 1998

Bathtub 1998

LE
GRAND
MOI-MOI

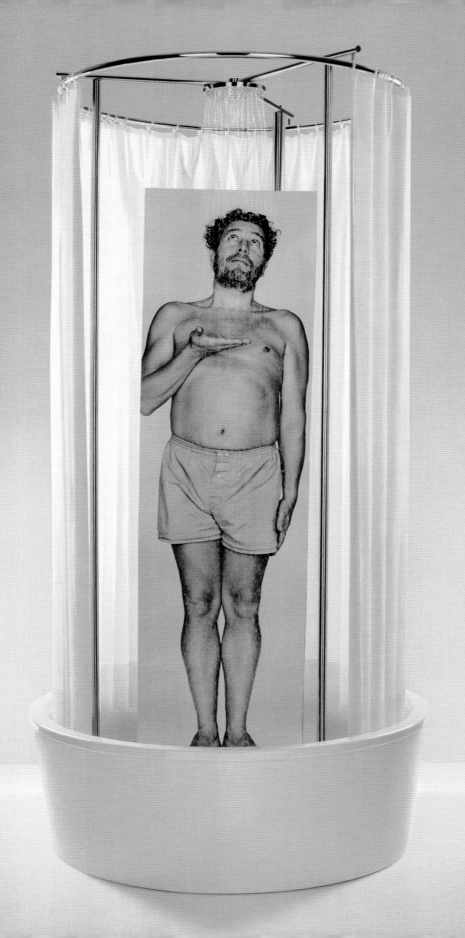

Shower 1998

Jelly Cube 2000

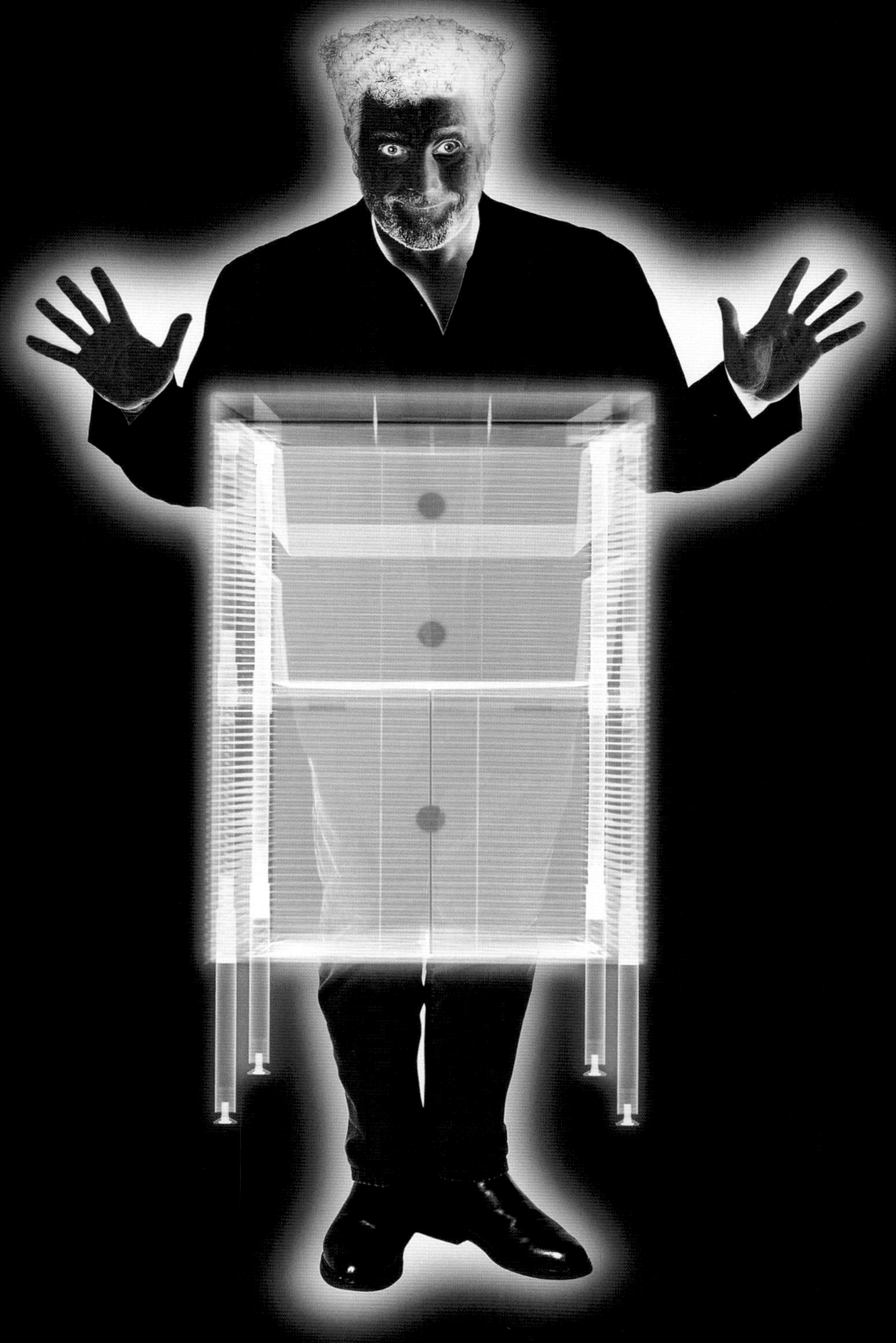

First 41 S5 Voilier L Coque 1989

First 35 S5 Voilier L Coque 1988

Ara III

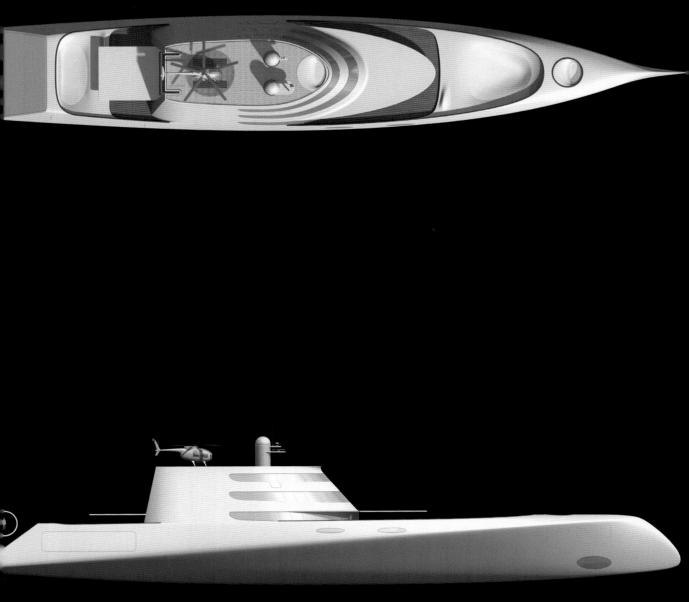

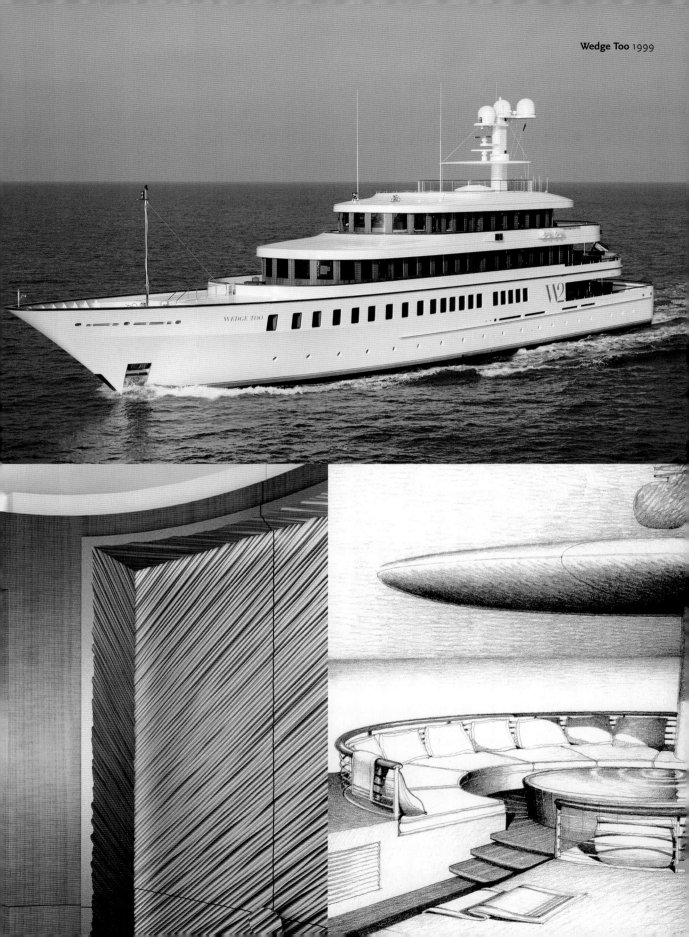

L'urgence est revenue

SAPEURS-POMPIERS
PERLY-CERTOUX
VÉHICULE DE COMMANDEMENT

Scooter Lama
(prototype) 1992

THOMSON

Remote Control 1994

De la technologie à l'amour

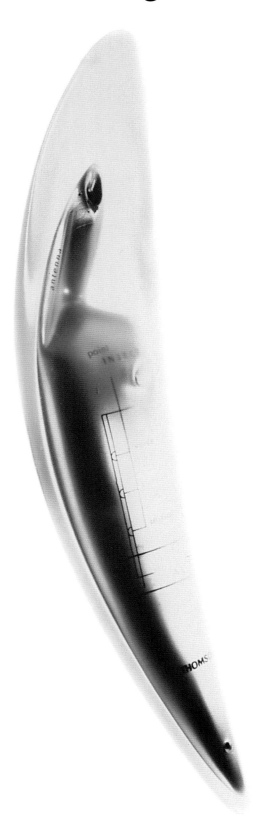

Plasmaa 1995

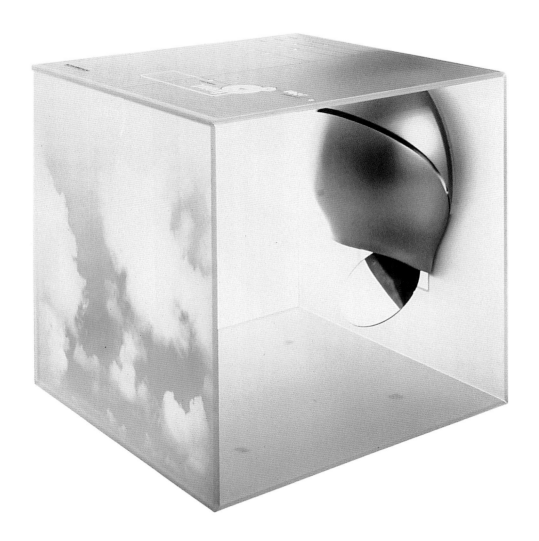

Cub 1996

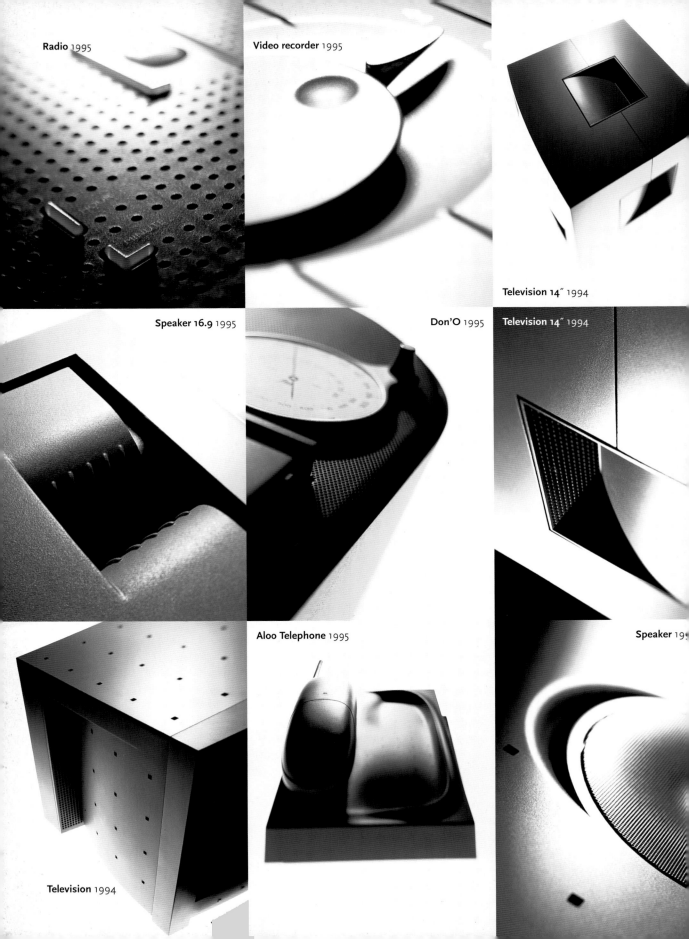

Radio 1995

Video recorder 1995

Television 14″ 1994

Speaker 16.9 1995

Don'O 1995

Television 14″ 1994

Aloo Telephone 1995

Speaker 19

Television 1994

Saba Television

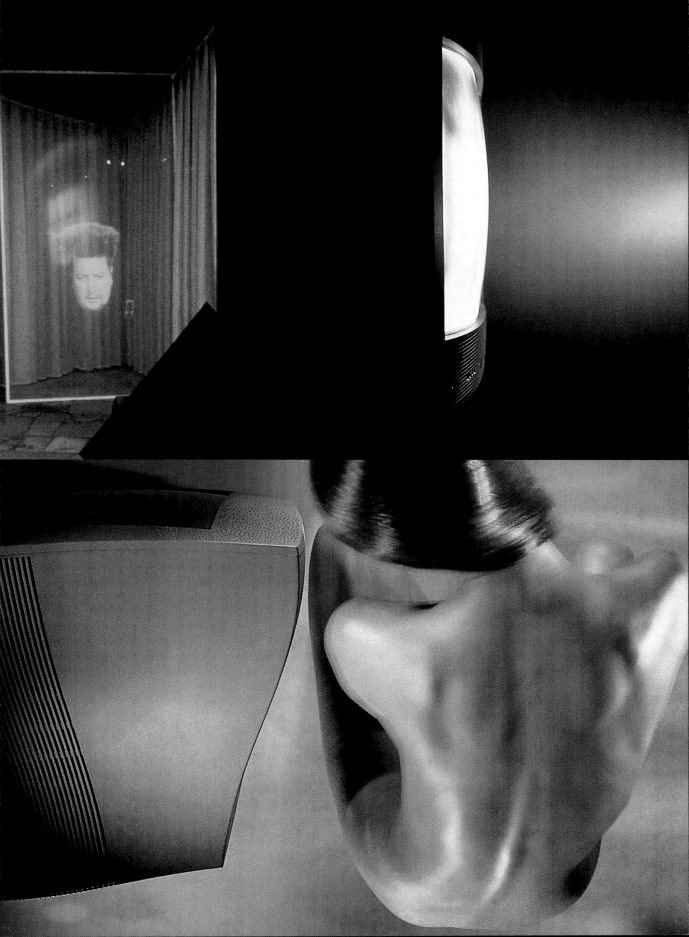

Oz TV 1994

Jim Nature TV 1994

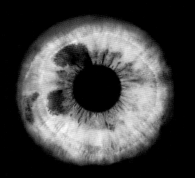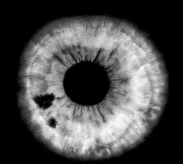

Remote Control Unit (M 5107) 1994

Remote Control Unit 1995

Remote Control Unit 1995

Torche radio 1996

Ola 1996

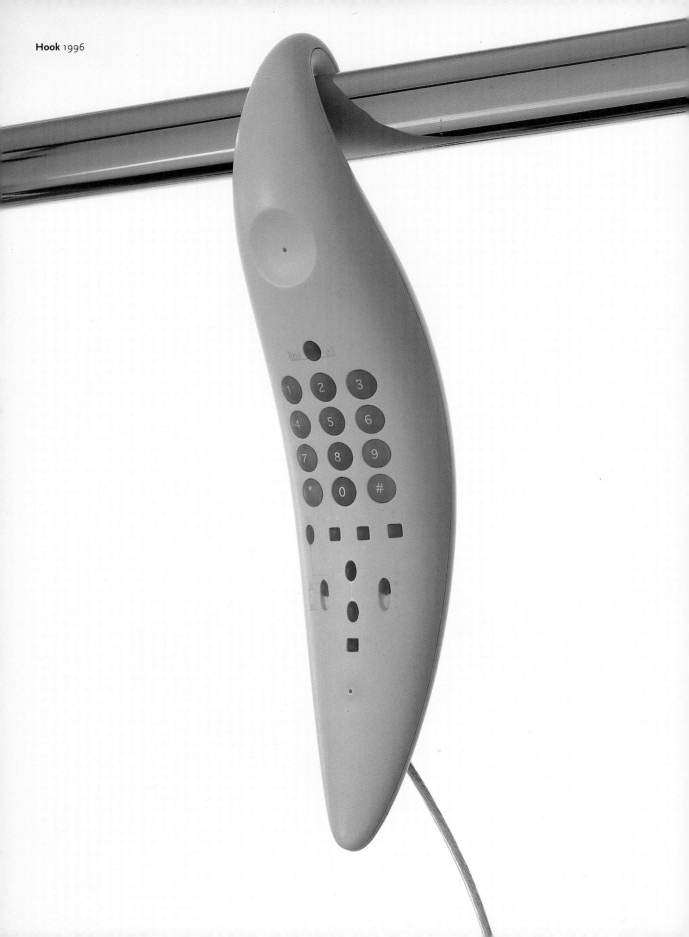

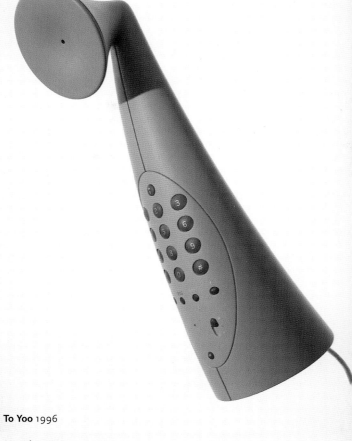

CooCoo 1996   **To Yoo** 1996

Poe 1996   **Moosk** 1996
(Design: Jérôme Olivet)

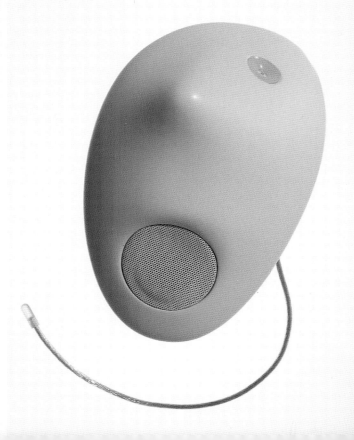

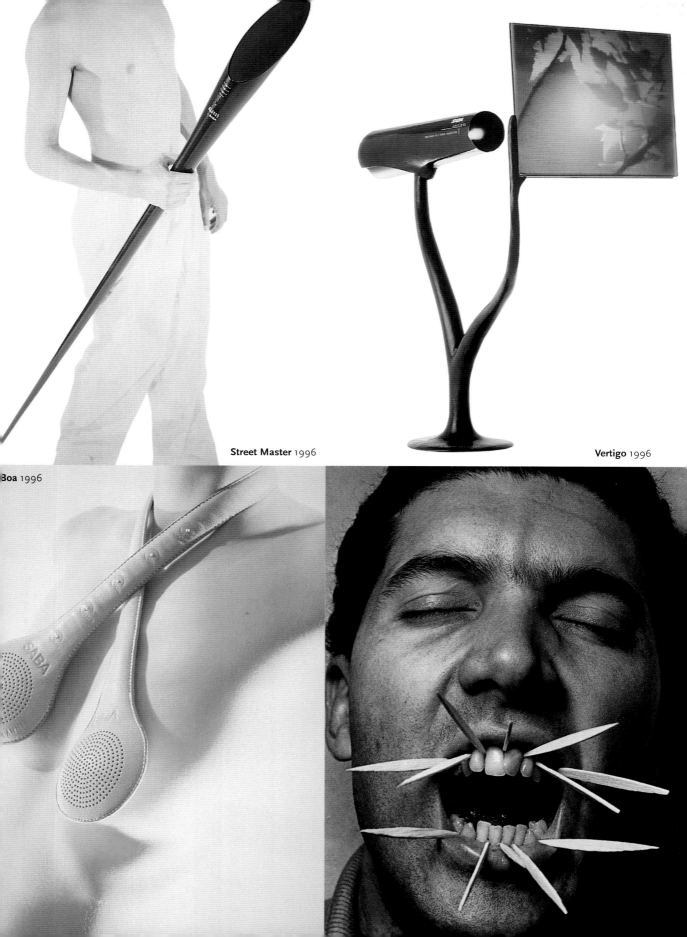

Street Master 1996

Vertigo 1996

Boa 1996

TV Partoo 1996

Icipari 1995

Lux Lux 1996

Comboo 1995

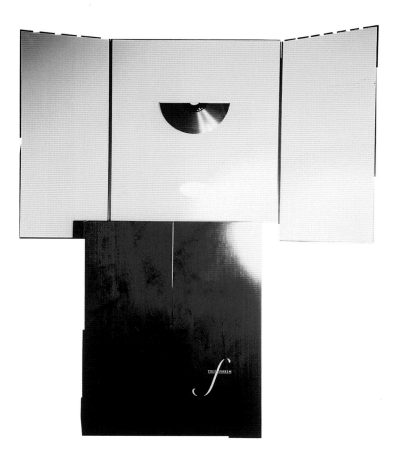

Toccata 1996

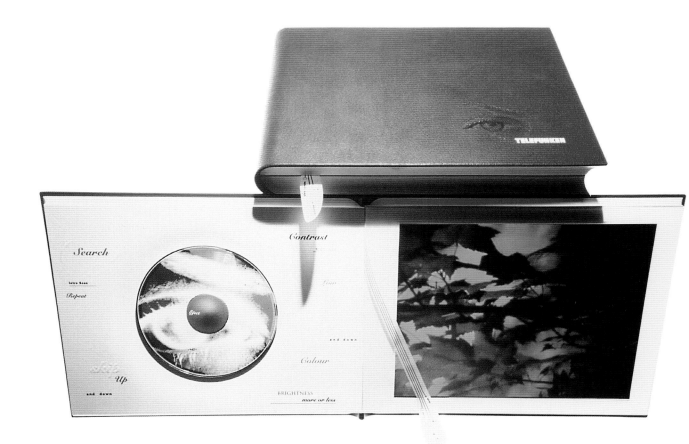

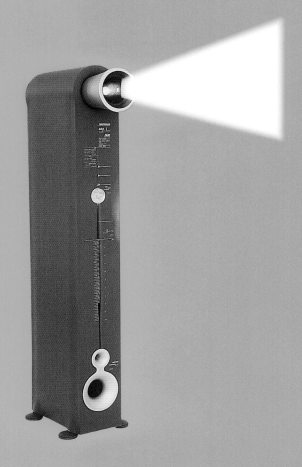

Les produits du groupe Thomson sont sous la direction artistique de Philippe Starck. Certains sont créés par lui-même, d'autres sont dessinés en collaboration ou par: Claude Bressan, Matali Crasset, Mike Davidson, Elsa Frances, Bernard Guerrin, Patrick Jouin, Michael Michalsky, Jérôme Olivet, Jean-Michel Policar, Andréa Quaglio, Manuela Simonelli, Gérard Vergneau

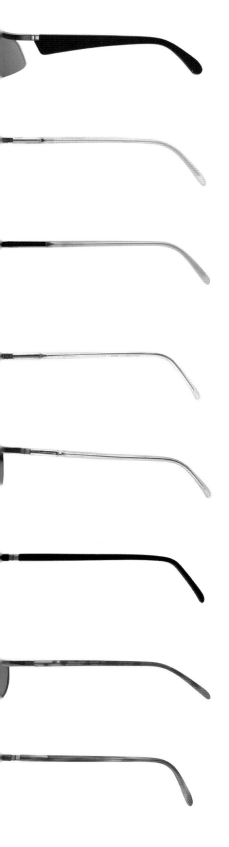

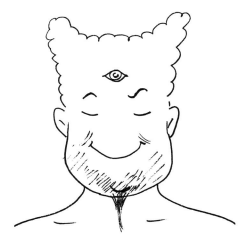

MOI
MOI s

STARK'3EYES

Demain sera moins

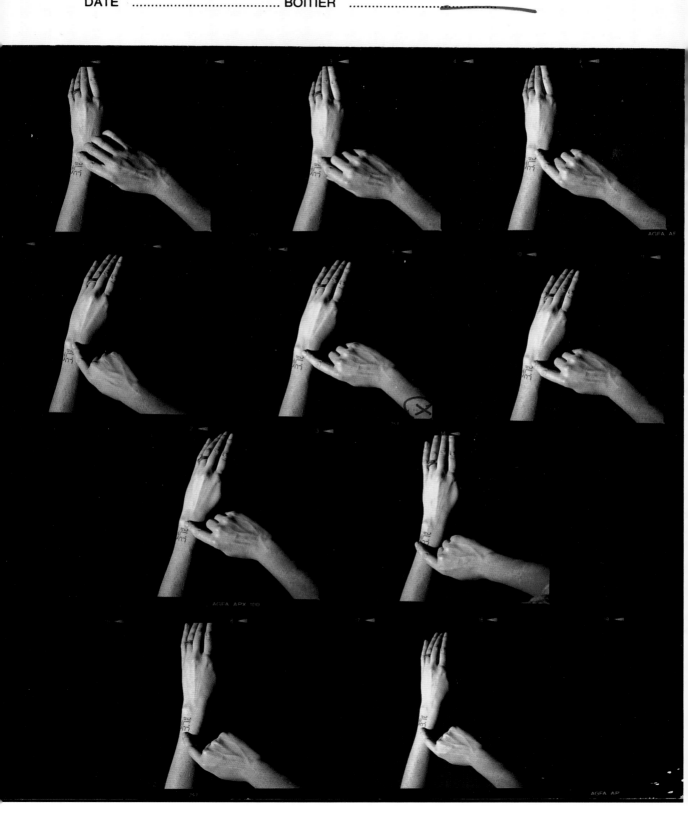

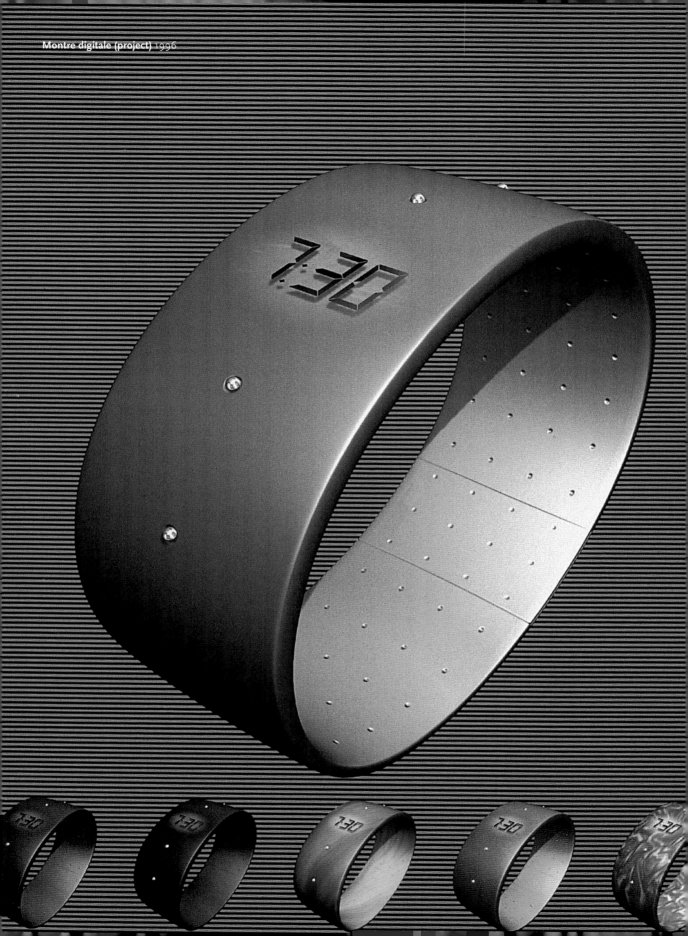

Low Cost Watch 1998

Walter Wayle 1989

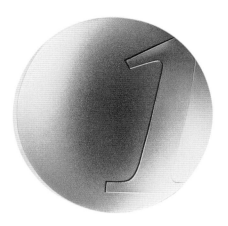

un ultime franc

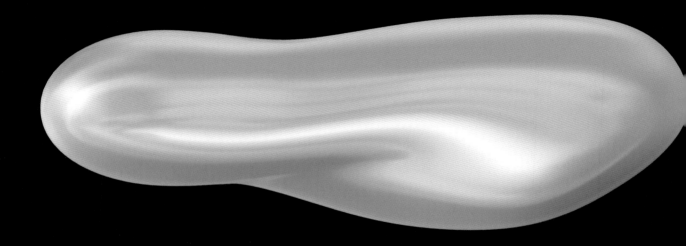

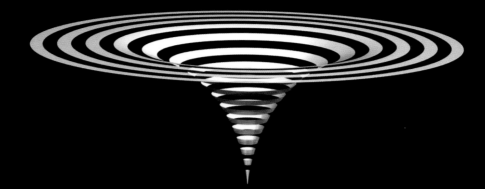

Nous  Us

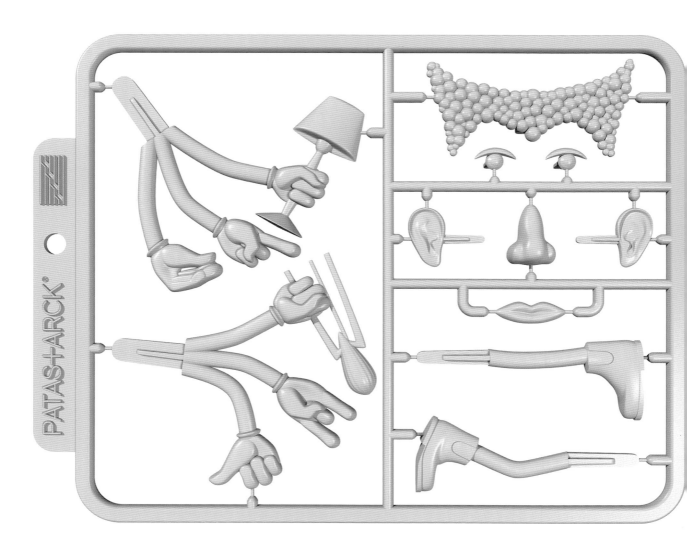

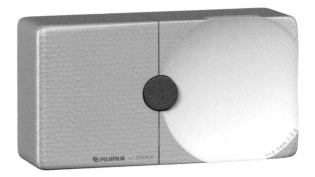

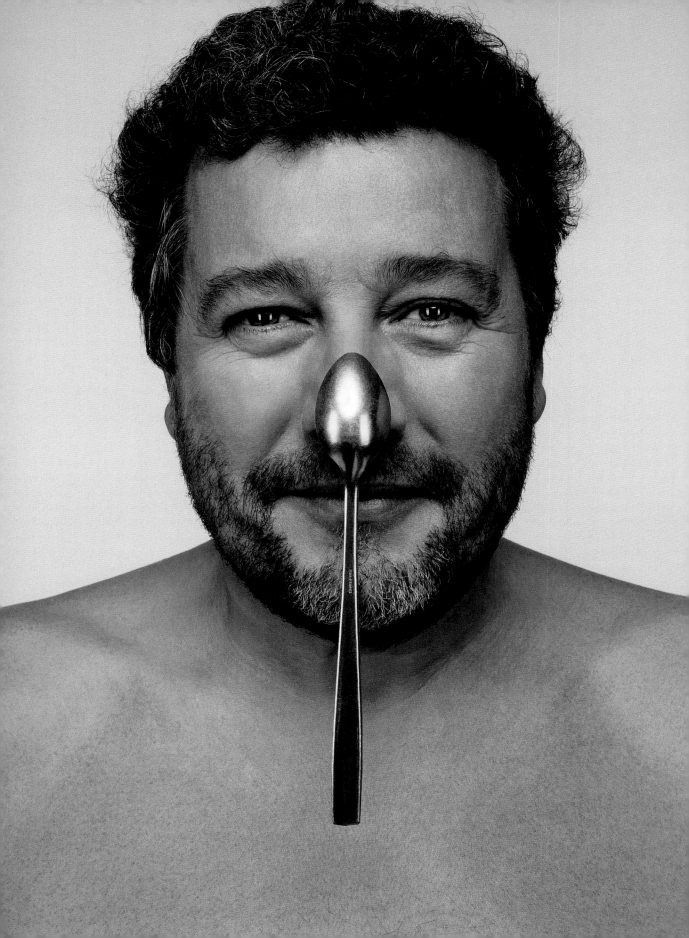

Pour la vie 1990

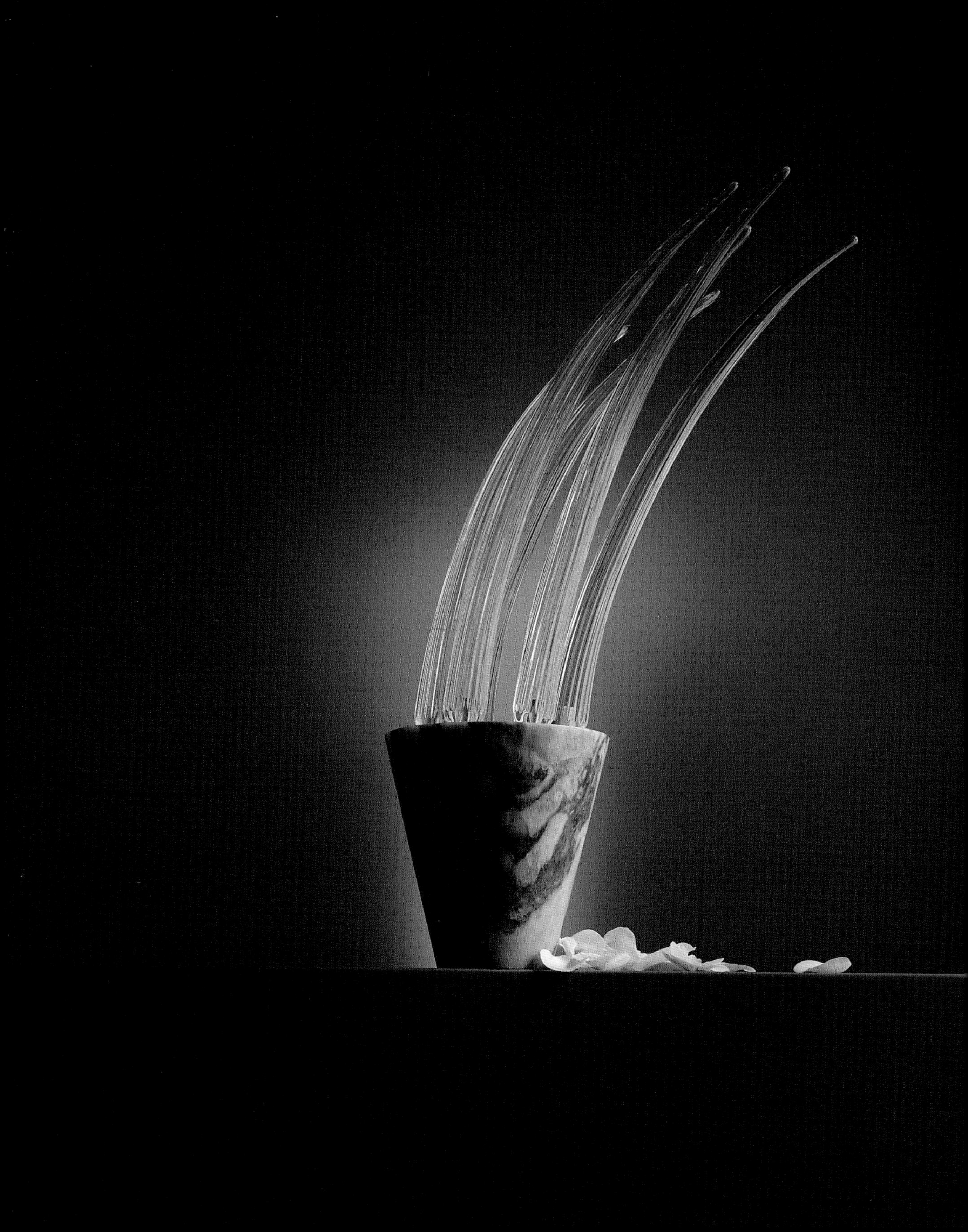

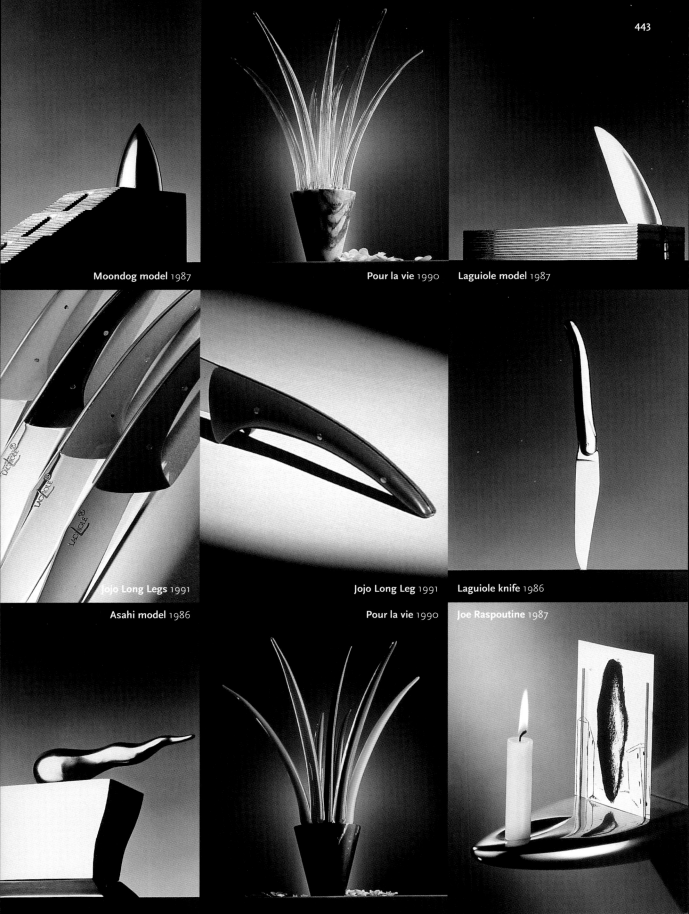

Moondog model 1987

Pour la vie 1990   **Laguiole model** 1987

Jojo Long Legs 1991

Jojo Long Leg 1991   **Laguiole knife** 1986

Asahi model 1986   **Pour la vie** 1990   **Joe Raspoutine** 1987

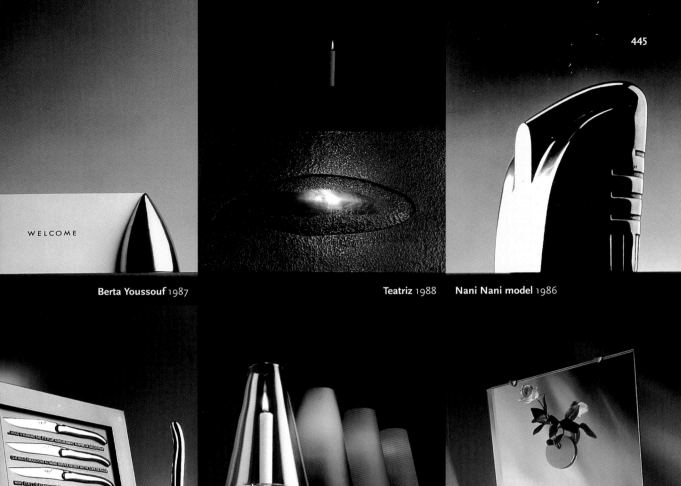

Berta Youssouf 1987

Teatriz 1988 Nani Nani model 1986

Laguiole Set 1986

O' Kelvin 1989 Paramount IV 1990

Miss Zenzen 1986

Paramount II 1990 Pointus 1986

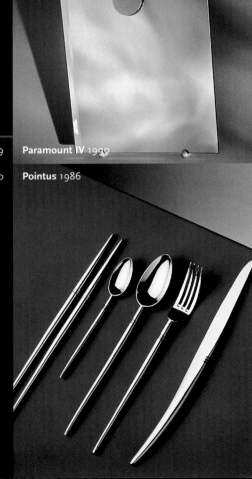

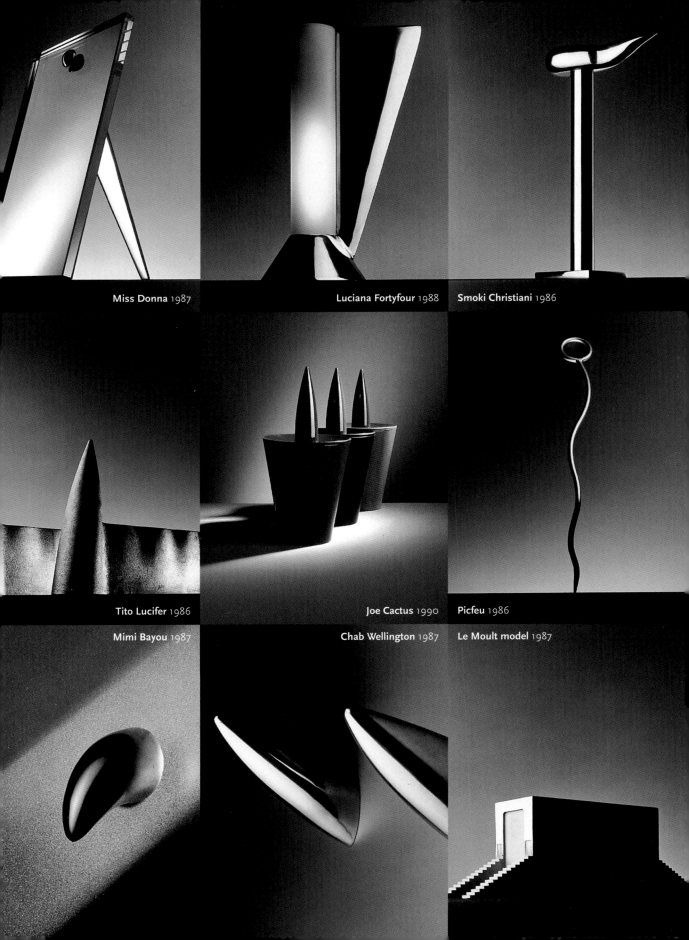

Miss Donna 1987

Luciana Fortyfour 1988

Smoki Christiani 1986

Tito Lucifer 1986

Joe Cactus 1990

Picfeu 1986

Mimi Bayou 1987

Chab Wellington 1987

Le Moult model 1987

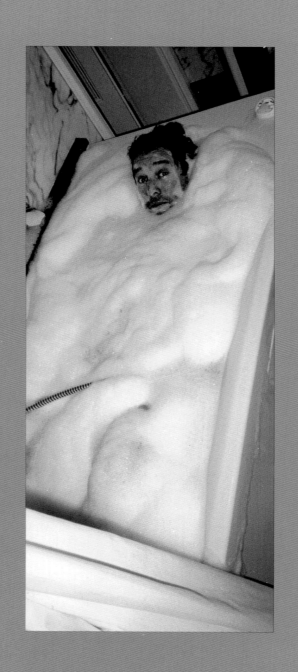

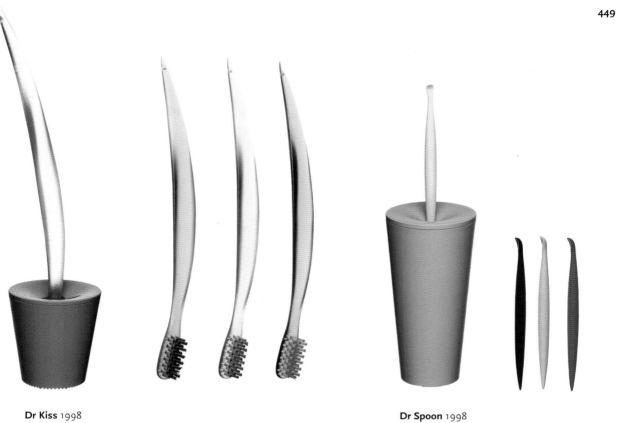

Dr Kiss 1998

Dr Spoon 1998

Dr Cheese 1998

Dr Kleen 1998

Curling Iron Set PS 603 2000   Tooth Brush PS 601 2000

Flosser PS 600 2000   Beard Trimmer PS 602 2000

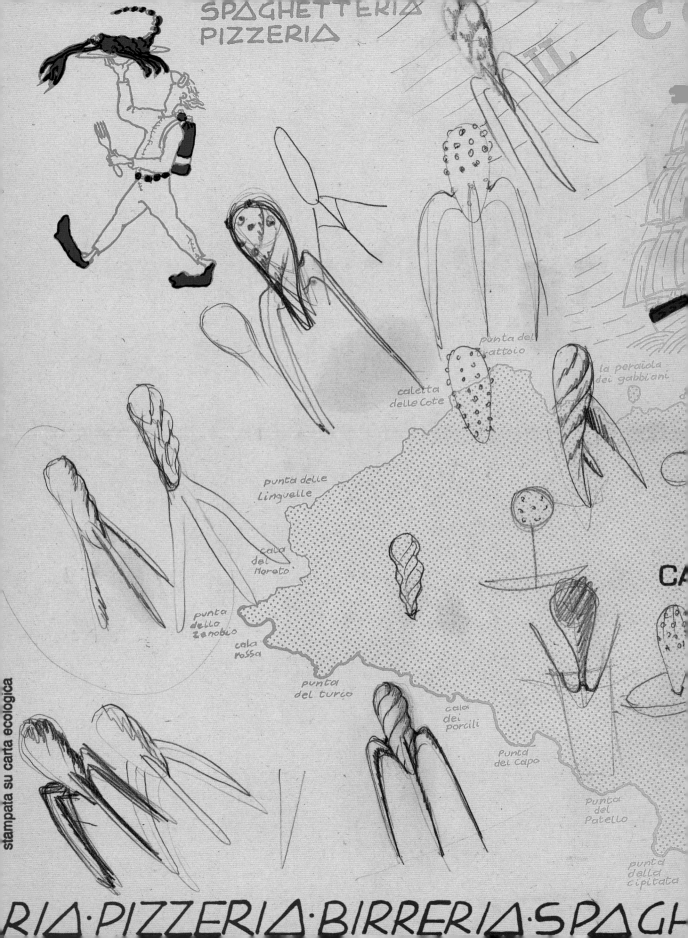

SPAGHETTERIA
PIZZERIA

IL

CA

punta del grattoio

caletta delle Cote

la peraiola dei gabbiani

punta delle Linguelle

cala del Moreto

punta dello Zenobio

cala rossa

punta del turco

cala dei porcili

punta del Capo

punta del Patello

punta della cipitata

stampata su carta ecologica

RIA · PIZZERIA · BIRRERIA · SPAGH

ZENTRO
GASTRONOMICO
SUBACQUEO

Seno
della
Perruccia

Punta
della Manza

Punta
della
Seccatoia

Punta
dell'Acquissucola

ISOLA

punta
della
teglia

cala
della
Mortola

porto
vecchio

Punta
della
Barbice

Punta
del
Vecchiaione

Punta
di Porto
vecchio

Punta
del
ferraione

cala
nuova

cala
dello
zurletto

Punta
della Fica

ERIA · PIZZERIA · BIRRERIA · SP

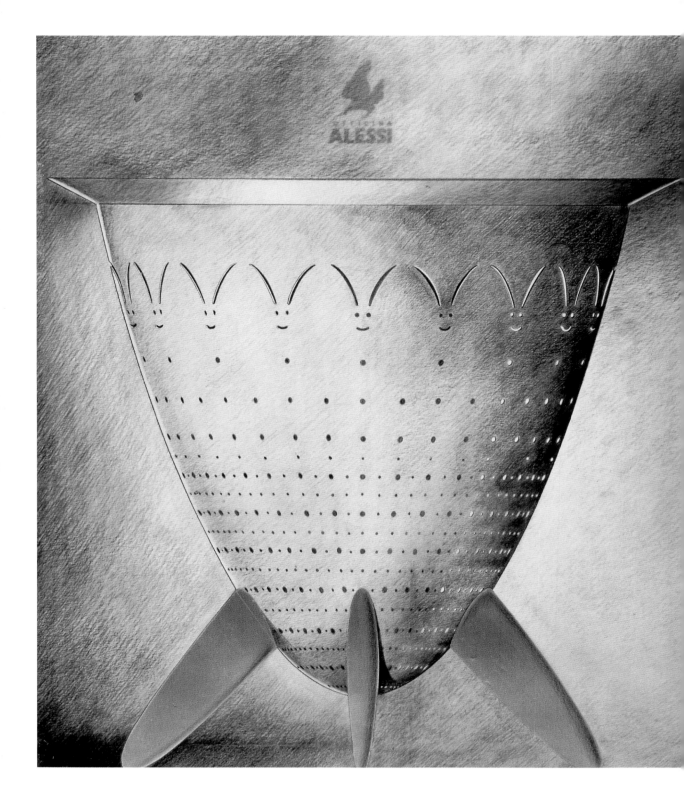

Max le Chinois 1990–1991

FRONT VIEW

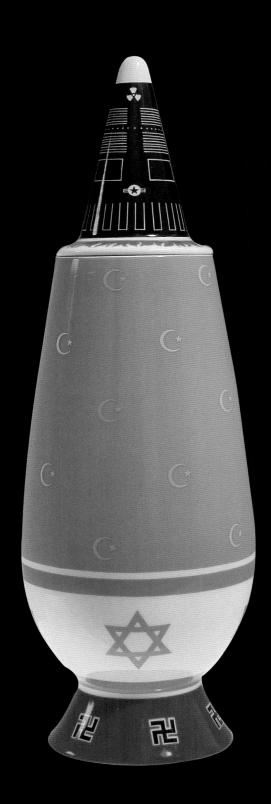

Olympic Flame 1992

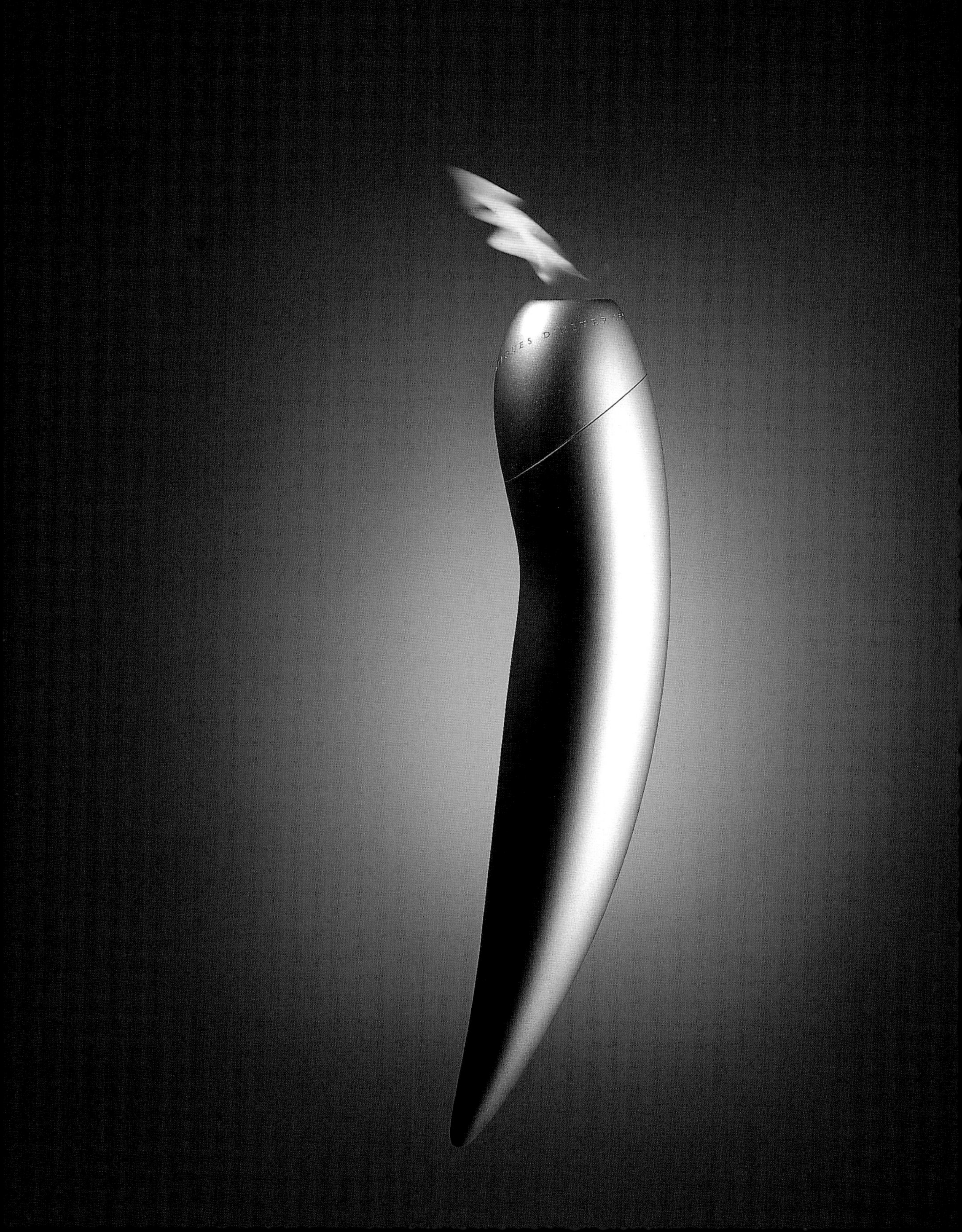

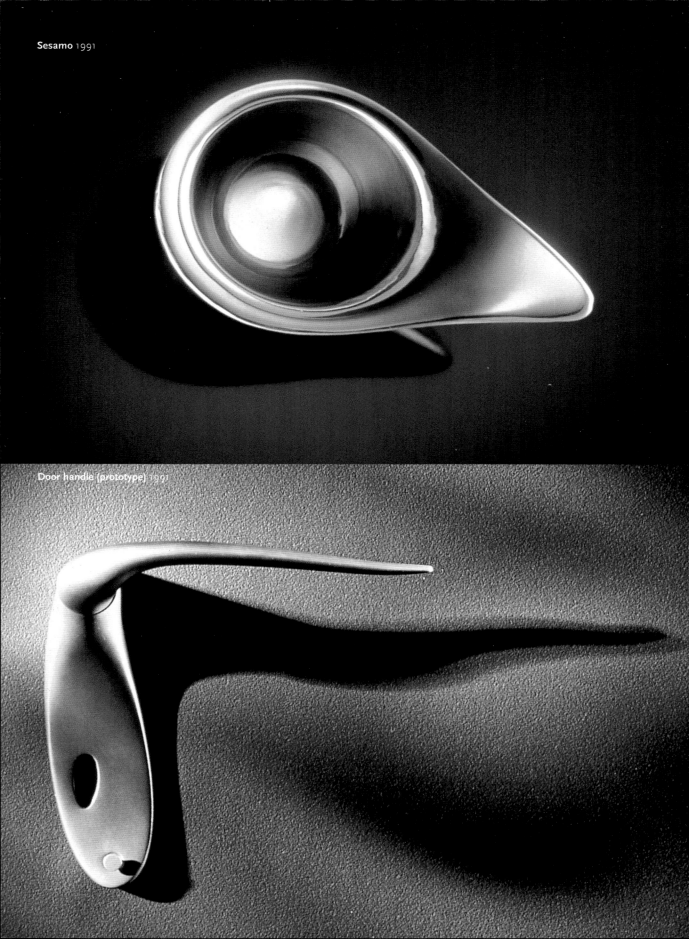

Sesamo 1991

Door handle (prototype) 1991

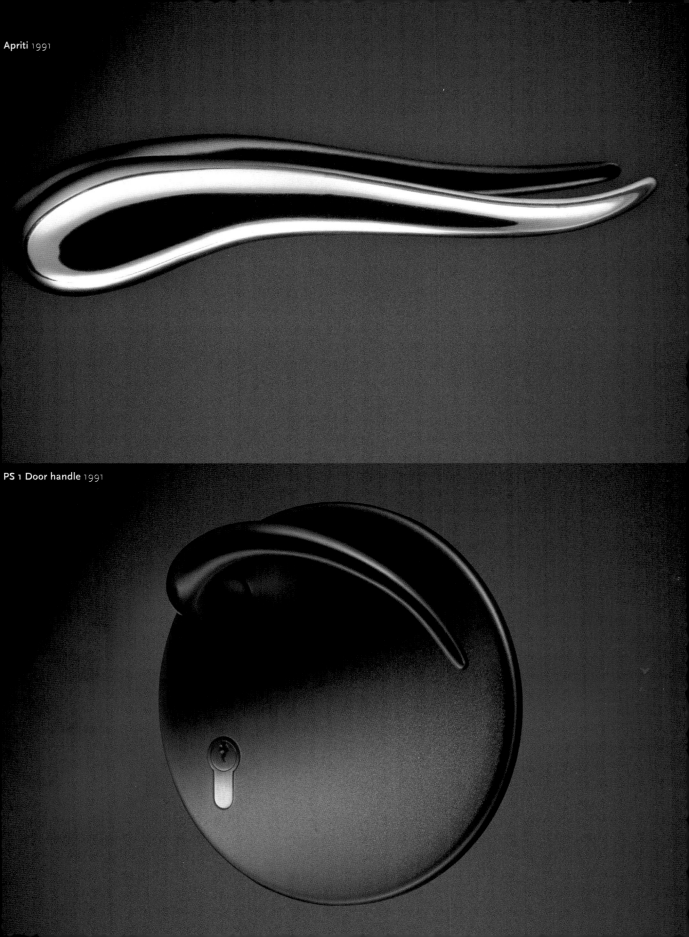

Apriti 1991

PS 1 Door handle 1991

Street lamp 1992

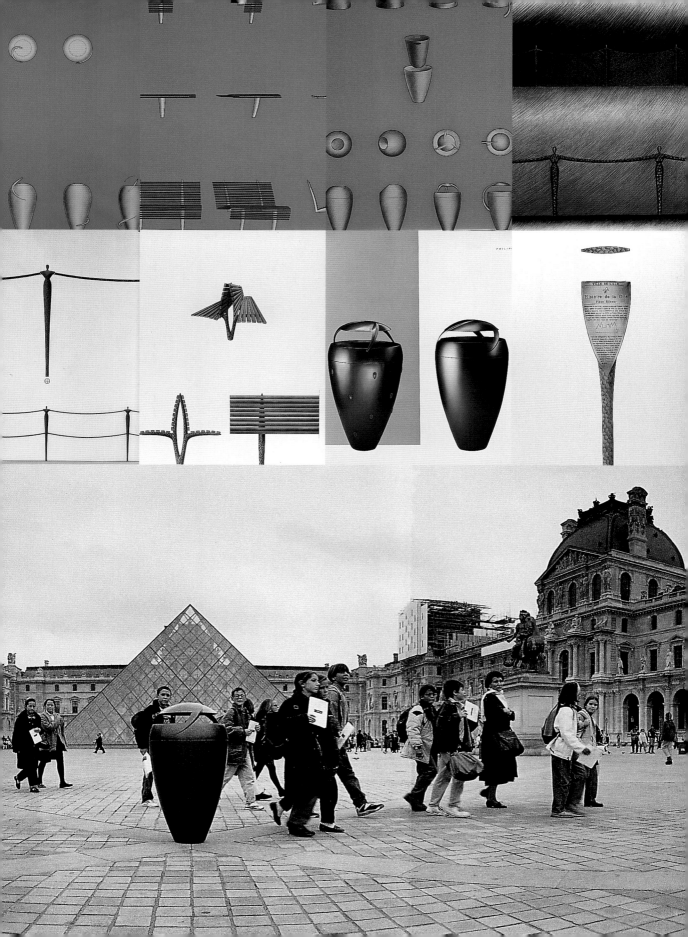

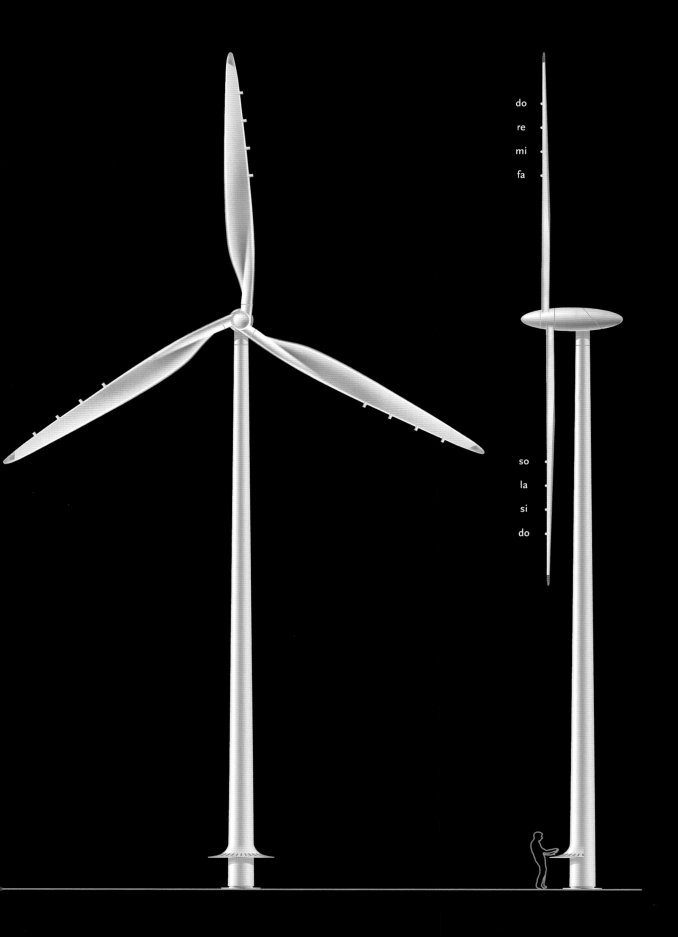

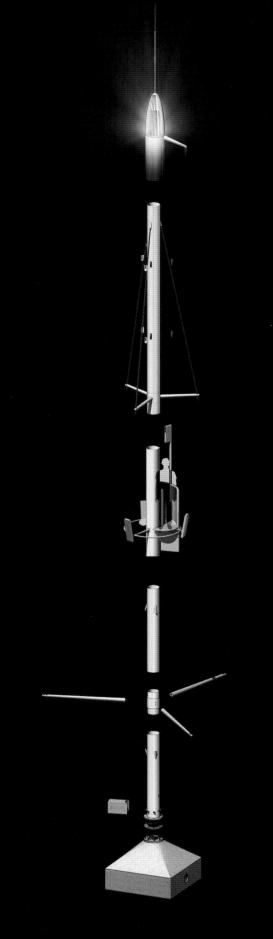

ARCHIVAL PRESERVERS
PO BOX 607638 · ORLANDO, FL 32860 · (407) 886-3100
INSERT EMULSION SIDE DOWN
ASSIGNMENT:

1	2 KODAK 5062 PX	3 KODAK 5062 PX	4 KODAK 5062 PX	5 KODAK 5062 PX

1	1A	2	2A	3	3A	4	4A	5	5A
6 KODAK 5062 PX	7 KODAK 5062 PX	8 KODAK 5062 PX	9 KODAK 5062 PX	10 KODAK 5062 PX

6	6A	7	7A	8	8A	9	9A	10	10A
11 KODAK 5062 PX	12 KODAK 5062 PX	13 KODAK 5062 PX	14 KODAK 5062 PX	15 KODAK 5062 PX

11	11A	12	12A	13	13A	14	14A	15	15A
16 KODAK 5062 PX	17 KODAK 5062 PX	18 KODAK 5062 PX	19 KODAK 5062 PX	20 KODAK 5062 PX

16	16A	17	17A	18	18A	19	19A	20	20A
21 KODAK 5062 PX	22 KODAK 5062 PX	23 KODAK 5062 PX	24 KODAK 5062 PX	25 KODAK 5062 PX

21	21A	22	22A	23	23A	24	24A	25	25A
26 KODAK 5062 PX	27 KODAK 5062 PX	28 KODAK 5062 PX	29 KODAK 5062 PX	30 KODAK 5062 PX

26	26A	27	27A	28	28A	29	29A	30	30A
31 KODAK 5062 PX	32 KODAK 5062 PX	33 KODAK 5062 PX	34 KODAK 5062 PX	35 KODAK 5062 PX

31	31A	32	32A	33	33A	34	34A	35	35A

L'intelligence est féminine

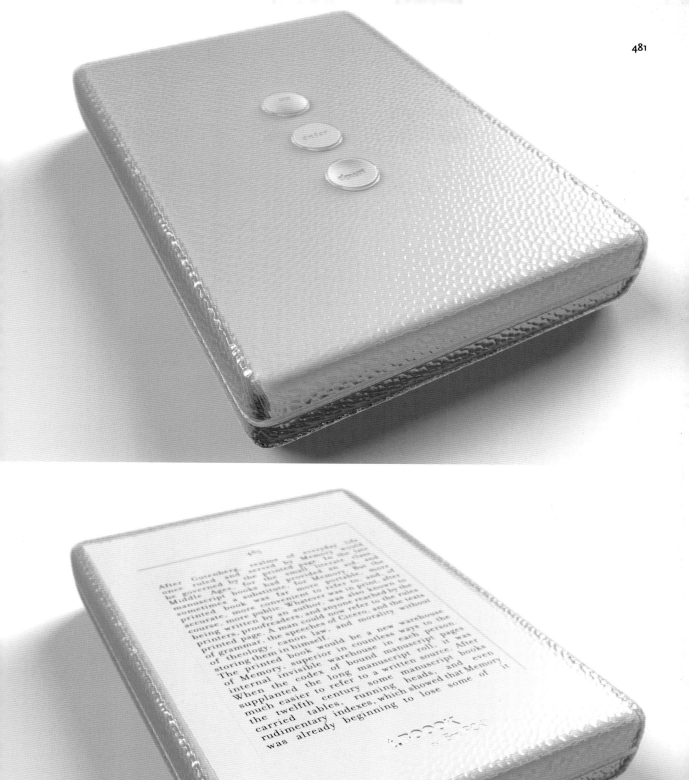

After Gutenberg, realms of wisdom once ruled and beyond by Memory in be governed by the primary literate Middle Ages. For the small literate class manuscript books had provided an ac- sometimes a substitute for memory, but printed book was far more reliable, more accurate, more convenient to refer to, and of course more public. Whatever was in print being written by an author was also known to printers, proofreaders, and anyone reached by the rules of grammar, the speeches of Cicero, and the texts storing them in himself.

The printed book would be a new warehouse of Memory, superior in countless ways to the internal invisible warehouse in each person. When the codex of bound manuscript roll it was much easier to refer to a written manuscript books the twelfth century some heads, and even carried tables, running indexes, which showed that Memory rudimentary beginning to lose some of it was already

Ball Point Pen 1998

Lead Refill 1998

Fluorescent Markers 1998

Retractable pencil 1998

Pencils 1998

Toothbrush 1998

Toothbrush for Children 1998

Hairbrush **Blow** 1998

X-Acto Knife 1998

Note Book 199

Tape Dispenser 1998

Eraser 199

Low Cost Clock 1998

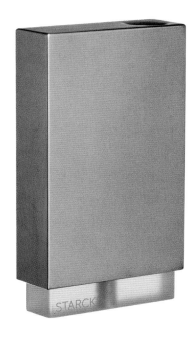

Lighter 1998

A. Echelle de secours//Escape ladder. Description: échelle câble acier galvanisé et barreaux tube duralumin, référence: 857.2127, prix: (1) taille

et buccal de secours, assure le "retournement" du porteur sur le dos, poignée de halage et sangle sous-cutale, référence: 581.4979, prix: 850 F/128,17 Euros.
D. Description: gilet Pocket Plastimo identique au modèle B mais dans une poche fermée portée à la ceinture, référence: 581.5258, prix: 575 F/

...quipements de protection provoquent souvent une réaction d'étonnement, ou d'inquiétude sur la santé mentale de celui qui s'en préoccupe. Je ...a ceinture de sécurité lorsque je suis en voiture, le casque lorsque je roule en moto, et cela ne m'a jamais gêné. Etre protégé de potentiels accidents ...ologiques, chimiques, biologiques ou radiologiques, ne relève, ni de la paranoïa, ni d'une prospective exagérément pessimiste. les exemples ...ents de ce type, en dehors de tout conflit militaire, seront malheureusement quotidiens et justifient certainement ces précautions. Banalement, on ...ra se limiter à répéter qu'il vaut mieux prévenir que guérir, surtout si on ne se guérit pas toujours.

...equipment often provokes a surprised reaction, not to mention doubts about the mental health of anyone who gives some thought to the matter. I ...always fasten my seatbelt when I'm in a car, I wear a helmet on a motorcycle and that doesn't bother me at all. To be safely equipped for any possi- ...ological, chemical, bacteriological, or radioactive mishap is neither a symptom of paranoia nor the sign of an excessively pessimistic nature. ...oles of this type of event, even in the absence of armed conflict, will unfortunately become routine occurrences, and certainly justify precautionary ...ures. An ounce of prevention is worth a pound of cure, especially where there's a risk of incurability.

61

M

N

O

P

Masque protection voies respiratoires (filtres vendus séparément)//Respirator mask (filters sold separately).

...scription: masque Giat dérivé du masque de protection de l'armée française, assure la protection des voies respiratoires en filtrant l'air en fonction des ...es utilisés, couvre-face à large visière panoramique souple qui s'adapte parfaitement aux formes du visage (2 tailles), 2 soupapes d'expiration, ...pet inspiratoire, demi-masque interne et système de ventilation de la visière évitant la buée, brides réglables, sangle de portage, poids 500g, livré sans ...ouche (vendues ci-dessous), références: taille femme 581.7099, taille homme 666.7430, prix: 1500 F/226,18 Euros.

Filtre protection accidents chimiques large spectre, grande autonomie//Broad-spectrum large-capacity filter for chemichal impurities.

...scription: cartouche filtrante Giat A2B2E2K2P3 combinée vapeurs organiques, vapeurs acides, dioxyde de soufre, ammo- ...che chimiques large spectre, grande autonomie, combinée vapeurs organiques, gaz et vapeurs inorganiques, vapeurs acides, dioxyde de soufre, ammo- ...que inspiratoire, poussières radiologiques comprises, ne produit pas d'oxygène, poids 370g, modèle plus performant que modèle O, référence:

Filtre protection accidents chimiques large spectre, capacité normale//Normal capacity filter for chemical impurities.

...scription: cartouche filtrante Giat A1B1E1K1P3 à large spectre spécifique, pour aérosols, gaz et vapeurs organiques, gaz et vapeurs inorganiques, ...7226, prix: 365 F/55,04 Euros.

Filtre poussières total (poussières radiologiques comprises)//Dust and particle filter (including radiological dust).

...xyde de soufre, ammoniac, filtre poussières total, ne produit pas d'oxygène, poids 240g, référence: 581.7200, prix: 325 F/49,01 Euros.

...scription: cartouche filtrante Giat P3 pour toutes les poussières, notamment poussières radiologiques, ne produit pas d'oxygène, référence: 581.7102 ...x: 155 F/23,37 Euros.

Description: avertisseur d'incen- ...Legrand, détecteur de fumée ...mestique avec sirène de forte ...ssance (85dB à 1m) et vo- ... lumineux, livré avec pile (9v) ...ccessoires de fixation, diamètre ...5cm, hauteur 3,8cm, référence: 596.5640, prix: 295 F/44,48 Euros.

L. Description: Radiatest Pekly, dé- ...tecteur de radio-activité de poche, alarme sonore et visuelle, très haute sensibilité, poids 150g, dimensions 102x60x26mm, référence:581.5444 prix: 1290 F/194,52 Euros.

...micro ...mo- ...touch ...prix:

...t micro ...Ericsson ...8, 788, ...rix: 329

Tous les équipements de protection dans ces deux pages en 24h chez vous: +80 F/12,06 Euros.

...cendie, ...xyde de ...radioacti- ..., gaz ...monoxide ...etector.

...seur mono- ..., fonctionne ...xe au mur à ...nd, détecte la ...de carbone, ...ence 895.2523, ...Euros.

...ecteur Legrand ...tique (butane, ...ille), signal visuel ...puissance (85dB à ...ecteur 9VDC/220v ...s 120x 60x28mm, ...730 prix: 590 F/88,96

J

L

JE SUIS SEREIN _____

I AM CALM

JE VOIS L'INVISIBLE _____

I SEE THE INVISIBLE

JE SUIS CURIEUSE _____

I AM CURIOUS

JE CONSOMME PEU _____

I USE SPARINGLY

JE SUIS SAGE _____

I AM WISE

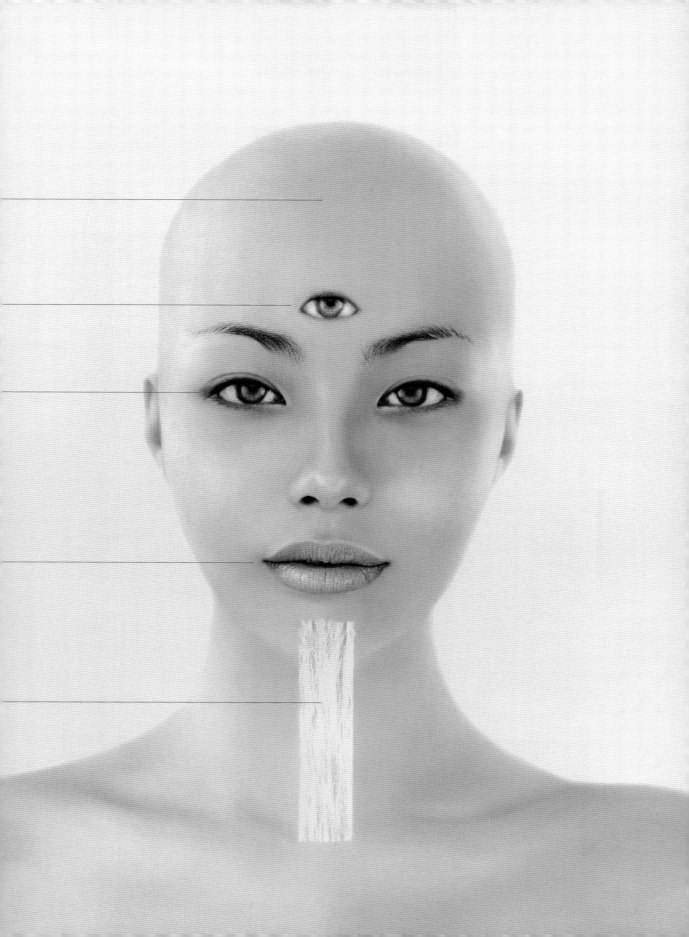

Non-products for non-consumers

One fine day, several million years ago, Ms Cromignonne and Mr Abominet fell in love with their offspring. A new era dawned. Madame strove to protect her infant, Monsieur to improve posterity. Together, the two of them – the pragmatic mother and the idealistic, visionary father – invented the naïve concept of Progress, which was to be expressed chiefly through the creation and manufacture of tools supposed to make our lives easier and even to contribute to our happiness. Much, much later – that is to say, in our times – it became evident that the most generous ideals tend to be the first to degenerate.

Man found himself many a time a slave to the tools he created to serve him. Although there are a few rare objects whose integrity, practicality, and sense of purpose has remained intact, a plethora of others exist only for themselves, without humour, love or fancy. Farewell, dreams of happiness... As I matured, I realized I could try to correct an injustice to which I was myself probably an accomplice.

Being neither a philosopher, nor a sociologist, nor a statesman, and lacking the intelligence to grapple with the problem on theoretical grounds, I decided to be pragmatic.

Grasping the wills and won'ts, the needs and desires of the citizen I would like to have as a friend and neighbour, I attempted to describe the equipment he or she is likely to carry, and maybe, through him or her catch a glimpse of the society in which I would like to see my children and those of my friends growing up. What a vast, pretentious and naive scheme.

I set about trying to find, collect, correct, or create (where necessary) objects which were honest, responsible, and respectful of people. Not necessarily beautiful objects, but good objects.

I soon realized I was facing an impossible task. After research and selection, very few products came up to my stringent standards. Yet, although the ones I approved were still far from my ideal of perfection, they did convey a certain spirit: an alternative direction, a new way of being.

Today, I am able to offer you a catalogue of these objects, a compendium I like to call a catalogue of "non-products for non-consumers." The non-consumer is an individual who is alert and wary, but also open, creative, enthusiastic, and finally extremely upstream and modern.

I hope that as you peruse these objects and the commentaries which accompany them, you will be able to recognize yourself as a member of the free and unincorporated tribe of non-consumers.

Further, I hope that you will be the ones to track down and create objects which, tomorrow morning, will constitute the future of the second compendium, so that, little by little, we can raise this collection to the level of our vision, and that the success of its "moral market", by setting an example, will mark out a new relationship between mankind, tools and their manufacture.

Cromignonne and Abominet could then see their dreams come true, and our children could at last go on new adventures.

To our future mistakes

Non-products are confronted with a grid of requirements based on criteria such as justification for existence, integrity of purpose, longevity, moral elaboration, didacticism, political significance, symbolic social significance, sexual significance, human responsibility, fair cost, fair price, creativity and, sometimes, humour, poetry and respect.

Naturally, none of the objects in this collection is fully satisfactory in each of the above respects. But each one is an endeavour, a mutation, an effort... This annual compendium, by definition immune to the whims of fashion, will therefore grow thicker as the years advance. Since it is impossible to be completely lucid, we shall make further mistakes – our mistakes will be the items which will be taken away from the catalogue. This page will give an account of these mistakes and make them into a constructive experience.

To our futures

This first catalogue is just a means of priming the pump. I am not a professional in mail-order merchandising, and, as a result, this first try is probably too personal. But the catalogue is a means to an end, a tool. You now possess it, put it to work. Take notes, make drawings, snap photos. Describe your needs and your dreams as catalyzed by what appears here. Send us your suggestions and ideas. You can also upload information to the Good Goods catalogue website at www.goodgoods.tm.fr. My mission here is about to end. Now it's up to you to destroy and reconstruct your future. Thank you.

Philippe Starck

Nicht-Produkte für Nicht-Konsumente

Eines schönen Tages, vor einigen Millionen Jahren, verliebten sich Frau Cromignonne und Herr Abominet in ihren Nachwuchs. Ein neues Zeitalter brach an. Madame wollte unbedingt ihr Kin beschützen; Monsieur die Nachwelt verbessern. Zusammen erfanden die beiden – die pragmatische Mutter und der idealistische, visionäre Vate – das naive Konzept des Fortschritts, das hauptsächlich durch die Erschaffung und Herstellung von Geräten zum Ausdruck gebracht wurde, die uns das Leben erleichtern und sogar zu unserem Glück beitragen sollten. Erst viel, viel später – in unserem Zeitalter – zeigte sich, daß die edelster Ideale oft die ersten sind, die zur Degeneration neigen.

Oft mußte der Mensch entdecken, daß er zum Sklaven der Geräte geworden war, die er erfunden hatte, damit sie ihm dienen. Zwar gibt es einige wenige Objekte, deren gute Qualität, Bedienbarkeit und Nützlichkeit erhalten geblieben sind, doch allzu viele andere sind reiner Selbstzweck, ohne Humor, Liebe oder Phantasie. Lebt wohl, Träume vom Glück ... Als ich heranreifte, erkannte ich, daß ich vielleicht ein Unrecht wiedergutmachen könnte, das ich wahrscheinlich selbst mitverschuldet hatte.

Weil ich weder ein Philosoph bin, noch ein Soziologe, noch ein Staatsmann, weil ich nicht intelligent genug bin, das Problem theoretisch anzugehen, beschloß ich, pragmatisch zu handeln. Ich versuchte, die Wünsche und Bedürfnisse me nes Mitbürgers, den ich gerne als Freund und Nachbarn hätte, zu erfassen – das, was er will und was er nicht will – und die Gegenstände zu beschreiben, mit denen er sich umgeben möchte um vielleicht durch ihn hindurch einen Blick auf eine künftige Gesellschaft werfen zu können, in der ich meine Kinder und die meiner Freunde au wachsen sehen möchte. Was für ein gewaltiges, prätentiöses und naives Programm.

Ich bemühte mich also darum, Objekte zu finder zu sammeln, zu verbessern oder (wenn nötig) z gestalten, die den Menschen gegenüber ehrlich, verantwortlich und respektvoll sind. Nicht unbedingt schöne Objekte, aber gute Objekte. Doch schon bald wurde mir bewußt, daß ich mir ein unerreichbares Ziel gesetzt hatte. Nach einem in tensiven Such- und Auswahlprozeß konnten nur sehr wenige Produkte meinen strengen Maßstäben genügen. Und selbst die Produkte, die mein Billigung fanden, waren meilenweit von meinem Ideal der Perfektion entfernt. Dennoch sprach aus ihnen eine gewisse Geisteshaltung, eine alternative Richtung, eine neue Lebensauffassung Heute kann ich Ihnen einen Katalog dieser Objekte anbieten, ein Kompendium, das ich als einen Katalog von »Nicht-Produkten für Nicht-Konsumenten« bezeichnen möchte. Der Nicht-

Konsument ist ein Mensch, der wachsam und argwöhnisch ist, aber auch offen, kreativ, enthusiastisch und schließlich äußerst fortschrittlich und modern. Ich hoffe, daß Sie sich als Mitglied der freien und ungebundenen Gruppe der Nicht-Konsumenten erkennen, wenn Sie sich diese Objekte ansehen und die Begleitkommentare lesen. Außerdem hoffe ich, daß Sie zu denen gehören werden, die weitere Objekte aufspüren und gestalten, so daß wir schon bald ein zweites Kompendium zusammenstellen und diese Sammlung Schritt für Schritt auf das Niveau unserer Vision anheben können. Der beispielgebende Erfolg dieses *moral market* würde ein neues Verhältnis zwischen Menschen, Geräten und ihrer Herstellung deutlich machen. Cromignonne und Abominet könnten dann ihre Träume verwirklicht sehen, und unsere Kinder könnten endlich neue Abenteuer erleben.

Zu unseren künftigen Fehlern

An Nicht-Produkte werden Anforderungen gestellt, die auf Kriterien wie den folgenden beruhen: Existenzberechtigung, Zweckdienlichkeit, Langlebigkeit, moralischer und didaktischer Anspruch, politische Bedeutung, symbolische gesellschaftliche Bedeutung, sexuelle Bedeutung, menschliches Verantwortungsbewußtsein, faire Kosten, faire Preise, Kreativität und manchmal Humor, Poesie und Respekt. Natürlich kann keines der Objekte in dieser Sammlung diesen Kriterien in jeder Hinsicht voll genügen. Aber jedes einzelne stellt eine Bemühung, einen Versuch dar. ... Dieses jährlich erscheinende Kompendium – gegen die Launen der Mode per definitionem immun – wird deshalb Jahr für Jahr umfangreicher werden. Weil immer die Gefahr besteht, daß man sich irrt und täuschen läßt, werden wir auch künftig Fehler machen – unsere Fehler werden die Objekte sein, die aus dem Katalog herausgenommen werden. Auf dieser Seite werden wir über unsere Fehler Rechenschaft ablegen und unsere Lehren daraus ziehen.

Zu unserer Zukunft

Dieser erste Katalog kann nur der Anfang sein. Ich bin kein professioneller Versandhändler, und deshalb ist dieser erste Versuch wahrscheinlich zu persönlich ausgefallen. Doch dieser Katalog ist ein Mittel zum Zweck, ein Werkzeug. Nutzen Sie ihn. Machen Sie Notizen, Zeichnungen, Fotos. Lassen Sie sich von den hier vorgestellten Objekten anregen, und beschreiben Sie Ihre Bedürfnisse und Träume. Schicken Sie uns Ihre Vorschläge und Ideen. Der Good-Goods-Katalog hat auch eine Internet-Adresse: www.goodgoods.tm.fr. Damit ist meine Mission fürs erste beendet. Jetzt liegt es an Ihnen, Ihre Zukunft zu zerstören und wiederaufzubauen. Vielen Dank.

Philippe Starck

Des non-objets pour des non-consommateurs

Un jour, il y a quelques millions d'années, Madame Cromignonne et Monsieur Abominet tombèrent amoureux de leur progéniture. C'était assez nouveau. Madame voulait protéger sa descendance, Monsieur voulait l'améliorer. A eux deux – elle pragmatique, lui théorique et visité – ils inventèrent l'idée naïve du progrès dont l'un des principaux moyens d'expression passa par la création et la production d'outils censés nous apporter une vie meilleure et même du bonheur. Bien plus tard – c'est-à-dire aujourd'hui – on peut s'apercevoir que les jolies idées sont généralement les premières à dégénérer.

L'Homme se retrouva bien souvent esclave d'outils créés pour le servir. Si certains rares objets auront l'honnêteté, la rigueur et le respect de leur mission, une pléthore d'autres ne rouleront que pour eux, sans humour ni amour, ni fantaisie. Adieu, rêves de bonheur. L'âge venant, je me suis dit que j'essaierais bien de corriger une histoire dont j'ai sûrement été moi-même complice.

N'étant pas philosophe, sociologue, politique... ni même assez intelligent pour attaquer le problème sur le plan théorique, j'ai décidé d'être pragmatique.

Par ses acceptations, ses refus, ses souhaits et ses nécessités nécessaires, j'ai tenté de décrire l'équipement du citoyen que j'aimerais avoir comme voisin et ami. Et, peut-être, entrevoir à travers celui-ci la société où j'aimerais voir grandir mes enfants, et les enfants de mes amis.

Vaste, prétentieux et naïf programme.

J'ai donc essayé de trouver, collecter, corriger, ou créer quand il le fallait, des objets honnêtes, responsables, respectueux de la personne. Des objets pas forcément beaux, mais des objets bons.

Je me suis vite aperçu que je m'attaquais à une mission impossible : après recherches et sélections, assez peu d'objets passèrent à travers ma grille d'exigence. De plus, les objets retenus étaient loin d'être aussi parfaits que je l'aurais voulu, mais on pouvait déjà y reconnaître un esprit, une nouvelle direction, une autre façon d'être.

Ces objets, je vous les propose aujourd'hui dans ce catalogue que j'aimerais appeler catalogue des « non-produits pour des non-consommateurs ». Des non-consommateurs conscients et suspicieux, mais aussi ouverts, créatifs, enthousiastes et finalement profondément à contre-courant, modernes.

J'espère qu'à travers ces objets et les commen-

taires qui les accompagnent, vous pourrez vous reconnaître comme membre de la tribu libre et infédérée des non-consommateurs. J'espère aussi que c'est vous qui débusquerez et créerez les objets qui, demain matin, constitueront le futur du deuxième recueil. Afin que, petit à petit, il soit à la hauteur de notre ambition et que, le succès de son *moral market* créant l'exemple, puisse apparaître une nouvelle relation entre l'Homme, la production et les objets.

Cromignonne et Abominet pourraient alors voir leurs rêves se réaliser, et nos enfants repartir – enfin – vers de nouvelles aventures.

A nos futures erreurs

Les non-produits doivent passer à travers une grille d'exigence dont les critères sont, entre autres, légitimité à exister, honnêteté du service, longévité, élaboration morale, didactisme, sens politique, sens de la représentation sociale, sens sexuel, responsabilité humaine, coût juste, prix juste, créativité et quelquefois, poésie, humour et respect.

Evidemment, aucun des objets de ce recueil ne satisfait en totalité aux exigences posées. Mais ils tentent, essaient, commencent. Ce recueil annuel, par définition à l'abri des modes et des démodes, ne fera ainsi que se compléter au fil des ans.

Parce qu'il est difficile de ne pas se laisser séduire, tromper, et de s'abuser soi-même, nous ferons encore des erreurs : nos erreurs seront les produits que nous ferons disparaître de ce recueil. Nous ne jouerons pas de l'oubli et cette page en rendra compte, afin que ces échecs nous soient utiles.

A nos futurs

Ce premier recueil n'est qu'une façon d'« amorcer la pompe ». Je n'ai pas vocation à faire du commerce par correspondance, et, pour cette raison, sa première version est sans doute trop personnelle. Mais ce catalogue n'est qu'un outil. Il est entre vos mains : servez-vous en. Notez, dessinez, photographiez, décrivez et signalez dans ces pages vos rêves, vos préoccupations. Envoyez-nous toutes vos suggestions, vos idées. Vous pouvez également expédier vos informations sur le site Internet du recueil Good Goods, www.goodgoods.tm.fr. Ma mission est ici sur le point de se terminer : c'est à vous qu'il appartient maintenant de détruire et reconstruire votre futur.
Merci.

Philippe Starck

N.C
NO CREATION
NO CHEMICAL

The N.C brand clothing and household linen I am bringing out satisfies two specifications. No Creation is a conscious effort to reject the creative approach. I want to summon up a prototype of a garment or piece of household linen with time-honoured qualities, a prototype already familiar to the collective memory, immune to the vagaries of fashion. No Chemical means that I am producing these goods using natural materials which have not undergone any chemical treatments or processing. The respect we owe the environment is above all respect we owe ourselves as human beings. Our line of N.C cotton garments made in Peru labeled Stop Cocaine Go Organic responds to moral need as well. The growth of organic cotton is been and encouraged by the Peruvian government as an incentive to farmers to quit growing coca (from which cocaine is made) as a cash crop. Currently, the inorganic cotton crop is responsible for 20% of the total pesticides used in agriculture. These chemicals are harmful to human health both in the field and later, when the inorganically grown cotton is in contact with the skin. The Skal (Eko label) attests to the exclusively organic quality of the cotton we use, which is grown and processed without the addition of chemicals. Skal is an international inspection agency recognized by the European Union, and its standards for ecological purity are the most demanding. The same is true for a pure alpaca wool or alpaca-wool blend garments: the quality of the yarns and natural hues (pure alpaca wool in a natural state is available in a wide variety of tints) enables us to offer clothing that is just as good as, if not better than, similar products which have been processed with chemical pollutants. For technical reasons certain N.C garments have not yet been awarded the Eko label from Skal. Nevertheless, they have been made respecting strict ecological standards.

A. **Produit:** Big Baby, **label:** N.C, **description:** grenouillère hiver et demi-saison 70% laine 30% alpaga, jauge 12, certificat Eko (Skal), **références:** noir 520.5298, camel 520.5212, anthracite 520.5220, **tailles:** 1 (S), 2 (M), 4 (XL), 5 (XXL), **prix:** 1290 F/194,52 Euros.

Tous les vêtements N.C des pages 10, 11, 12, 13, **en 24 heures chez vous:** +80F/12,06 Euros.

A

Design: Patricia Bailer, produit: 9 months T-Shirts, label: N.C, fabricant: Bo Weevil, date de conception: 1997, date de production: 1998, description: série de 8 T-Shirts pur coton couleur blanc naturel où est imprimé un fœtus aux différentes étapes de son développement, taille: le T-Shirt est de plus en plus grand pour s'adapter à la morphologie de la femme enceinte, référence: 857.4421, prix: 900 F/135,71 Euros les 8 T-Shirts, en 24h chez vous: +80 F/12,06 Euros.

N.C. Political T-Shirts. L'expérience et la réflexion m'ont conduit à synthétiser quelques conclusions élémentaires.Elles sont devenues de courtes phrase qui appartiennent, à mon sens, au registre de l'évidence. J'ai choisi d'imprimer 8 de ces phrases sur un T-Shirt, un support simple et efficace, pour rappeler à ceux qui les porteront, ou les liront, que nous ne pouvons pas toujours faire l'économie de la responsabilité et de l'action. Le coton de ces T-Shirts est nat cultivé et traité sans produits chimiques ni pesticides, qualité garantie par le label Eko (Skal).

N.C. Political T-Shirts. Experience and contemplation have led me to draw certain basic conclusions. Expressed in the form of short maxims, they belor what I see as the realm of universal wisdom. I have decided to print eight of these statements on a T-Shirt, a simple and direct form of communication, to rer all those who will wear or read them that we cannot always afford the luxury of irresponsibility and inertia. The natural unbleached cotton in these T-Shi grown and processed without chemical additives or pesticides, according to Eko (Skal) standards.

Design: Philippe Starck, **produit:** Political T-Shirts, **label:** N.C, **fabricant:** Bo Weevil, **date de conception:** 1997, **date de production:** 1998, **description:** T-Shirt pur coton blanc naturel, message imprimé en noir, **références:** God is...858.0006, Le civisme...853.7950, Nous n'avons...854.5685, Tomorrow...851.8300, Moral...852.6745, L'amour...851.8866, Nous sommes...851.9609, We are...853.3016, **tailles:** 1 (S), 3 (L), 5 (XXL), **prix:** 150 F/22,62 Euros, **en 24h chez vous:** +80 F/12,06 Euros.

A

B

OAO: nous sommes ce que nous mangeons. L'homme est un écosystème où l'esprit est indissociable du corps et de sa nourriture, dans une relation d'intim[e] interdépendance. S'il est largement admis que l'alimentation a une influence sur la santé du corps, il est tout de même curieux que l'on ne reconnaisse pas aus[si] communément son rôle vis-à-vis de la qualité de la pensée. La gamme de produits OAO est un accès créatif à une nourriture organique moderne. Son intégrit[é] biologique est garantie par le laboratoire Lima Expert, précurseur de l'alimentation organique, qui assure depuis plus de 40 ans une sélection rigoureuse de se[s] aliments biologiques. L'alimentation biologique sera – hélas – une mode, mais elle laissera un acquis important: une nouvelle norme de qualité alimentaire[.] Lorsque l'on peut manger de la nourriture ayant poussé dans un sol non traité aux engrais industriels et n'ayant subi aucun adjuvant chimique, il ne faut pa[s] hésiter. Meilleurs pour la santé, les produits bio nous permettent aussi de retrouver des goûts que l'on avait tendance à oublier. OAO, mangeons intelligent.

OAO: We are what we eat. Man is an ecosystem in which mental synergy is an integral part of the body and its food; a web of intimately interdepender[t] and intertwined processes. Oddly enough, although it seems to be commonly accepted that diet has an influence on physical health, people are reluctan[t] to acknowledge its impact upon mental energy. The OAO product line is a creative approach to modern organic self-care. Its biological integrity has bee[n] tested by Lima Expert laboratories, foundation-layers for quality health foods. For over 40 years, Lima has been setting standards for organically grow[n] naturally processed foods. Unfortunately the "health-food craze" will turn out to be a mere passing fad. But it will have left an imprint on the way we eva[l]-uate what we eat. When it is possible to obtain products free of any chemical additives, which have been grown in soil uncontaminated by industrial fe[r]-tilizers, we should not hesitate. You will find that organic foods are not only healthier, they are tastier as well. OAO, eat smart.

A. Produit: huile d'olive Sei Colli OAO, **partenaire:** Lima Expert, **description:** huile à base d'olives issues de l'agriculture biologique récoltées à la main[,] première pression à froid, **contenance:** 1 x 75cl, **référence:** 968.3577, **prix:** 99 F/14,93 Euros (prix au litre 132 F/l - 19,91 Euros/l).

B. Produit: huile d'olive San Vito OAO, **partenaire:** Lima Expert, **description:** huile à base d'olives issues de l'agriculture biologique récoltées à la main[,] première pression à froid, plus rare et délicate que la Sei Colli, **contenance:** 1 x 75cl, **référence:** 968.3585, **prix:** 119 F/17,94 Euros (prix au litr[e] 159 F/l - 23,98 Euros/l).

C

C. Produit: riz thaï mi-complet OAO, **partenaire:** Lima Expert, **description:** riz thaï mi-complet issu de l'agriculture biologique, **poids:** 6 boîtes x 500g, **référence:** 956.3954, **prix:** 89 F/13,42 Euros (prix au kilo 29,67 F/kg - 4,47 Euros/kg).

D

D. Produit: riz basmati complet OAO, **partenaire:** Lima Expert, **description:** riz basmati complet issu de l'agriculture biologique, **poids:** 6 boîtes x 500g, **référence:** 956.3717, **prix:** 89 F/13,42 Euros (prix au kilo 29,67 F/kg - 4,47 Euros/kg).

E

E. Produit: spaghetti mi-complets OAO, **partenaire:** Lima Expert, **description:** spaghetti mi-complets issu de l'agriculture biologique, **poids:** 12 boîtes x 500g, **référence:** 956.4187, **prix:** 119 F/17,94 Euros (prix au kilo 19,83 F/kg - 2,99 Euros/kg).

F

F. Produit: pâtes semini mi-completes OAO, **partenaire:** Lima Expert, **description:** pâtes semini, à base de blé dur semi-complet issu de l'agriculture biologique, **poids:** 12 boîtes x 500g, **référence:** 956.7747, **prix:** 119 F/17,94 Euros (prix au kilo 19,83 F/kg - 2,99 Euros/kg).

G

G. Produit: sel de s´same OAO, **partenaire:** Lima Expert, **description:** condiment à base de graines de sésame grillées issues de l'agriculture biologique et de sel marin, **poids:** 6 pots x 100g, **référence:** 956.6746, **prix:** 75 F/11,31 Euros (prix au kilo 125 F/kg - 18,85 Euros/kg).

H

H. Produit: sel marin OAO, **partenaire:** Lima Expert, **description:** sel marin récolté à Noirmoutier, **poids:** 6 x 200g, **référence:** 968.5529, **prix:** 59 F/8,90 Euros (prix au kilo 49,17 F/kg - 7,42 Euros/kg).

I. Produit: poivre noir en grains OAO, **description:** poivre noir de Madagascar issu de l'agriculture biologique, **poids:** 6 pots x 80g, **référence:** 969.3335, **prix:** 75 F/11,31 Euros (prix au kilo 156,25 F/kg - 23,56 Euros/kg).

I

E. **Gel nettoyant moussant Starck with Bioderma™.** Très doux (sans savon), émollient et filmogène, il permet le nettoyage efficace du visage et du corps tout en évitant le dessèchement et la fragilisation. Il est adapté à tous les types de peaux (homme, femme, enfant), ne pique pas les yeux et peut même être utilisé comme shampooing pour les très jeunes enfants ou les nourrissons. Sans parfum.

Starck with Bioderma™ foaming cleansing gel. This extremely mild, detergent-free gel cleans the face and body without dehydrating and leaves the skin with a silky glow. It is safe for people of all ages, even children, does not sting the eyes, and can be used even as a shampoo for infants or very young children. Fragrance free.

Produit: gel nettoyant moussant Starck with Bioderma™, **description:** flacon-pompe 250ml, **référence:** 689.1934, **prix:** 85 F/12,82 Euros (34 F/dl – 5,13 Euros/dl).

Tous les Starck with Bioderma **en 24h chez vous:** +80 F/12,06 Euros.

E. **Ginseng+++ Starck with Europ-Labo.** Complexe fortifiant, dynamisant et stimulant général de l'organisme, tant sur un plan physique que psychique. Un concentré de substances naturellement prodigieuses: ginseng, guarana, gelée royale et lécithine de soja.

Starck with Europ-Labo ginseng+++. A complex which fortifies, energizes, and stimulates the organism, on both a psychic and physical level. It is a concentration of naturally powerful substances: ginseng, guarana, royal jelly, lecithin.

Produit: Ginseng+++ Starck with Europ-Labo, **contenance:** 55 gélules, **référence:** 701.6140, **prix:** 95 F/14,32 Euros, **en 24h chez vous:** +80F/12,06 Euros.

F. **Gélules de propolis Starck with Europ-Labo.** Tonique général et revitalisant. Riche en flavonoïdes, en essences et en acides naturels, elle est un remarquable soutien pour stimuler les défenses naturelles, lutter efficacement contre les agressions extérieures et favoriser la résistance cellulaire et la vitalité de l'organisme.

Starck with Europ-Labo propolis capsules. Propolis, a general revitaling tonic, rich in bioflavinoids, essences and natural acids. Propolis boosts the body's resistance to disease, arms it against outside agression, and promotes the organism's vitality and cellular resilience.

Produit: Gélules de propolis Starck with Europ-Labo, **contenance:** 75 gélules, **référence:** 705.4980, **prix:** 65 F/9,80 Euros, **en 24h chez vous:** +80F/12,06 Euros.

G. **Gelée royale fraîche Starck w** Labo. Reconstituant et stimulant, défenses naturelles de l'organisme. tre des éléments vitaux et convient Particulièrement recommandée aux périodes de croissance, aux convale personnes âgées, aux personnes stressées, déprimées.

Starck with Europ-Labo fresh ro tonic and stimulant, it reinforces the ral defenses. This concentrate of vitali beneficial to people of all ages, bu cially recommended for young pe growth spurts, convalescents, elde and anyone who feels tired, depressi ject to stress.

Produit: Gelée royale fraîche Starck Labo, **contenance:** 65 capsules, 704.4496, **prix:** 95 F/14,32 Euros, **e** vous: +80F/12,06 Euros.

H. **Gel d'aloes Starck with Europ-Labo.** Gel hydratant*. L'aloe vera, ou aloès, est une plante grasse des régions chaudes et arides qui renferm feuilles un suc amer utilisé depuis l'Antiquité pour ses vertus médicinales. Gel cosmétique qui convient à toutes les peaux, particulièrement re en cas de fragilité cutanée, en cas d'irritations, de piqûres d'insectes, d'exposition au soleil. Il aide la peau à retrouver élasticité et souplesse en sensation de fraîcheur. Propriétés apaisantes et cicatrisantes. Bénéfique après le rasage. *Hydratation des couches supérieures de l'épiderme.

Starck with Europ-Labo aloe vera gel. A moisturizing gel*. Aloe Vera is a succulent plant which grows in hot, arid regions. Its leaves contain a which has been used for medicinal purposes since Antiquity. This gel treatment is suitable for all skin types, and is especially recommended for skin irritation due to chapping, insect bites, sunburn, or windburn. It restores the skin's elasticity and softness leaving a refreshing feeling. Healin properties. A good after shave treatment. *Moisturization of the skin's outer layer.

Produit: Gel d'aloes Starck with Europ-Labo, **contenance:** 50ml, **référence:** 739.5205, **prix:** 45 F/6,79 Euros (prix au décilitre: 90F/dl), **en 24h** +80F/12,06 Euros.

Starck with Bioderma™. La gamme Starck with Bioderma™ est le résultat de ma rencontre avec Annie Vinche, à la tête du laboratoire Bioderma™. Une scientifique rare, animée d'un authentique sentiment humaniste. Je suis sensible aux mêmes priorités, mais malheureusement tout à fait dénué de talents dermatologiques. Depuis longtemps utilisateur de ses produits, j'ai décidé de créer avec elle une gamme de soins préventifs essentiels et simples. Essentiels: indispensables quotidiennement, sans parfum ajouté qui pourrait dénaturer l'odeur originelle de la peau. Simples: d'utilisation aisée, contenant un minimum d'ingrédients, d'une présentation honnête et pratique. L'épiderme est soumis à des agressions multiples (pollution, soleil, vent, froid, chauffage...) responsables de la sécheresse qui fragilise la peau et entraîne un vieillissement prématuré. Adaptés à tous les types de peaux et de cheveux, les produits de la gamme Starck with Bioderma™ respectent leur structure et reconstituent le film hydrolipidique qui les protège. Les composants, soigneusement limités en nombre, ont été choisis afin de minimaliser les risques allergiques. Leur efficacité et leur haute tolérance ont été testées en milieu hospitalier dermatologique.

Starck with Bioderma™. This range is the result of my encounter with Annie Vinche, head of Bioderma™ Laboratories. She is an exceptional scientist, inspired by genuinely humanistic motivations. Although I am driven by the same prerogatives, I am forced to admit that I lack the dermatological talents. As a longtime user of Bioderma™ products, I decided to create, with her, a line of essential, preventive skin care products, an indispensable daily routine without artificial perfumes liable to mask the skin's natural fragrance. Simple products, easy to use, containing few ingredients and packaged in an honest, practical manner. Skin is subjected to a variety of attacks from pollution, sun, wind, cold, central heating and so on, leading to dehydration and premature ageing of the skin. Adapted to all skin and hair types, Starck with Bioderma™ products respect the epidermal structure and restore the hydrolipidic film which protects it. The ingredients, carefully screened down to a bare minimum, have been chosen for their hypoallergenic properties. Their effectiveness and safety have been clinically tested.

A. **Produit:** muesli aux fruits OAO, **partenaire:** Lima Expert, **description:** mélange équilibré à base de fruits et de noix (raisins secs, noisettes, pommes sèches), épeautre (céréale à valeur nutritive élevée), pétales de maïs et Sarrasin, issus de l'agriculture biologique, **poids:** 6 boîtes x 375g, **référence:** 958.9708, **prix:** 129 F/19,45 Euros (prix au kilo 57,33 F/kg - 8,64 Euros/kg).

B. **Produit:** galettes multicéréales OAO, **partenaire:** Lima Expert, **description:** galettes à base de riz et de céréales mélangées issus de l'agriculture biologique, **poids:** 12 paquets x 100g, **référence:** 968.0578, **prix:** 75 F/11,31 Euros (prix au kilo 62,50 F/kg - 9,42 Euros/kg).

C. **Produit:** sirop de blé OAO, **partenaire:** Lima Expert, **description:** sirop de blé (sucres lents) issu de l'agriculture biologique, pour sucrer les aliments, les boissons, ou à tartiner, **contenance:** 6 flacons x 420g, **référence:** 969.6083, **prix:** 119 F/17,94 Euros (prix au kilo 42,22 F/kg - 7,12 Euros/kg).

D. **Produit:** lait d'avoine et de riz OAO, **partenaire:** Lima Expert, **description:** boisson rafraîchissante végétale à base d'avoine et de riz complet issus de l'agriculture biologique, aromatisée à la vanille, substitut idéal, froid ou chaud, du lait ou du filtrat de soja, **contenance:** 12 briques x 1l, **référence:** 967.8670, **prix:** 169 F/25,48 Euros (prix au litre 14,08 F/l - 8,12 Euros/l).

E. **Produit:** biscuits aux céréales et éclats de chocolat OAO, **partenaire:** Lima Expert, **description:** biscuits préparés à base de céréales (flocons d'avoine, de maïs) et de cacao issus de l'agriculture biologique, **poids:** 14 paquets x 150g, **référence:** 968.0934, **prix:** 189 F/ 28,50 Euros (prix au kilo 90 F/kg - 13,57 Euros/kg).

F. **Produit:** pâte à tartiner aux noisettes OAO, **partenaire:** Lima Expert, **description:** à base de noisettes sélectionnées issues de l'agriculture biologique, **poids:** 6 pots x 250g, **référence:** 970.0552, **prix:** 169 F/ 25,48 Euros (prix au kilo 112,67 F/kg - 16,99 Euros/kg).
G. **Produit:** pâte à tartiner au chocolat OAO, **description:** goût exceptionnel, à base de noisettes et de cacao issus de l'agriculture biologique, **poids:** 6 pots x 250g, **référence:** 970.0560, **prix:** 219 F/ 33,02 Euros (prix au kilo 146 F/kg - 22,01 Euros/kg).

Champagne. Depuis 1992, Jean-Pierre Fleury cultive l'ensemble de son vignoble en bio-dynamie: un choix de culture qui respecte l'écosystème et e totalement les engrais industriels, remplacés par des traitements à base végétale et minérale. Initiée par Jean-Pierre Fleury et son ami Poirrier, cette profondément moderne fait appel au respect, à l'honnêteté et à l'amour de la personne qui consommera ce produit. Outre son goût plus authentique pagne est le prototype des nouveaux rapports qu'il est possible d'entretenir avec la production, son environnement, et soi-même. Consommé avec m c'est un grande source de bonheur. Produit sur une petite surface, ce champagne biologique n'est malheureusement proposé qu'en série limitée et n

Champagne. In 1992, Jean-Pierre Fleury converted his entire vineyard to biodynamic farming techniques. This venture respects the ecosystem by the usual industrial fertilizers and pesticides, and using plant- and mineral-based treatments instead. Initiated by Jean-Pierre Fleury and his friend Poirrier foundly modern approach based on an appeal to the integrity, honesty, and discernment of the people who will later consume the product. This chan only tastes more genuine, it is also a model for the new synergy developing between production techniques, nature, and the soil: imbibed in moder great source of pleasure. However, because this organic champagne is grown in small quantities, it is available only as a limited edition of numbered bo

H. **Produit:** Champagne Jean-Pierre Fleury, sélectionné par OAO, **partenaire:** Lima Expert, **description:** Champagne brut issu de raisins de l' biologique, mis en bouteille au domaine, **contenance:** 75cl, **référence:** 970.8057, **prix:** 200 F/30,16 Euros (prix au litre 266,67 F/l - 40,21 Euros

I. **Produit:** Château Jarr 1997 OAO, **partenaire:** Lima Expert, **description:** Bordeaux blanc sec, issu de raisins de l'agriculture biologique, appell trôlée, produit et mis en bouteille au domaine, **contenance:** 75cl, **référence:** 970.7603, **prix:** 59 F/8,90 Euros (prix au litre 78,67 F/l - 11,87 Euro
J. **Produit:** Château le Barradis 1995 OAO, **partenaire:** Lima Expert, **description:** Côtes de Bergerac rouge, appellation contrôlée, vin issu de l'agriculture biologique, mis en bouteille au château, **contenance:** 75cl, **référence:** 970.3713, **prix:** 89 F/13,42 Euros (prix au litre 118,67 F/l - 17,8
K. **Produit:** Domaine de Barbarossa 1997 OAO, **partenaire:** Lima Expert, **description:** vin de Corse rouge issu de raisins de l'agriculture biologique lation contrôlée, mis en bouteille au domaine, **contenance:** 75cl, **référence:** 970.0692, **prix:** 59 F/8,90 Euros (prix au litre 78,67 F/l - 11,87 Euros
L. **Produit:** Domaine de Coulée 1997 OAO, **partenaire:** Lima Expert, **description:** Chardonnay, vin blanc de pays de la Hte vallée de l'Aude, issu de l'agriculture biologique, mis en bouteille au domaine, **contenance:** 75cl, **référence:** 970.7891, **prix:** 69 F/10,40 Euros (prix au litre 92 F/l - 13,87 Eu

Tous les produits alimentaires des pages 6 à 9 **en 24h chez vous:** +99 F/14

L'abus d'alcool est dangereux pour la santé, consommez avec modération.

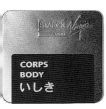

CD **Thème Starck with Virgin.** J'ai eu le bonheur de naître dans la musique, et de pouvoir continuer à y vivre. Elle est certainement l'un des éléments qui influe le plus sur mon travail créatif. J'ai toujours une mélodie dans la tête. J'aime avant tout le son, quelle que soit sa nature, sa culture ou son époque, pour la diversité des émotions fondamentales auxquelles il donne accès. En recueillant dans quatre disques les compositions musicales pour lesquelles j'ai le plus de gratitude, j'ai voulu transmettre différents sentiments, correspondants à des moments et des envies distincts de l'existence de chacun. Ces quatre disques marquent le début d'une collection qui se prolongera dans notre catalogue suivant, avec de nouveaux enthousiasmes. Je veux aussi remercier ici tous les artistes et les maisons de disques qui ont accepté de nous céder leurs titres pour ces quatre compilations. Sans eux et leur musique, je ne serais rien. Starck with Virgin theme CD. It was my good fortune to be born musically, and to have been able to continue my life that way. There's always a tune dancing through my mind, and I'm sure this is one of the most significant elements influencing my creative work. Above all, I love sound, regardless of its cultural or epochal source, for the simple reason that it opens the listener to such a broad spectrum of emotions. My purpose in assembling these four records of musical compositions to which I owe the most gratitude, is to convey the various feelings which resonate within all of us at distinct moments in our individual experience. These four discs are the starting point of a collection which will expand as new enthusiasms are added in the catalogue to follow. I would like to thank all the artists and recording companies who were willing to participate in putting together these four anthologies. Without them and their music, I would be nothing.

A. Conscience – nous rappeler que tout est politique, que des artistes se préoccupent toujours de militantisme et d'engagement//Conscience – reminding us that every act is political, that artists draw their inspiration from a commitment to an ideal.
Conscience*: Patti Smith (People Have the Power), Curtis Mayfield (New World Order), Pato Banton (Pato Banton 's Opinion PT2), Carlos Puebla (Hasta Siempre - Che Guevara), Lou Reed (Swords of Damocles), John Lennon (Instant Karma), David Bowie (Heroes), Leslie Winner (John Says), Latcho Drom (Balada Conducatoruili), Ben Harper (Oppression), P.I L (Acid Drop), Pascal Comelade (La Bella Ciao)...
Produit: CD Thème Conscience Starck with Virgin, référence: 592.3875, prix: 149 F/ 22,47 Euros.

B. Tête – une aide à la concentration et au rêve//Mind – the seat of concentration and reverie.
Tête*: Hiroshi Fujiwara (Hard Boiled Dub), Alpha (My Things), Robert Wyatt (Maryan), Michael Nyman (The Promise), Marianne Faithfull (Sleep), Philip Glass (Secret Agent), David Byrne/Brian Eno (Regiment), Nusrat Fateh Ali Khan/Michael Brook (Lament, extrait de Night Song), Moon Dog (Bird's Lament), Lou Reed/John Cale (A Dream), Laurie Anderson (The Night Flight From Houston), Pascal Comelade (Oh Caroline).
Produit: CD Thème Tête Starck with Virgin, référence: 592.3867, prix: 149 F/ 22,47 Euros.

C. Cœur – l'intention de vous faire pleurer comme une midinette, à chaque note et sans scrupules//Heart – urging us to sob like overwrought teenyboppers at each note, unashamedly.
Cœur*: Robert Wyatt (Sea Song), The Velvet Underground with Nico (Femme Fatale), Lou Reed & John Cale (Hello It's Me), Nilsson (Everybody's Talkin' – B.O. Midnight Cowboy), PJ Harvey/Pascal Comelade (Love Too Soon), Lou Reed (Street Hassle), Nusrat Fateh Ali Khan (Yeh Jo Halka Saroor Sae), Marianne Faithful (Times Square), Manna (Who Changed The Order), Nico Faquito (Al Veiven De Mi Carreta), Bonga (Mona ki n'Gixica), Pascal Comelade (Ti Amo)...
Produit: CD Thème Cœur Starck with Virgin, référence: 592.2950, prix: 149 F/ 22,47 Euros.

D. Corps – sans préjugés culturels, son seul but est de faire bouger. Un caillou n'y résisterait pas//Body – free of cultural bias, its single goal is to bring about motion. A pebble would not, could not, remain inert.
Corps*: Liquid Liquid (Cavern), L'orchestre National de Barbès (Alaoui), Dillinger (Funky Punk), Billy Idol (Dancin'with Myself), Urban Dance Squad (Deeper Shade Of Soul), Lou Reed (Sweet Jane), U-Roy (Jah Son Of Africa), P.I.L (Warrior), Iggy Pop (NightClubbing), The Fun Lovin' Criminals (Fun Lovin' Criminals), Paul Simon (The Obvious Child), Waldeck (Wake Up), Manna (Hoggin 'A' Dub), Pascal Comelade (Rock Del Veneno)...
Produit: CD Thème Corps Starck with Virgin, référence: 592.3859, prix: 149 F/ 22,47 Euros.

*Liste des titres provisoire, sous réserve de l'accord des ayants-droit.

A

Amin Zaoui

Je raconte à Hélène

...vaisselle concentré Starck with Ecover. Il serait inconséquent de croire que la nature puisse tirer profit d'un liquide vaisselle, comme elle le fait ...ou des fourmis. Mais puisque nous ne pouvons pas encore nous passer de détergents, la politesse minimale est de chercher sérieusement à li... ...gâts. Les détergents entraînent notamment une modification de la tension superficielle de l'eau, ce qui leur permet de nettoyer facilement, mais ...uelle l'asphyxie des insectes, de la faune et de la flore aquatiques. Comme si, pour l'homme, l'air était brusquement remplacé par de l'eau. La ...selle Starck with Ecover est efficace, mais il s'emploie à rétablir aussi vite que possible la tension superficielle de l'eau par l'utilisation de com... ...urels et de combinaisons chimiques plus élémentaires. Notre responsabilité ne doit pas s'arrêter au bouchon de l'évier.
... Ecover concentrated dishwashing liquid. It would be naïve to believe that the ecosystem could benefit from a dishwashing liquid the way it ...trees or ants. But since we human parts still require clean utensils, the least we can do is limit the damage we wreak in pursuit of hygiene. The ...gents alter the surface tension of the water to promote cleaning, which, in passing, asphyxiates insects, the aquatic fauna and flora, as if, with... ...the air we breathe became water. Concentrated dishwashing liquid Starck with Ecover is efficient, but it also restores natural water surface ten... ...kly as possible, by using natural components and elementary chemical compounds. Our responsibilities will not go well beyond the sink drain.
...uide vaisselle concentré Starck with Ecover, description: flacon-pompe 250ml, référence: 540.5718, prix: 45 F/6,79 Euros (180 F/l - 27,16 Euros/l)

...ssant en poudre Starck with Ecover. Ce blanchissant en poudre s'utilise pour les textiles blancs en complément de la lessive Starck with Ecover. ...ni azurants optiques, il respecte la peau. La compatibilité dermatologique de tous les produits Starck with Ecover est maximale.
... Ecover whitening additive. This powdered whitener can be added to white loads in conjunction with Starck detergent with Ecover. Free of ...eners and bleach, it respects the skin. All Starck products with Ecover display maximal dermatological compatibility.
...anchissant en poudre Starck with Ecover, description: 250g x 2, référence: 540.6706, prix: 30 F/4,52 Euros le lot de 2 boîtes (60 F/kg - ...kg)

B

C

UN DÉTERGENT BON POUR L'HOMME! Les tablettes pour lave-vaisselle ECOVER sont sans phosphates et sans chlore. [...]

STARCK WITH ECOVER TABLETTES POUR LAVE-VAISSELLE

...es pour lave-vaisselle Starck with Ecover. Les tablettes pour lave-vaisselle Starck with Ecover sont sans phosphates et sans chlore. Au lieu des ...s pétrochimiques classiquement employés, Ecover choisit des matières premières organiques, végétales ou minérales, renouvelables (ici, des ...dérivés du sucre). Ecover recherche la meilleure dégradabilité finale, et non la biodégradabilité primaire telle que définie par la loi, qui est insuf... ...tests sont le plus souvent effectués par les fabricants de détergents classiques dans une eau à 20 degrés, sur des bactéries "professionnelles" ...aux détergents, donc dans des conditions très éloignées d'une situation authentique. La dégradation secondaire, préférée ici, s'attache à ce que ...uisse faire disparaître plus facilement tous les éléments nuisibles encore présents après la perte du pouvoir lavant des produits détergents.
... Ecover tablets for automatic dishwashers. These dishwashing tablets are free of phosphates and bleach. Instead of the petrochemical com... ...nally found in such products. Ecover opts for organic raw materials from renewable plant or mineral sources (in this case, detergents derived from ...ver is formulated to achieve the best final biodegradability, instead of the primary biodegradability as defined by law, which is insufficient. In ...re usually conducted by manufacturers of conventional detergents at water temperatures of 70 degrees Fahrenheit, on "professional" bacteria ...detergent. These simulated conditions thus bear little resemblance to real-life situations. The purpose of measuring secondary degradation, as ...make it easier for nature to eliminate all the harmful elements which linger after the detergent has exhausted its washing power.
...lettes pour lave-vaisselle Starck with Ecover, description: 25 pastilles x 20g, référence: 746.7087, prix: 75 F/11,31 Euros (150 F/kg - 22,62 Euros/kg).

A. Diluant Starck with Biofa. Produit diluant à base d'essences naturelles (écorces d'agrumes et minérales). Il permet de diluer la laque et de nettoyer les instruments et pinceaux ayant été en contact avec laques et vernis, sans entraîner de dommages pour la santé et l'environnement. Les matières premières organiques et minérales des produits Starck with Biofa se décomposent rapidement dans le milieu naturel en éléments inoffensifs. Ce diluant accomplit même la prouesse de sentir naturellement bon.
Starck with Biofa thinner. A paint thinner made of natural essences (minerals and citrus peels). It is designed to thin varnish and clean brushes and rollers which have been used to apply varnish and gloss, with no adverse effects on health or the environment. The organic and mineral raw materials used in the Starck Biofa product line break down rapidly as products harmless to the natural environment. Moreover, this thinner even passes the odor test with flying colors.
Produit: diluant Starck with Biofa, contenance: 0,75l, référence: 532.2626, prix: 45 F/6,79 Euros (prix au litre : 60 F/l / 9,05 Euros), en 24h chez vous: +149 F/22,47 Euros.

B. Laque Starck with Biofa. Laque satinée pour la protection et la décoration du bois, du plâtre et des métaux. Les peintures de cette gamme offrent un niveau d'efficacité comparable, sinon supérieur, aux peintures à composants pétrochimiques: rendement élevé, odeur agréable, qualité de couleurs et sont sans danger pour la santé. Elles ont en revanche un temps de séchage partiellement plus long. Les peintures naturelles Starck with Biofa, en remplissant parfaitement leurs fonctions, sans polluer ni l'homme ni la nature, démontrent qu'un produit efficace n'est pas nécessairement nocif. Le nécessaire respect de l'environnement est d'abord respect de l'homme.
Starck with Biofa varnish. Satin-finish varnish for the protection and decoration of wood, plaster, and metal surfaces. The varnishes in this range display performances equal to or even greater than those available with petrochemical-based paints: high yield, pleasant odour, and colour quality, while presenting absolutely no health hazard. They merely require slightly longer drying times. Starck natural paints with Biofa fulfill their purpose admirably without damaging either the environment or human beings. A product does not have to be harmful to be effective.
Produit: laque Starck with Biofa, contenance: 0,75l, références: voir en page 45, références 31 à 35 prix: 95 F/14,32 Euros (prix au litre : 126,67 F/l / 19,09 Euros), en 24h chez vous: +149F/22,47 Euros.

C. Peinture Starck with Biofa. Peinture murale naturelle, satinée, diluable à l'eau, sans solvant. A la différence des peintures classiques elle ne contient pas de substances chimiques (solvants notamment) susceptibles d'avoir des incidences sur la santé. Le Toluol (benzène méthylique), classiquement utilisé dans les peintures, peut entraîner une pollution des habitats 5 fois plus élevée que dans la rue. Les composants naturels (matières premières organiques et minérales) des peintures Starck with Biofa respectent la santé de l'homme. Cette gamme de couleur exclusive est une proposition fondée sur l'une de mes compétences majeures: la maîtrise du sens et des implications physiologiques des couleurs. Mais ce n'est qu'un conseil, certainement pas une directive de décorateur.
Starck with Biofa paint. Natural, water-soluble, satin-finish emulsion wall paint. Unlike conventional paints, it contains none of the chemical solvents or substances which are liable to manifest their toxicity to the human organism. Toluene, the methyl benzene ordinarily used in paint, can raise the pollution level in the private dwelling to nearly fivefold the level in the street. The natural components used to manufacture the Starck with Biofa paints (raw materials from mineral and organic sources) respect human health. The exclusive colour range is a suggestion based on one of my most highly developed skills, an expertise in the meaning and physiological implications of colors. However, it is meant to be taken only as advice and not as a decorator's edict.
Produit: peinture Starck with Biofa, références: voir en page 45, références 1 à 30 prix: 1l - 55 F/8,29 Euros, 4l - 195 F/29,40 Euros, 10l - 450 F/67,85 Euros, en 24h chez vous: +149 F/22,47 Euros.

A

Wet Elegance Starck with K-Way. La ligne Wet Elegance est conçue pour rendre un pur service, mais de façon différente. Il m'a semblé en effet remarqu une malédiction du vêtement "de sport", ayant la triste destinée de polluer les paysages avec des couleurs offensantes. Le "fun" ne m'a jamais fait rire. Il m semblé aussi possible que nécessaire de proposer des vêtements parfaitement fonctionnels, mais dans un autre registre, se référant plutôt à une élégan urbaine et moderne. Wet Elegance est une ligne au dessin classique, "nettoyé", d'un prix abordable, ayant les mêmes compétences pratiques que ses équiv lents: légereté, imperméabilité, coupe-vent. Une matière de synthèse est, pour le moment, seule en mesure de satisfaire à ces critères. Avec K-Way, marq emblématique, inventeur du coupe-vent, nous avons développé un tissu à reflets changeants, à la fois imperméable, respirant, et facile d'entretien. Nous sommes pas condamnés à la vulgarité.

Starck with K-Way Wet Elegance. The Wet Elegance line was embarked upon to right a long-neglected wrong. I must not be the only one to have noticed th casual clothing is beset by a curse, compelling it to pollute the scenery with offensive colors. Garish hues have never amused me. I also felt it was both pos ble and necessary to make available completely functional clothing which takes its cue from an urban, modern concept of elegance. Wet Elegance is chara terized by purity and classicism, at an affordable price range and with the same practical virtues as its peers: lightweight, waterproof, a windbreaker. Synthe fibres are the only choice which fulfills these criteria at the moment. Working with K-Way, whose name is synonymous with windbreakers in France, we ha developed a waterproof, air permeable fabric with a wet look finish, easy to maintain. We are not doomed to vulgarity.

Design: Philippe Starck, **produits:** ligne Wet Elegance Starck with K-Way, **fabricant:** K-Way, **date de conception:** 1997, **date de production:** 199
A. Produit: Wet Lord Starck with K-Way, **description:** veste imperméable coupe-vent, trois boutons, mixte, trois poches passepoilées dont une poitrine, c
fermé par bouton-pression, capuche, fournitures métal hypoallergeniques, composition 60% polyamide, 40% polyester, **références:** ext. gris/int. jau
808.3096, ext. anthracite/ int.gris 808.3827, **tailles:** 1 (S), 2 (M), 4 (XL), 5 (XXL), **prix:** 790 F/119,12 Euros.

Tous les Starck with K-Way en 24h chez vous: +80 F/ 12,06 Euro

ayak Starck with Rotomod. Dans le sport, on est passé du trois mâts à la planche à voile, de l'automobile aux patins à roulettes, de la paire de ski au mono-
:i. Cette marche vers le minimum est l'évidence d'un progrès. Mais en même temps qu'ils se réduisaient, beaucoup de ces objets voyaient leur difficulté
emploi augmenter. Quoi de plus beau qu'un surfer dans les vagues? Quoi de plus difficile aussi? Ce mouvement de simplification a récemment touché le
ayak. Avec la nouvelle génération "seat-on-top" – double avantage de ne plus enserrer la taille et d'être équipé d'un cockpit autovideur – les néophytes peu-
ent se permettre l'exploration du milieu aquatique en toute sécurité. Avec Rotomod, l'un des meilleurs fabricants du marché, nous avons décidé de ne pas
écorer ce kayak de la trop commune panoplie de fluorescences: elles le transforment en injure visuelle, en contradiction avec l'intimité vis-à-vis du milieu
aturel qu'il permet. Equilibré, très résistant, facile d'utilisation, d'un prix abordable, assez léger pour être porté sur l'épaule ou sur le toit d'une voiture.
ayak Starck with Rotomod. From the galleon to the windsurfer, from the automobile to the roller skate, from the ski to the snowboard: obviously, the
ture of transportation lies in minimalization. But many of these conveyances require greater skill to pilot as they are pared down to the bare essentials. A
irfer riding a wave is a thrilling sight, but not all of us can accomplish this feat. Recently, the kayak has also been simplified, and as a result the new seat-
n-top generation is easier to paddle than its ancestors – the waist is no longer confined and the cockpit is self-draining. Neophytes can now explore the
quatic world safely. Rotomod, one of the leading manufacturers on the market, consented to forego decorating this model with the usual dayglo palette
at I find so displeasing. The kayak should blend in with the natural environment as the first step towards leading you to become acquain-ted with it. Sturdy,
alanced, and easy to paddle: it is well priced and lightweight enough to be carried on one shoulder or on a car roof.
roduit: Kayak Starck with Rotomod, fabricant: Rotomod, description: kayak multi-usage (en mer, rivière et torrent), insubmersible, autovideur (évacua-
ɔn automatique de l'eau par 4 trous de vidange), siège réglable, cale-pieds intégrés, maniable et stable (coque type "aile de mouette", étravée sur toute
longueur), léger (18kg), empilable, cadenassable, sans entretien (P.E haute-densité, traité anti-UV), recyclable, livré avec pagaies, dimensions
80x0,78x0,34m, référence: 675.1784, prix: 3500 F/527,76 Euros, en 24h chez vous: +299 F/45,09 Euros.

A. TeddyBearBand. La mutiplication des jouets me paraît favoriser l'infidélité: l'enfant ne s'attache en définitive à aucun, zappant de l'un à l'autre d'auta
plus vite que les jouets sont nombreux. Il n'y a pas de raison pour que, plus tard, il se comporte différemment avec les gens, ami ou amant. Partisan d
amour unique, j'ai rêvé d'un jouet unique, une sorte d'entraînement à un attachement durable. Jouet surréaliste, TeddyBearBand fait aussi appel à l'ima
nation, bien plus loin que le simple ours en peluche. Il permet de placer l'amour et l'amitié en dehors du champ de la consommation.

TeddyBearBand. In my opinion, an overabundance of toys fosters infidelity. Instead of forming a lasting attachment to one toy, the child flits ever fas
from one to another, the greater the number of toys, the more frantic the pace. There is no reason that, later on, he or she should treat people, a friend
a lover any differently. As an advocate of the one-true-love approach, I dreamt of a single toy that would serve as an apprenticeship for the lasting hum
relationships that await our children. A surreal toy, TeddyBearBand stimulates the imagination considerabily more than any mere plush bear. It removes lc
and friendship from the realm of disposable emotions.

Design: Philippe Starck, **éditeur:** Moulin Roty, **produit:** TeddyBearBand, **date de conception:** 1997, **date de production:** 1998, **description:** animal
peluche à tête d'ours, dont 3 membres sont terminés par des têtes différentes, chien, chèvre, lapin, et membre inférieur droit comme une patte, hauteu
37cm, **tissu:** trame polyester, dessus coton, **bourrage:** 100% polyester, **référence:** 761.1897, **prix:** 275 F/41,47 Euros, **en 24h chez vous:** +80 F/12,06 Eurc

A

B

B. Voiture à pédales. L'automobile est une chose ennuyeuse. Etrangement, les jouets qui la représentent n'essaient pas d'en changer les règles du je
ils se font le relais de l'erreur sémantique initiale. Pour éviter la petite auto qui ne serait qu'une simple caricature de la voiture inepte de papa, mon a
Ferdinand Amat de Vinçon m'a proposé cette essence d'automobile: la voiture de la mémoire collective. Cette voiture à pédales est malheureuseme
chère, et produite en série limitée. Mais, peut-être, sa qualité lui permet-elle aussi de servir d'exemple, pour ne pas acquérir la manie de changer plus ta
de voiture tous les ans. Quand une voiture est vraiment bonne, on peut l'aimer et la garder longtemps.

Pedalcar. Automobiles are a tiresome subject. Oddly, toys which represent them make no effort to improve on the rules of the game they merely echo t
initial semantic error. To offer an alternative to the expensive little caricature of Daddy's inept conveyance, my friend Ferdinand Amat de Vinçon suggest
this distillation of four-wheeled mythology, the automobile of our collective memory. Unfortunately, this pedalcar is expensive and produced as a limited e
tion. But perhaps its standards of quality will elevate it to the rank of revered archetype. Perhaps its owners will not become like those silly adults who pu
chase a new car every year. When an automobile is truly good, it can be loved and kept for a long time.

Produit: Voiture bleue, **fabricant:** Vilac, **description:** voiture à pédales, série limitée à 500 exemplaires, numérotée sur le volant, capot bois laqué ble
volant bois massif, siège réglable en matière plastique jaune, roues plastique, dimensions 1,20x1,055x0,50m, fabrication française (Jura), **référenc**
685.4800, **prix:** 2200 F/331,73 Euros, **en 24h chez vous:** +299 F/45,08 Euros.

12 Architecture

74 Interiors

190 Furniture

296 Industrial Design

510 Magma

518 Words

542 Overview

574 A–Z

1967

1993 1993

1984 1982

1997

1997

1980 1969 1984 1981

1979 1967

1982

1997

1984 1985 1994 1994

1967 1967 1983 1984

1987

1987 1987 1984 1984 1993

1988 1970 1983 1987

1994 1985 1987

1987 1992

1984 1978 1996 1992

1996

1987 1994

1987 1984 1995

1984 1986 1987

1967 1988 1995

1988 1969

1988

1994 1983 1986 1994

1970 1988 1991

1970 1988

12 Architecture

74 Interiors

190 Furniture

296 Industrial Design

510 Magma

518 Words

542 Overview

574 A–Z

arck says he spent his childhood under his father's drawing boards: hours spent sawing, cutting, gluing, sanding, dismantling bikes, motor cycles and other
jects. →Endless hours – a whole lifetime – spent taking apart and putting back together whatever comes to hand, remaking the world around him. →Several
rs and several prototypes later, the Italians have asked him to renew the notion of furniture, he has transformed life in the Elysee Palace (at President Mitterand's
quest), Café Costes has become Le Café, he has turned the Royalton and Paramount in New York into the first classics of the new hotel world, and strewn Japan
th the architectural tours de force that make him the leading exponent of Expressionist architecture. →His respect for the environment and for humankind has
o been recognized in France, where he has designed the Ecole Nationale Supérieure des Arts Décoratifs in Paris, the control tower at Bordeaux airport, and a
ste recycling plant in the Paris metropolitan area. →Abroad, he continues to shake up the traditions and culture of major cities around the world. He has designed
e restaurant Felix in Hong Kong and the Teatron in Mexico. The United States is dotted with the new worlds of the imagination constituted by his hotels: the
lano in Miami, the Mondrian in Los Angeles, the Hudson in New York and the Clift in San Francisco. In London, the new Jean-Paul Gaultier gallery will join the
nderson and St Martin's Lane hotels. Other architectural projects now in progress, in Australia, Turkey, Mexico and elsewhere will transform these sites too into
ractions where the pleasurable and the unexpected come together. →An honest, enthusiastic citizen of today's world, he considers it his duty to share with us his
bversive vision of a better world, which is his alone and yet fits us like a glove. He tirelessly changes the realities of our daily life by bringing to bear on them our
epest roots and wellsprings. He captures the essential spirit of the sea for Bénéteau, turns the toothbrush into a noble object, the garden gnome into an item of
rniture, squeezes lemons upside-down, and even contrives to make our TV sets friendlier by introducing a little more humanity into Thomson's electronic world.
e also finds time to transform our pasta, ash-trays, lamps, toothbrushes, door handles, cutlery, candlesticks, luggage, kettles, knives, vases, clocks, scooters,
otorbikes, desks, beds, taps, baths, bathrooms, and toilets... in short, our entire life. A life that he finds increasingly fascinating, leading him ever closer to the
man body itself, with clothes, underwear, shoes, glasses, watches, food, toiletries, and so on. And he remains determined that all his designs should respect the
ture and the future of mankind. →The world's museums haven't missed out. Paris, New York, Munich, London, Chicago, Kyoto, Barcelona – all exhibit his work as
t of a master. →Prizes and awards are showered on him in France, the United states and Italy: Designer of the Year, Grand Prix for Industrial Design, the Oscar for
sign, Commandeur des Arts et des Lettres, Compasso d'Oro, amongst many others. →Always and everywhere, he seems to understand better than anyone else
r dreams, desires, and needs, and our responsibility to the future, not to mention the requirement that he respect his fellow citizens by making of his work a
litical and civic act. →Crazy, warm, yet terribly lucid, he draws incessantly, as though driven by a sense of urgent necessity, for himself and for others. His fine,
elligent work touches us, by all means, but touches us above all because he puts his heart into that work, creating objects that are good first, and beautiful
erwards. →→→→→Seine Kindheit habe er unter den Zeichentischen seines Vaters verbracht, erinnert sich Starck. Stundenlang zerlegt er, schneidet aus, sägt, klebt
sammen und schmirgelt ab – alles, was ihm in die Finger kommt, auch Fahrräder, Motorräder und andere Dinge. →Schon als Kind besteht sein Leben darin, die
nge, die ihn umgeben, auseinander zu nehmen und so die ihn umgebende Welt neu zu gestalten. →Einige Jahre und viele Prototypen später lassen die Italiener
n ihm Möbel entwerfen, bittet ihn der französische Präsident François Mitterrand, den Élysée-Palast umzugestalten und erringt das Café Costes den Titel Le Café.
t dem Royalton und dem Paramount Hotel in New York setzt er einen neuen Standard für Hotels; Japan überzieht er mit architektonischen Monstern, die ihn als
ponenten expressionistischer Architektur ausweisen. Starcks Respekt vor der Umwelt und den Menschen ermutigt Frankreich, ihn mit Entwürfen für die École
tionale Supérieure des Arts Décoratifs in Paris, für den Kontrollturm des Flughafens von Bordeaux und für eine Müllverwertungsanlage in der Nähe von Paris zu
auftragen. →In den Metropolen der Welt bringt er Tradition und fest verwurzelte Kultur ins Wanken: Er gestaltet das Restaurant Felix in Hongkong, das Teatron in
exiko. Seine Hotels markieren eine neue Dimension auf dem amerikanischen Kontinent: das Delano in Miami, das Mondrian in Los Angeles, das Hudson in New
rk, das Clift in San Francisco. In London bildet die neue Galerie von Jean Paul Gautier in diesem Jahr eine Ergänzung zum Hotel Sanderson und dem St. Martin's
ne. Weitere noch nicht abgeschlossene Architekturprojekte in Australien, in der Türkei, in Mexiko und anderswo verwandeln die Räume, die man ihm anvertraut,
Begegnungsschauplätze zum Wohlfühlen und für die Sinne. →Als enthusiastischer und ehrlicher Weltbürger macht Starck es zu seiner Pflicht, seine subversive
rsion von einer gerechteren Welt an seine Mitmenschen weiterzugeben – eine Version, die sein geistiges Eigentum ist und doch so gut zu uns allen paßt. →Indem
beständig unsere Wurzeln und unsere Sehgewohnheiten sublimiert, verändert er unermüdlich unseren Alltag. Er entwirft zeitlose Segelboote für Bénéteau, adelt
e Zahnbürste, kreiert einen Gartenzwerg-Hocker, kehrt das Zitronenauspressen einfach um, und es gelingt ihm sogar, dass wir unsere Fernsehgeräte sympathi-
her finden, indem er seinen »Emotional Style« in die elektronische Welt der Thomson-Gruppe einführt. Aber Starck findet auch noch Zeit, unsere Nudeln, Aschen-
cher, Lampen, Zahnbürsten, Türgriffe, Bestecke, Kerzenleuchter, Koffer, Wasserkessel, Messer, Vasen, Uhren, Motorroller, Büros, Betten, Wasserhähne, Bade-
nnen und Toiletten – kurzum unser ganzes Leben zu verändern ... unser Leben, das ihn mehr und mehr fasziniert, wie seine aktuelle Beschäftigung mit dem
nschlichen Körper zeigt: Ob in seinen Designs für Kleidung und Unterkleidung, Schuhen, Brillen, Uhren, Nahrung oder für Hygieneprodukte und anderes mehr,
allen seinen Schöpfungen folgt Starck seinem Credo, die Natur und die Zukunft des Menschen zu respektieren. →Das wissen auch die Museen: New York,
inchen, London, Chicago, Kyoto, Barcelona, Paris: überall werden ihm Ausstellungen gewidmet. In Frankreich, in den USA und in Italien wurde Starck mit zahl-
chen Preisen und Auszeichnungen geehrt: Er ist Créateur de l'Année (Designer des Jahres in Frankreich), erhielt den Grand Prix pour le Design Industriel (Großer
eis für Industriedesign), den Oscar du Design (den Oskar für Design) den Titel Officier des Arts et des Lettres, den Compasso d'Oro und viele andere Auszeich-
ngen. →Immer und überall präsent, scheint Starck wie kein anderer unsere Träume, Sehnsüchte, Bedürfnisse und unsere Verantwortung gegenüber der Zukunft
verstehen, und sieht aus Respekt für seine Mitmenschen in seiner Arbeit eine gesellschaftspolitische Aufgabe. →Verrückt und genial und dabei gnadenlos
llsichtig wie kein zweiter, kreiert er unaufhörlich, als sei es eine Notwendigkeit für ihn selbst und die anderen. Er berührt uns mit seinem Schaffen, weil es ehrlich
 und intelligent, aber auch und vor allem, weil es von Herzen kommt und Objekte erfindet, in denen die Qualität noch vor der Schönheit kommt.→→→→→Starck
rappelle avoir passé son enfance sous les tables à dessin de son père, d'heures employées à scier, découper, coller, poncer, décortiquer vélos, motos et autres
jets. →Des heures, une vie, à défaire et faire tout ce qui le touche, à refaire le monde qui l'entoure. →Quelques années et quelques prototypes plus tard, les
liens lui confient notre mobilier, le Président François Mitterrand lui demande de changer sa vie à l'Élysée, le café Costes devient Le café. Il fait du Royalton et du
ramount de New York les premiers classiques d'une nouvelle hôtellerie. Il parsème le Japon de monstres architecturaux qui en font le chef de file de l'architecture
pressionniste. Son respect de l'environnement et des humains touche aussi la France qui lui confie la réalisation de l'École Nationale Supérieure des Arts
coratifs à Paris, la Tour de contrôle de l'Aéroport de Bordeaux et l'usine de retraitement de nos déchets en région parisienne. →A l'étranger, il continue de
usculer les traditions et les cultures des grandes métropoles. En réalisant le restaurant Felix à Hong Kong, le Teatron à Mexico. Ses hôtels ponctuent d'un nouvel
aginaire le territoire américain : le Delano à Miami, le Mondrian à Los Angeles, le Hudson à New York, le Clift à San Francisco. A Londres, la nouvelle galerie Jean
ul Gaultier répondra cette année aux hôtels Sanderson et St Martin's Lane. D'autres projets architecturaux en cours de réalisation, en Australie, en Turquie, au
xique et ailleurs, transformeront aussi ces endroits qu'on lui confie en des lieux d'attraction, de plaisir et de rencontres. →Citoyen enthousiaste et honnête, il se
t un devoir de nous faire partager sa vision subversive d'un monde plus juste qui seul lui appartient et qui pourtant nous va si bien. →Et il n'a de cesse de changer
tre quotidien, en y sublimant toujours nos racines et nos sources profondes. Il retrouve un éternel de la marine avec Bénéteau, anoblit la brosse à dents, fait un
uble du nain de jardin, presse les citrons mais à l'envers, en arrive même à rendre nos télévisions amicales en faisant entrer plus d'humanité dans le monde
ctronique de Thomson. Mais il prend aussi le temps de changer nos pâtes, nos cendriers, nos lampes, nos brosses à dents, nos poignées de porte, nos couverts,
s bougeoirs, nos valises, nos bouilloires, nos couteaux, nos vases, nos horloges, nos scooters, nos motos, nos bureaux, nos lits, nos robinets, nos baignoires, nos
its-coins, notre Vie enfin... notre vie qui le passionne de plus en plus, au point de se rapprocher maintenant du corps humain avec les vêtements, les sous-
ements, les chaussures, les lunettes, les montres, la nourriture, ainsi que les produits d'hygiène et autres, avec le souhait déterminé de respecter par toutes ses
ations, la nature et l'avenir de l'homme. →Les Musées ne s'y trompent pas. New York, Munich, Londres, Chicago, Kyoto, Barcelone, Paris : tous l'exposent et le
nsacrent. →Il a été récompensé de tous les prix et awards, en France, aux Etats-Unis ou en Italie. Créateur de l'Année, Grand Prix du Design Industriel, Oscar du
sign, Commandeur des Arts et des Lettres, Compasso d'Oro, et bien d'autres. →Toujours et partout présent, il semble comprendre mieux que quiconque nos
es, nos désirs, nos besoins, et notre responsabilité vis à vis du futur, ainsi que la nécessité de respecter ses concitoyens en faisant de son travail un acte politique
civique. →Fou, génial mais aussi terriblement lucide, il dessine sans répit, par nécessité, par urgence, pour lui et les autres, nous touchant par un travail juste et
elligent, certes, mais aussi et surtout parce qu'il y met du cœur, créant des objets bons bien avant que d'être beaux. →Ed Mae Cooper

What I'd like to offer here is a distillation of certain images. These are patterns, conclusions that I have reached, but they don't amount to a system. I shall probably get around to adding to them. They are the materials of a conversation conducted while still on the road.

(...) I no longer wish to talk about design. Objects are no longer a concern; they are more like an unavoidable secretion of a slightly shameful kind, like sweat or ear-wax. I never stop producing. You might say I produce out of sheer idleness. Nowadays, it's mainly the broad outlines of things that interest me. But the outlines are entirely personal, and all but fantastical. They have no claim to truth, except for me, as tools. Thought-bubble by bubble, an instrument of greater or lesser coherence is constructed, allowing me to continue my enterprise: the exploration of our wonderful animal space.

Here I put before you some of the tools of my work.

Contradiction?

I have grown closer to the stars by acknowledging the little hillock of mud on which I stand.
As a major producer, I am alert to the nauseous side of that role. It helps prompt the desire to see what else there is. Access to matter immediately triggers the desire for non-matter. That's where I am coming from. I'm aware of the apparent paradox. But no one more intensely aspires to honesty than the robber, no one covets austerity so fiercely as the rich man, no one desires wealth as unconditionally as the poor man.
History abounds in those infinitely perverted beings whose sole motivation is a quest for the ideal.
Instead of denying these apparent contradictions, we must use them to accede to some elsewhere.
I know that what made me originates in family heritage and the contingencies of professional life: self-transcendence by creation, religious upbringing leading to abstraction, and career happenstance leading to production. No doubt the production derives from some sense of lack.
The configuration of these three parameters makes for a profile apparently paradoxical, but in my eyes extremely coherent.

Duty

As a producer, I'd be ashamed to find myself satisfied by mere production. If, designing a toothbrush, I thought of nothing but the toothbrush, I'd be dumb or venal. I try to be neither: that's the duty I recognise. I have to think of the mouth this brush will enter; I have to acquaint myself with its owner. I need to know the kind of society that has given rise to this life. I need to acquaint myself with the species of animal that created this civilisation.
On the species level, we find broad outlines, major obstacles, dead-ends and challenges. It's beyond my power to sweep them away, but the sight of them at least aids comprehension. On longer contemplation, I can come back down the ladder, and grasp why the plan is thus and not contrariwise. In everything I produce, I try to apply this procedure.

Idleness

Dreaming is a form of action. Idleness is a form of action. The idle man stares at the sky and sees what constitutes our eternal ceiling. The sky is one of the things that constructs us, one of our constants. But it is not what people believe. What we see no longer is: the moon's image takes eight seconds to reach us, the sun's three minutes. The stars, and the sun in particular, are incessantly in movement. In the image of stars located 12 million light-years away, we may see bodies that have long since ceased to exist. What constructs and in part defines us may therefore have already ceased to exist. This is a considerable shock.
On the basis of a rudimentary acquaintance with physical chemistry – everything around us is reducible to different assemblages of the same molecules or combinations of atoms – we come to the simple conclusion that there is little enough that is solid or eternal.
Ours is an endless shipwreck. Like children paddling to keep their heads above water, we need to catch hold of something that floats.
The only thing that I find real, tangible, and quantifiable is the "electric" relations between humans. This is of course still more striking when the relation is one of physical love.
Now my gaze no longer lingers on the visible, it discerns only the tubes by which we are connected, individual to individual.
These are links of different qualities, resistance, porosity and elasticity.
In my head, I have replaced perception of the visible with vision of the real.
I now live in a different structure, one composed not of bolts, solder, structure and collage, but of entities linked by vectors of energy.

Dimensions

In general, all of life takes place in two dimensions, and is populated by flat, banal, prefabricated images. But it can be radically transformed the moment one begins to have lightning visions in three dimensions. Only in the transition to the real, to the carnal, can the notion of infinity at last be grasped. And from that moment on, things are no longer the same.

Beyond, there are other visions. Beyond three dimensions begins the analysis of structure, of what is behind the scenes: impulses, architectures, intimate dynamics. Nowadays, I refuse to see the finished product; my ambition is to see only that of which it is made. This involves a constant effort to ennoble – through understanding – the components of things. Combined with a neo-scientific way of working, this allows one to learn humane and practical lessons; I try to apply to the must humble of quotidian routines what I observe in these thought-experiments. I call this attitude "reductive nobility".

Science

I didn't study science, but it's the only thing that interests me. Through theoretical rudiments, I seek the first flickering of comprehension, moving toward an understanding of everything that surrounds us. There lies the aristocracy of thought, there is our nobility. I understand science as an intuition that can, perhaps, be verified. My interest in verification is limited, unlimited my interest in approaching intuition. A strange gymnastics of the mind is required, a sort of hygienic functioning, allowing it to garner every day a new dimension.

Mutation

To avoid the random, to avoid shipwreck, it is important to understand that we are not an isolated segment but a stage. We are the snapshot of a movement that has a point of departure and a point of arrival. We should understand ourselves as action not state. This is essential.

We should undertake a little memory exercise: remembering the humility of our condition, that of a bacteria ignorant even of reproduction, which copies clay crystals. You see what level we were at.

Our transformation into fish, batrachian. The fundamental stage of coming ashore, the transition to terra firma, which allowed the egg a stable bed. The ape-stage, and finally that of the super-ape that we have become today.

But this is not a final state. It's no longer in duration than a flash of lightning.

The vision of the previous voyage is sufficient proof of this. Our extraordinary mutation is a sample of what is possible, and shows us what must follow: the continuation of the voyage. Confronted with the splendour of the first part, one longs to see the next. There is magic, too, in the paucity of clues about the nature of this "sequel". It holds a fascination greater than any mysticism. Will we become a cloud? A vibration, a note of music, an aerosol, a wavelength? No doubt something else again.

The obligation to continue the story of our mutation is not merely a poetic duty, but a technical necessity. In 4.2 billion years, the implosion of the sun will cause us to vitrify. We shall have to move on. A radical change of state is therefore necessary prior to that event. We can attain it by completely accepting and integrating our mutant state. If we don't, if we prove unable to maintain our speed of evolution, our civilisation is doomed.

Vigilance in relation to maintaining the speed of evolution is fundamental. We have one or two clues to what happens if we neglect it: revolutions.

Stripped of their concomitant romantic imagery, revolutions are undesirable. They are costly, and may delay matters. Revolutions merely compensate for a slow-down in evolution.

Participation

No one will be condemned for lacking genius, but we all have a duty of participation: we aren't required to bring a mountain to our civilisation, but contributing a grain of sand is mandatory. Birth is a gift whose reciprocity requires this minimal tribute to civilisation. Each brings what she can. There is an exercise that is at once a form of gift and an entry ticket: the angle-of-vision obligation. It's a schematic example. If you look at your feet, you're an idiot. Training your gaze a little further ahead adds some security if you don't want to trip. A little further ahead again makes the attainment of a form of intelligence possible, but one is not yet in a position to give. Close to the horizontal, some progressive life-solutions may come to light.

As soon as our gaze has moved above the horizon, attaining the horizontal, we are in the domain of intelligence and able to fulfil certain duties toward society. The gaze goes beyond earth and matter. This is vision: the eye is no longer confined by the line of the horizon, and exploration of space and time

can commence. At 45°, genius begins, able to grasp certain elements fundamental to understanding our species. As we come closer to the vertical, we enter the divine. But it's a snake in the game of snakes and ladders, a well shaft in its own axis, a trap. The seductive mystical dimension is also an escape route into the regressive, the useless, and even into danger.

Beyond the vertical, behind one, the past begins. Retrospect is an attitude structurally disadvantageous to our strategy of mutation. The last quarter between the vertical and the horizontal is that of schizophrenia. Back at the horizontal, madness strikes one down. Everyone can accomplish this minimal exercise: raising one's eyes.

One can prolong the exercise of vision on the horizontal plane: by looking in front of oneself, like everyone else, one remains within the normal boundaries of thought. One should cease to think "in general terms"; that is not where one's duty is accomplished. It's only beyond this point, in original thought – exploration, the attempt to turn a little bit aside – that life becomes interesting. And this should be quantified. 45° is a broad, panoramic vision – the necessary vision.

If one attains 90° on either side, thought again becomes unserviceable. Facing about, looking back, leads back to the past: to self-negation, to the negation of the species. This whole, made of vertical and horizontal together, creates a cone: I call it the "cone of obligatory vision". This is the first thing that even the most indigent can afford.

For Jean-Luc Godard, television is lowering one's eyes, cinema is raising one's gaze. What is implied here is the highly symbolic nature of one's angle of vision.

What we know

In our civilisation, there are permanent forms which are part of every epoch and every culture.

They are not especially difficult to detect. A minimal knowledge of physics, astrophysics, and perhaps mathematics, brings to light certain patterns that make these subjects easier to understand.

It is striking to see the extreme similarity between these scientific propositions and the forms that recur in all times, places and civilisations.

One example among many is the general form of the vase, the amphora. The curves it describes represent the proportions of the universe with some accuracy.

In the pre-Big Bang, we find the plinth. The Big Bang is the foot.

The swelling body of the vase is that of the expanding universe.
Its neck is a slight contraction followed by a weak expansion.
Moreover, experiments show that the retinal persistence of a multitude of human faces creates a single face not unlike that of the Mona Lisa, a picture almost universally esteemed the canonic Western representation of humanity.
These clues – mingled with children's suggestions and compared with physicists' remarks – might tend to prove the existence of a single unconscious comprehension, at work worldwide, along with a structural harmony between human functioning and the laws governing it.
Clues.

Renaissance

The elements linking me to Venice are many, and the links more coherent than this succession of fragments might suggest. In my love for the city is also my desire for a return to mud, fertile mud. I find myself again in that primordial soup whence arose the modernity of the Renaissance. My inspiration is perhaps the merest spectre of a dream, but in all my preoccupations there is a tacit intention, that of establishing a form of society enrooted in the example of the Venetian Republic. A city peopled with scientists, philosophers and enlightened traders. A prototype that gave birth to a paradigm of civilisation.
In the race to the lagoon, I see a possible antidote to that eternal threat, the return of barbarity.

Poetry

Strangely enough, it has taken me 50 years to understand that "poetry" is an important word, in its abnormal, active, subversive aspect. My lack of interest in finished poetry is matched only by my interest in tracking it down and casting light on its manifestations through the different scales of matter or time.
I should like to close this circle by turning over in my bed and scrutinising the stars. Scientific publications are a good lens to place between ourselves and the sky. In them, I have found two pieces of information that leave me ultimately happy and optimistic: the discovery, in space, of a monolithic green diamond, as large as the earth, and that of an asteroid resembling a dog's bone, the size of the state of New Jersey.
Thus begins the discovery of Surrealist stellar bric-à-brac on a very large scale.

One good reason to wake up in the morning with a smile...
(...)

Le Devoir de Vision

Ich möchte an dieser Stelle in geraffter Form einige bildliche Vorstellungen entwickeln. Es sind Schemata und Schlussfolgerungen, zu denen ich gelangt bin, die aber keine Summe ausmachen. Diesen Materialien aus einem unterwegs geführten Gespräch werde ich sicher noch einige Elemente hinzufügen müssen.

(...) Ich möchte nicht mehr über Design reden. Der Gegenstand ist für mich so gut wie kein Anlass zur Beschäftigung mehr, sondern so etwas wie eine unwillkürliche, beinahe peinliche Sekretion, etwa wie Schweiß oder Ohrenschmalz. Ich produziere unaufhörlich. Ich könnte sagen, ich produziere aus Faulheit. Heute interessieren mich an den Dingen vor allem die großen Umrisse. Sehr persönliche, fast phantasmagorische Umrisse. Sie beanspruchen nicht einmal wahr zu sein, sondern brauchen nur für mich zu gelten, als Arbeitswerkzeuge. Im Schweifen der Gedanken entsteht ein mehr oder weniger kohärentes Instrumentarium, mit dem ich ein Abenteuer weiterführen kann: die Erforschung unserer wunderbaren tierischen Spezies.

Was ich hier vorlege, sind also Bausteine für ein solches Instrumentarium.

Widerspruch?

Ich habe mich den Sternen genähert und mich zugleich auf meinem Misthaufen wiedergefunden. Meine Rolle als Vielproduzierender gibt mir die Möglichkeit, den Ekel daran zu begreifen. Sie gestattet mir, den Wunsch zu nähren, mich anderswo umzuschauen. Der Zugang zur Materie ruft unmittelbar Sehnsucht nach Nichtmaterie hervor. Von diesem Standpunkt aus spreche ich. Ich bin mir der offensichtlichen Paradoxie der Situation bewusst. Aber nach meiner Überzeugung ist schwerlich mehr Wille zur Ehrlichkeit zu finden als beim Dieb, mehr Wunsch nach Kargheit als bei dem, der im Überfluss lebt, mehr Streben nach Reichtum als beim Allerärmsten.

In der Geschichte mangelt es nicht an jenen unendlich pervertierten Gestalten, die nur von der Suche nach einem Ideal beseelt sind. Anstatt diese offensichtlichen Widersprüche zu leugnen, gilt es sich ihrer zu bedienen, um anderswohin zu gelangen.

Ich bin mir völlig bewusst, dass das, was mich geprägt hat, seinen Ursprung in einem Familienerbe und in einem beruflichen Zufall findet: die Überschreitung seiner selbst durch die schöpferische Arbeit, das Absehen von sich selbst durch die religiöse Erziehung sowie die zufälligen Umstände, die mich, zweifelsohne um ein Gefühl des Mangels auszugleichen, zum Produzieren geführt ha-

ben. Die Zusammensetzung dieser drei Parameter ergibt heute eine Figur, die paradox erscheinen mag, die ich jedoch für sehr kohärent halte.

Notwendiges Vorgehen

Wenn ich mich in meiner Stellung als Produzierender ganz damit begnügte, zu produzieren, fände ich dies beschämend. Wenn ich beim Entwerfen einer Zahnbürste nur an sie dächte, wäre ich ein Idiot oder käuflich. Ich versuche, weder das eine noch das andere zu sein: Das halte ich für ein notwendiges Vorgehen. Es kommt darauf an, sich den Mund vorzustellen, der diese Bürste aufnehmen wird, den Menschen, dem dieser Mund gehört. Ich muss mir Fragen nach dem Leben dieses Menschen stellen. Ich muss wissen, wie die Gesellschaft aussieht, die dieses Leben hervorgebracht hat. Ich muss die tierische Spezies kennen, die diese Zivilisation geschaffen hat.

Was nun diese Spezies angeht, zeichnen sich große Umrisse, viele Verriegelungen, Mauern und Herausforderungen ab. Es steht nicht in meiner Macht, sie zu beseitigen, aber ich kann sie, wenn ich sie sehe, ein wenig zu verstehen versuchen. In gelassenerer Stimmung kann ich die Treppe in umgekehrter Richtung hinabsteigen, verstehen, warum ein Entwurf so aussieht und nicht wie sein Gegenteil. Diesen Gedankengang versuche ich in allen meinen Produktionen umzusetzen.

Faulheit

Eine Form des Handelns ist die des Träumers, des Faulenzers. Der Faulenzer betrachtet den Himmel und sieht, was unser ewiges Dach ausmacht. Der Himmel ist eines der Dinge, die uns strukturieren, eine unserer Konstanten. Und doch ist er nicht das, für das man ihn hält. Was wir sehen, ist bereits nicht mehr das, was ist. Acht Sekunden benötigt das Bild des Mondes, um bei uns anzukommen. Drei Minuten das der Sonne. Die Gestirne, und letztgenanntes im Besonderen, sind ständigem Wandel unterworfen. Handelt es sich um zwölf Millionen Lichtjahre entfernte Sterne, sehen wir manchmal Himmelskörper, die es gar nicht mehr gibt. Es kommt also vor, dass das, was uns strukturiert und uns zum Teil bestimmt, bereits nicht mehr existiert. Das ist eine wichtige, aufrüttelnde Erkenntnis.

Mit Hilfe einiger elementarer Kenntnisse in Physik und Chemie – alles, was uns umgibt, lässt sich auf verschiedene Zusammensetungen der gleichen Moleküle oder Atom-ombinationen zurückführen – kommt man u dem Schluss, dass es in dem Ganzen nicht iel Ewiges oder Festes gibt. Wir sind dauer-afte Schiffbrüchige. Als Kinder, die wir uns aum über Wasser halten können, müssen ir uns an etwas Schwimmendes klammern. Das Einzige, was mir wirklich, fasslich, quan-ifizierbar erscheint, ist die »elektrische« Be-iehung zwischen den Menschen. Diese fällt atürlich stärker aus, wenn es sich um eine iebesbeziehung handelt.

ch habe mir angewöhnt, meinen Blick nicht ehr auf dem Sichtbaren ruhen zu lassen, ondern nur noch die Kanäle wahrzuneh-en, die die Einzelnen miteinander verbin-en. Es sind Kanäle unterschiedlicher Qua-täten, Festigkeiten, Porositäten und lastizitäten. In meinem Kopf habe ich die Vahrnehmung des Sichtbaren durch das Se-en der Wirklichkeit ersetzt. Seither lebe ich einem anderen Gefüge, das nicht aus chrauben, Schweißnähten, Gerüsten oder erklebungen besteht, sondern aus Verbin-ungen zwischen Wesen mit Hilfe von Ener-iekanälen.

Dimensionen

m Allgemeinen spielt das ganze Leben sich n zwei Dimensionen ab, bevölkert von vor-efertigten, platten Bildern. Doch kann es ich an dem Tag von Grund auf verändern, n dem dreidimensionale Anschauungen ufblitzen. Erst im Übergang zum Wirkli-hen, zum Fleischlichen, kann der Begriff es Unendlichen verstanden werden. Und on diesem Augenblick an sind die Dinge icht mehr dieselben.

Darüber hinaus gibt es weitere Sichtweisen. Diesseits der drei Dimensionen beginnt die Analyse der Strukturen, dessen, was man icht sieht, der Triebfedern, der Architektu-en, der inneren Dynamiken: Ich lehne es eute ab, das fertige Produkt zu sehen, son-ern versuche wahrzunehmen, woraus es ich zusammensetzt. Es handelt sich um ine unaufhörliche Veredelungsarbeit durch as Verständnis eben der Elemente, die die Dinge konstituieren. Mit Hilfe einer neo-wis-enschaftlichen Denkweise lassen sich daraus enschliche und praktische Lehren ziehen: ch versuche auf den allerbescheidensten All-ag anzuwenden, was ich in diesen Untersu-hungen beobachte. Ich möchte hinsichtlich ieser Haltung von einem »Adel des Herab-tufers« sprechen.

Wissenschaften

ch habe keine wissenschaftlichen Studien etrieben, aber Wissenschaften sind das Ein-zige, was mich interessiert. Mit Hilfe rudi-mentärer Theoriekenntnisse suche ich nach ersten Erkenntnissen auf dem Weg zu einem Verständnis all dessen, was uns umgibt. Hierin liegt die Aristokratie des Denkens, hierin unser Adel. Ich begreife die Wissen-schaft als eine potentiell verifizierbare Intui-tion. Zwar bin ich an der Verifizierung nur zum Teil interessiert, wohl aber an der Annäherung mittels Intuitionen. Dazu bedarf es einer besonderen Akrobatik des Geistes, einer Art Hygiene der Denkhaltung, die es gestattet, an jedem Tag eine Dimension hin-zuzugewinnen.

Mutation

Um Irrwege oder gar Schiffbrüche zu vermei-den, kommt es darauf an zu verstehen, dass wir kein isoliertes Segment, sondern eine Entwicklungsstufe sind. Wir sind die Mo-mentaufnahme einer Bewegung, die einen Ausgangs- und einen Ankunftspunkt hat. Wir müssen uns als Handlung, nicht als Zu-stand auffassen. Das ist von grundlegender Wichtigkeit.

Dazu muss man einer kleinen Gedächtnisü-bung nachgehen und sich der Bescheiden-heit unseres Daseins erinnern. Man sollte an die Bakterie zurückdenken, die nicht fort-pflanzungsfähig ist und ihre Struktur aus der Kopie von Tonkristallen gewinnt. Man sieht, auf welcher Stufe wir uns einmal befunden haben. Man erinnere sich an die Verwand-lung zum Fisch, zum Lurch. An die entschei-dende Phase der Landung, des Übergangs auf das Festland, durch den es möglich wurde, Eier an gesicherter Stelle abzulegen. An den Stand des Affen und schließlich den des Überaffen, den wir heute erreicht haben. Aber das ist kein ein für alle Mal gesicherter Zustand, nur ein Wetterleuchten.

Der Blick auf die zurückgelegte Reise genügt, um uns davon zu überzeugen. Diese außer-ordentliche Metamorphose zeigt uns ein Muster dessen, wie die Reise fortgeführt wer-den kann und muss. Die prachtvolle Schön-heit des ersten Teils macht einem Lust, die Fortsetzung zu erleben. Eine gewisse Magie liegt auch in der Spärlichkeit der Hinweise, die uns hinsichtlich der Art und Weise dieser Fortsetzung zur Verfügung stehen. Diese Frage ist und bleibt erregender als alle Mysti-zismen.

Werden wir zu einer Wolke werden? Einer Vibration, einer Musiknote, einem Aerosol, einer Wellenlänge? Gewiss noch zu ganz anderem.

Die Verpflichtung zur Fortsetzung der Muta-tionsgeschichte ist nicht nur eine poetische Aufgabe, sondern auch eine technische Not-wendigkeit. In 4,2 Milliarden Jahren wird uns die Implosion der Sonne in Glas verwandeln. Wir werden umziehen müssen. In der Zwi-schenzeit ist also ein radikaler Wandel der Verhältnisse vonnöten. Diesen können wir erreichen, wenn wir unser Mutantendasein einbeziehen und vollständig akzeptieren. Ak-zeptieren wir es dagegen nicht und zeigen uns unfähig, den Takt unserer Evolutionsge-schwindigkeit aufrechtzuerhalten, so heißt dies, unsere Zivilisation zum Tode zu verur-teilen. Die Konstanz der Evolutionsgeschwin-digkeit zu beachten ist fundamental. Sollte dies nicht geschehen, kennen wir einige Hin-weise auf das Nachfolgende: Revolutionen. Und Revolutionen sind, einmal abgesehen von den romantischen Bildern, die sie um-ranken, nicht wünschenswert. Sie sind teuer und zudem ein Zeitverlust. Revolutionen sind nur Aufholbewegungen, die Geschwin-digkeitseinbußen der Evolution wettmachen.

Beteiligung

Keiner wird sich dafür tadeln lassen müssen, dass er kein Genie ist, aber wir alle haben eine Pflicht zur Beteiligung: Wir brauchen keinen Berg zu unserer Zivilisation beizutra-gen, geboten ist aber, ein Körnchen Sand hinzuzufügen. Geborenwerden bringt im Gegenzug diesen Minimaltribut an die Zivili-sation mit sich. Jeder trägt dazu bei, was er kann. Es gibt eine Übung, die eine Art Ge-schenk und zugleich eine Eintrittskarte dar-stellt: die Verpflichtung auf den Blickwinkel. Es handelt sich um ein schematisches Bei-spiel. Wenn man auf seine Füße schaut, ist man ein Idiot. Den Blick etwas weiter nach vorn zu richten bringt eine gewisse Sicher-heit, nicht zu stolpern. Ihn noch ein wenig höher zu heben, ermöglicht bereits eine be-stimmte Form von Intelligenz, aber man ist noch nicht in der Lage, etwas zu geben. Bei Annäherung an die Horizontale können Lösungen für einen Fortschritt des Lebens zutage treten.

Sobald der Blick über den Horizont, über die Horizontale hinausgelangt, befindet man sich im Bereich der Intelligenz und ist in der Lage, bestimmte Aufgaben gegenüber der Gesellschaft zu erfüllen. Der Blick reicht über die Erde und die Materie hinaus. Man ge-langt in die Dimension der Vision: Das Auge steht nicht mehr im Bann der Horizontlinie, und die Erkundung von Raum und Zeit kann beginnen. Bei 45° erreicht man die Stufe des Genies und wird fähig, bestimmte für das Verständnis unserer Gattung fundamentale Elemente zu erkennen. In der Annäherung an die Vertikale tritt man ins Göttliche ein. Doch ist dies zugleich ein Spiel, eine Falle. Die mystische Dimension ist verführerisch, aber auch eine Ausflucht regressiver und nutzloser, wenn nicht sogar gefährlicher Art. Jenseits dieser Vertikale, hinter einem, beginnt die Vergangenheit. Diese Haltung einzunehmen ist hinsichtlich unseres Mutationsverlaufs strukturell weniger nützlich.

Im letzten Viertel zwischen der Vertikalen und der Horizontalen liegt das Stadium der Schizophrenie. In der rückwärtigen Horizontalen stürzt man in den Wahnsinn ab.

Zu der minimalen Übung, die Augen zu heben, ist jeder imstande.

Die Sichtübung lässt sich horizontal weiterführen: Wenn man wie alle Welt vor sich schaut, bleibt man im normalen Denkstrom. Wer immer »im Allgemeinen« denkt, erfüllt seine Aufgabe nicht mehr. Erst jenseits, im eigenen Denken, im erkundenden Sehen, indem man versucht, ein wenig Abstand nach rechts oder links zu gewinnen, wird es interessant. Aber man muss Maß halten.

Bei 45° eröffnet sich eine große, panoramatische, notwendige Vision.

Bei 90° nach jeder Seite, wird das Denken erneut unbrauchbar. Den Blick zurückzuwenden, nach hinten zu schauen, führt zurück in die Vergangenheit, in die Selbstverneinung und die Negation unserer Spezies.

Beide, Vertikale und Horizontale zusammen, bilden einen Kegel, den ich einmal »obligatorischen Sichtkegel« nenne. Das ist das Erste, was auch der Ärmste zu bieten hat.

Jean-Luc Godard hat davon gesprochen, dass Fernsehen bedeutet, die Augen zu senken, während das Kino verlangt, den Blick zu heben. Welchen Blickwinkel man einnimmt, ist ein hochsymbolischer Akt.

Wir wissen

In unserer Zivilisation lässt sich das Fortbestehen von Formen beobachten, die Bestandteil aller Epochen und Kulturen sind. Das lässt sich ziemlich leicht feststellen. Aus einigen physikalischen, astrophysikalischen, vielleicht auch mathematischen Erkenntnissen ergeben sich Schemata, die das Verständnis dieses Phänomens erleichtern. Es ist verblüffend, dass zwischen solchen wissenschaftlichen Aussagen und den über die Orte, Zeiten und Zivilisationen hinweg wiederkehrenden Formen äußerste Ähnlichkeit herrscht.

Ein Beispiel dafür ist die Grundform der Vase, der Amphore, an der man auf sehr präzise Weise einen Kurvenverlauf erkennt, der die Proportionen des Universums aufgreift. Im Sockel erkennt man die Phase vor dem Urknall. Der Urknall entspricht dem Fuß. Der gewölbte Körper der Vase stellt die Ausdehnung des Universums dar.

Ihr Hals bildet eine leichte Kontraktion, gefolgt von einer schwachen Ausdehnung.

Experimente zeigen übrigens, dass sich beim Sehen zahlreicher menschlicher Gesichter durch Netzhauteinzeichnung ein einziges Gesicht herausbildet, das stark an die Mona Lisa erinnert – ein Bild, das nahezu weltweit als kanonische westliche Darstellung des Menschen anerkannt ist.

Solche Hinweise könnten, verbunden mit Vorschlägen von Kindern und verglichen mit Anmerkungen von Physikern, tendenziell die Existenz eines globalen unbewussten Verständnisses und einer strukturellen Harmonie zwischen dem menschlichen Verhalten und den es regelnden Gesetzen belegen. Hinweise, immerhin.

Renaissance

Auf kohärentere Weise, als diese Abfolge von Fragmenten denken lassen könnte, verbindet mich vieles mit Venedig. Meine Liebe zu dieser Stadt deckt sich mit meiner Neigung, zum fruchtbaren Urschlamm zurückzukehren. Ich finde mich in der Ursuppe wieder, aus der die Modernität der Renaissance hervorgegangen ist. In der Art meiner Beschäftigungen, die möglicherweise dem Schreckbild eines Traumes folgt, liegt ein unausgesprochener Wille zur Errichtung eines Gesellschaftsmodells, das seine Wurzeln aus der Republik Venedig bezöge. Eine Stadt, bevölkert von Wissenschaftlern, aufgeklärten Händlern und Philosophen. Ein Prototyp, der ein Zivilisationsmodell hervorgebracht hat. In der Flucht zur Lagune sehe ich ein mögliches Gegengift zur Barbarei, dieser stets drohenden Gefahr.

Poesie

Merkwürdigerweise habe ich 50 Jahre gebraucht, bis ich wirklich begriffen habe, dass »Poesie« ein wichtiges Wort ist: in seiner anormalen, gleichsam subversiven Bedeutung. Sowenig ich an bereits fertiger Poesie interessiert bin, sosehr liebe ich es, ihre Spuren zu entdecken und ihre Erscheinungsformen durch die verschiedenen Stufungen der Materie oder der Zeit hindurch zutage zu fördern.

Ich möchte den Kreis schließen, indem ich in mein Bett zurückkehre und ausgiebig in die Sterne schaue.

Wissenschaftliche Veröffentlichungen bilden eine gute Linse zwischen dem Himmel und uns. Ich habe darin zwei Informationen gefunden, die mich unbedingt glücklich und optimistisch stimmen: Im Weltraum ist ein monolithischer grüner Diamant entdeckt worden, so groß wie die Erde. Sowie ein Asteroid, der einem Hundeknochen ähnelt und die Ausmaße des Staates New Jersey hat.

Der Anfang zur Entdeckung eines großen surrealistischen stellaren Krimskrams ist gemacht.

Grund genug, morgens aufzuwachen und zu lächeln (...)

La Conscience Globale

Je voudrais proposer ici un condensé de quelques images. Ce sont des schémas et des conclusions auxquels je suis parvenu, mais ils ne constituent pas une somme. J'aurais sûrement encore quelques éléments à ajouter. Ce sont les matériaux d'une conversation que l'on prend en cours de route. (...) Je voudrais ne plus parler de design. L'objet n'est quasiment plus une préoccupation, sinon comme une secrétion automatique presque honteuse, un peu comme la sueur, ou le cérumen. Je produis sans cesse. Je pourrais dire que je produis par paresse. Aujourd'hui, ce sont surtout les grandes lignes des choses qui m'intéressent. Des lignes très personnelles, presque fantasmagoriques. Elles ne cherchent même pas à être vraies, sinon pour moi, en tant qu'outils. Bulle après bulle, se construit un outil plus ou moins cohérent qui me permet de continuer une aventure : l'exploration de notre merveilleuse espèce animale.
Je livre ici des fragments d'outils de travail.

Contradiction ?

Je me suis rapproché des étoiles en me retrouvant sur mon tas de boue.
Mon rôle de grand producteur me donne la possibilité d'en comprendre la nausée. Il me permet de stimuler une envie d'aller voir ailleurs. L'accès à la matière génère immédiatement le désir de non-matière. C'est de cet endroit-là d'où je parle. Je suis conscient du caractère apparemment paradoxal de la situation. Mais je crois qu'il est difficile de trouver plus de volonté d'honnêteté que chez le voleur, de désir de dénuement que chez l'opulent, de richesse que chez le plus pauvre. L'Histoire ne manque pas de ces êtres infiniment pervertis, seulement animés d'une quête d'idéal.
Au lieu de nier ces apparentes contradictions, il est nécessaire de s'en servir, pour aller ailleurs. Je suis totalement conscient que ce qui m'a fait trouve son origine dans un héritage familial et un hasard professionnel. Le dépassement de soi-même par la création, l'abstraction par l'éducation religieuse, et ces circonstances aléatoires qui m'ont amené à produire, assurément pour pallier un manque. Le résultat de l'assemblage de ces trois paramètres dessine aujourd'hui une silhouette qui peut sembler paradoxale, mais que je crois très cohérente.

Démarche obligatoire

Dans ma position de producteur, si je me satisfaisais exclusivement de produire, j'en concevrais de la honte. Si, en dessinant une brosse à dents, je ne pensais qu'à elle, je serais idiot, ou vénal. J'essaie de n'être ni l'un ni l'autre : c'est la démarche obligatoire. Il faut penser la bouche qui va accueillir cette brosse, connaître le propriétaire de cette bouche. Je dois me poser des questions à l'égard de la vie de cette personne. Il faut que je sache à quoi ressemble la société qui a accouché de cette vie. Il faut que je connaisse l'espèce l'animale qui a créé cette civilisation.
Du point de vue de notre animalité se dessinent de grandes lignes, des grands verrous, des murs et des défis. Je n'ai pas la puissance de les balayer, mais, en les voyant, je peux essayer de les comprendre un petit peu. Avec plus de quiétude, je peux redescendre l'escalier en sens inverse, comprendre pourquoi le dessin est celui-là et non l'inverse. Je tente de mettre en œuvre ce schéma de réflexion dans toutes mes productions.

Paresse

Une forme d'action consiste à être un rêveur. Etre un paresseux. Le paresseux regarde le ciel et voit ce qui constitue notre éternel plafond. Le ciel est l'une des choses qui nous construit, l'une de nos constantes. Il n'est pourtant pas ce que l'on croit. Ce que nous voyons n'est déjà plus ce qui est. Huit secondes seront nécessaires à l'image de la lune pour nous parvenir. Trois minutes pour celle du soleil. L'agitation des astres, de celui là en particulier, est incessante. Lorsqu'il s'agit d'étoiles, situées à 12 millions d'années-lumière, nous voyons parfois des corps qui ont déjà cessé d'exister. Ainsi il arrive que ce qui nous construit, et nous définit en partie, n'existe déjà plus. C'est un choc important.
A partir de connaissances élémentaires de physique chimie – tout ce qui nous entoure se résume à différents assemblages des mêmes molécules ou des combinaisons d'atomes –, on en arrive à la conclusion simple qu'il n'y a pas beaucoup d'éternel ou de solide là-dedans.
Nous sommes des naufragés permanents. Enfants, surnageant à peine, nous avons besoin de nous raccrocher à quelque chose qui flotte.
La seule chose que je trouve réelle, tangible, quantifiable, est la relation ‹ électrique › entre les humains. C'est évidemment plus remarquable encore lorsqu'il s'agit d'une relation amoureuse.
J'ai pris l'habitude de ne plus arrêter mon regard au visible, pour ne plus distinguer que ces tubes qui relient les individus. Des liens

e différentes qualités, duretés, porosités, asticités.

Dans ma tête, j'ai remplacé la perception du isible par la vision du réel.

e vis désormais dans une autre structure ui n'est pas de boulons, de soudures, de tructures ou de collages, mais de liaisons ntre des entités au moyen de tubes 'énergie.

Dimensions

n général, toute la vie se passe en deux di- mensions, peuplée d'images préfabriquées t plates. Mais elle peut être bouleversée le our où l'on commence à avoir ces éclairs de isions en trois dimensions. C'est seulement ors du passage au réel, au charnel, que la otion d'infini peut être comprise. Et les hoses, de cet instant, ne sont plus jamais es mêmes.

u-delà, il y a d'autres visions. En deçà des rois dimensions commence l'analyse des tructures, ce que l'on ne voit pas, les res- orts, les architectures, les dynamiques in- mes : je refuse aujourd'hui de voir le pro- uit fini pour tenter de ne voir que ce qui le ompose. Un travail incessant d'anoblisse- ent par la compréhension des éléments mêmes qui constituent les choses. A partir 'un fonctionnement d'ordre néo-scienti- que, on peut en tirer des enseignements umains et pratiques : je cherche à appliquer u quotidien le plus humble ce que j'observe ors de ces enquêtes. A l'égard de cette atti- ude, j'aimerais pouvoir ici parler d'une ‹no- lesse du rabaisseur›.

Sciences

e n'ai pas fait d'études scientifiques, mais s sciences sont la seule chose qui m'inté- esse. Au moyen de rudiments théoriques, je echerche les balbutiements de la compré- ension, vers l'intelligence de tout ce qui ous entoure. C'est là que se situe l'aristo- ratie de la pensée, là que se trouve notre oblesse. La science, je l'entends comme ne intuition potentiellement vérifiable. Si je e suis que partiellement intéressé par la vé- fication, je le suis par l'approche des intui- ons. Une gymnastique singulière de l'esprit st nécessaire, une sorte d'hygiène de fonc- onnement, qui permet tous les jours de ga- ner une dimension.

Mutation

our éviter l'errance et même le naufrage, il st important de comprendre que nous ne ommes pas un segment isolé, mais que ous constituons une étape. Nous sommes

l'instantané d'un mouvement qui a un dé- part et une arrivée.

Nous devons nous comprendre comme une action, non comme un état. C'est fonda- mental.

Il faut se livrer à un petit exercice de mémoire : se rappeler l'humilité de notre condition, celle de la bactérie qui ne sait même pas se reproduire, copie les cristaux d'argile. On voit à quel niveau on se trouvait. La transformation en poisson, en batracien. L'étape fondamentale de l'accostage, le pas- sage sur la terre ferme, qui va permettre que l'œuf soit posé de manière stable. L'état de singe, et enfin celui de sursinge que nous avons aujourd'hui atteint.

Mais ce n'est pas un état acquis, juste un éclair.

La vision du voyage passé suffit à nous en convaincre. Cette extraordinaire métamor- phose nous montre un échantillon de ce qui peut, et doit, devenir la continuation du voyage. Devant la beauté splendide de la pre- mière partie, on a envie de voir la suite. Il y a aussi une magie dans la maigreur des in- dices dont nous disposons quant à la nature de cette suite. Et cela reste plus passionnant que tous les mysticismes.

Deviendrons-nous une nuée ? une vibration, une note de musique, un aérosol, une longueur d'onde ? Sûrement autre chose encore.

L'obligation de la continuation de l'histoire de la mutation est non seulement un devoir poétique, mais une nécessité technique.

Dans 4,2 milliards d'années, l'implosion du soleil nous conduira à la vitrification. Il nous faudra déménager. Un changement d'état ra- dical est donc nécessaire entre temps. Nous pouvons y parvenir par l'intégration et la complète acceptation de notre état de mu- tant. Si en revanche nous ne l'acceptons pas, si nous montrons une incapacité à maintenir le rythme de notre vitesse d'évolution, cela revient à condamner notre civilisation.

La vigilance vis-à-vis de cette constance de vitesse d'évolution est fondamentale. Sans elle, nous avons quelques indices de ce qui se passe : des révolutions.

En dehors de l'imagerie romantique qui les entoure, elles ne sont pas souhaitables. Coû- teuses, elles font aussi perdre du temps. Les révolutions ne sont que le rattrapage d'une baisse de vitesse d'évolution.

Participation

Personne ne se verra blâmé de n'être pas génial, mais nous avons tous un devoir de participation : nous ne sommes pas obligés d'apporter une montagne à notre civilisa- tion, mais y ajouter un grain de sable est en

revanche une obligation. Naître implique, en échange, ce tribut minimal à la civilisation. Chacun apporte ce qu'il peut.

Il existe un exercice, tout à la fois une forme de cadeau et de ticket d'entrée : l'obligation de l'angle de vision. C'est un exemple sché- matique. Si l'on regarde ses pieds, on est un idiot. Porter le regard un peu devant soi ajoute un peu de sécurité, pour ne pas trébu- cher. Un peu plus loin en avant encore per- met déjà d'atteindre une forme d'intelli- gence, mais on ne se trouve pas encore en position de donner. A l'approche de l'hori- zontale, ce sont quelques solutions de pro- grès de vie qui peuvent se faire jour.

Dès que le regard a dépassé l'horizon, à l'ho- rizontale, on se situe dans l'intelligence et en mesure de remplir certains devoirs vis-à-vis de la société. Le regard va au-delà de la terre et de la matière. On est dans la vision : l'œil n'est plus arrêté par la ligne d'horizon, l'ex- ploration de l'espace et du temps peut com- mencer. A 45°, on est dans l'ordre du génie, à même d'entendre certains éléments fonda- mentaux pour la compréhension de notre es- pèce. A l'appoche de la verticale, on entre dans le divin. Mais c'est une case du jeu de l'Oie, un puits à la verticale de soi-même, un piège. La dimension mystique, séduisante, est aussi une échappatoire de l'ordre du ré- gressif et de l'inutile, sinon du danger.

Au-delà de cette verticale, derrière soi, com- mence le passé. Une attitude structurelle- ment moins utile à l'égard de notre dé- marche de mutation.

Dans le dernier quart entre la verticale et l'horizontale, c'est le stade de la schizophré- nie. A l'horizontale, en arrière, on entre dans la folie. On tombe.

Tout le monde peut accomplir l'exercice mi- nimal de lever les yeux.

On peut prolonger l'exercice de vision, sur le plan horizontal : en regardant devant soi, comme tout le monde, on reste dans le cou- rant normal de pensée. Il ne faut plus penser ‹ en général ›, où l'on ne fait plus son devoir. C'est seulement au-delà, dans la pensée originale, l'exploration, où l'on tente de s'éloigner, un peu plus à droite ou plus à gauche, que cela devient intéressant. Mais il faut le mesurer.

A 45°, c'est une grande vision, panoramique, nécessaire.

Si l'on atteint 90° de chaque côté, une fois de plus la pensée devient inutilisable. Re- tourner le regard, regarder derrière, ramène au passé, à la négation de soi et de notre espèce.

Le tout, vertical et horizontal associés, crée un cône. Je l'appellerai ‹cône de vision obli- gatoire›. C'est la première chose que même le plus démuni peut offrir.

Ce que Jean-Luc Godard exprime en considérant que la télévision c'est baisser les yeux, quand le cinéma implique d'élever le regard. L'angle du regard est un acte hautement symbolique.

On sait

Il est possible de noter dans notre civilisation des permanences de formes, qui participent de toutes les époques et de toutes les cultures.

C'est assez aisément remarquable.

Quelques connaissances de physique ou d'astrophysique, peut-être mathématiques, font émerger certains schémas qui permettent d'en simplifier la compréhension.

Il est frappant de voir l'extrême similitude entre ces propositions scientifiques et des formes récurrentes à travers les lieux, les temps et des civilisations.

Un exemple parmi d'autres en serait la forme générale du vase, de l'amphore, où l'on repère cette même écriture de courbes qui reprend assez précisément les proportions de l'univers.

Dans le pré-big-bang, on trouvera le socle. Le big-bang sera le pied.

Le corps enflé du vase est celui de l'expansion de l'univers.

Son col est une légère contraction suivie d'une faible expansion.

Par ailleurs, des expériences montrent que la vision par persistance rétinienne d'une multitude de visages humains conduit à la constitution d'un visage unique qui n'est pas sans rappeler celui de la Joconde, un tableau à peu près universellement reconnu comme représentation occidentale canonique de l'humain.

Ces indices, mêlés à des suggestions d'enfants, comparés à des remarques de physiciens, pourraient tendre à prouver l'existence d'une compréhension inconsciente globale, et d'une harmonie structurelle, entre le fonctionnement humain et les lois qui le régissent.

Des indices.

Renaissance

D'une manière plus cohérente que cette succession de fragments ne pourrait le laisser penser, beaucoup d'éléments me rattachent à Venise. Mon amour pour la ville est aussi celui d'un retour à la boue féconde. Je me retrouve dans la soupe primordiale d'où sortit la modernité de la Renaissance. Guidée peut-être par le spectre d'un rêve, il y a dans la nature de mes préoccupations une intention non-dite d'instauration du modèle d'une société qui tirerait ses racines de cette république de Venise. Une ville peuplée de scientifiques, de commerçants éclairés et de philosophes. Un prototype qui a accouché d'un modèle de civilisation.

Dans la fuite vers la lagune, je vois un antidote possible au retour de la barbarie, une menace toujours présente.

Poésie

Bizarrement, j'ai mis 50 ans pour vraiment comprendre que 'poésie' était un mot important. Dans son côté anormal, actif, subversif. Autant je suis peu intéressé par la poésie déjà finie, autant j'aime en pister les indices et en mettre à jour les manifestations à travers les différentes échelles de la matière ou du temps.

Je voudrais fermer la boucle en retournant sur mon lit et en regardant bien dans les étoiles.

Les publications scientifiques constituent une bonne lentille entre le ciel et nous. J'y ai rencontré deux informations qui me rendent définitivement heureux et optimiste : la découverte, dans l'espace, d'un diamant vert, monolithique, gros comme la terre. Et celle d'un astéroïde ressemblant à un os de chien, aux dimensions de l'Etat du New Jersey. C'est le début de la révélation d'un grand bric-à-brac stellaire surréaliste.

Une raison suffisante pour se réveiller le matin, et sourire (...)

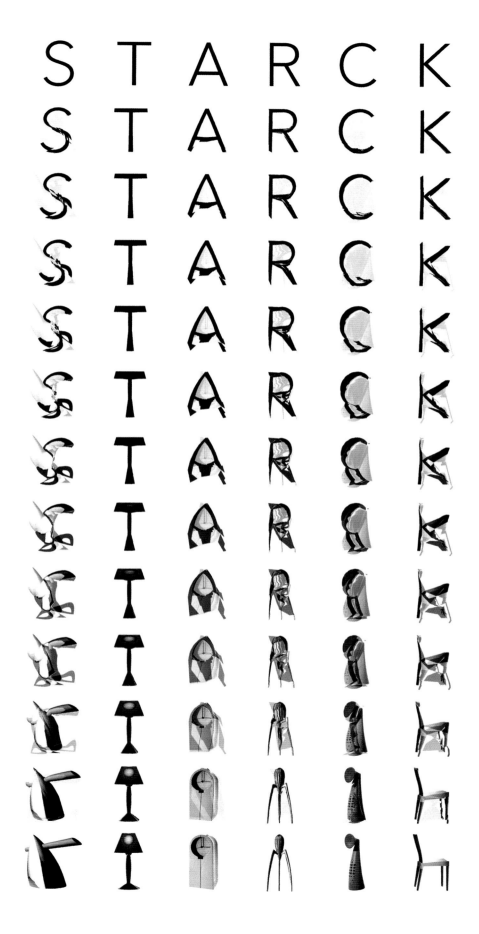

Extract of a conversation with Elisabeth Laville (in August 1998), originally published in a special issue of *La Lettre d'Utopies* / "Responsible Design"

We have to replace beauty, which is a cultural concept, with goodness, which is a humanist concept

Philippe Starck spent a Saturday morning answering our questions in the peace and calm of his house in Formentera (Spain) – a house "in the middle of nowhere, without water or electricity, facing the Mediterranean", where he goes to "give thanks to God until the end of time for portables" – meaning both telephones and computers, thanks to which he can work there just as efficiently as if he were in his Paris offices. The result is what he calls "management through absence." There, he can remain completely detached and think creatively when making decisions, because of the distance between him and the "fever" and the "backroom problems" which are handled by his small and "extremely competent" team in Paris.

In your opinion, what is the role of the designer today?

In the 1950s, one of the fathers of design, Raymond Loewy, invented a slogan which was responsible both for his own success and, in part, for that of the design movement: "ugliness doesn't sell well." At that time, he may have been right, but I'm afraid that this formula was already structurally flawed. We have to escape from this flaw, we have to kill the word of the father... We have to understand that "ugliness doesn't sell well" means that design is simply the slave of industry and production, that its role is to help things sell. Structurally, that is no longer what we do. Today, the problem is not to produce more so you can sell more. The fundamental question is that of the product's right to exist. And it is the designer's right and duty, in the first place, to question the legitimacy of the product, and that is how he too comes to exist. Depending on what answer he comes up with, one of the most positive things a designer can do is refuse to do anything. This isn't always easy. He should refuse, nevertheless, when the object already exists and functions perfectly well. Simply to repeat it would be a venal act, and one which would have serious consequences, impoverishing the wealth of the Earth, and impoverishing and dulling the minds of people, because afterwards his act will be picked up and carried further by those services which browbeat people until they buy something. I mean advertising, and the press in general...

How then should one judge of an object's right to exist?

The essential thing to do is to test it in relation to a number of more or less strict criteria.

The first quite strict criterion is to do nothing which could cause harm to man. This is a rather simplistic criterion, but we must respect it nevertheless, and sometimes that means losing a lot of money. So we don't work for the arms industry, we don't work for hard spirits, we don't work for tobacco, we don't work for religion, and we don't work for anything which involves money from dubious sources, which is getting more and more complicated. It's quite possible that we could end up accepting dirty money which has been laundered through one kind of business or another. I had to refuse a fabulous contract in East Berlin, because of such doubts, and in fact, now, in all our contracts, we have a clause which says that our clients must declare the sources of their financing. If it turns out that they lied to us, the contract is automatically void. So those are the most immediate demands, the necessary moral rules, which are just obvious.

After that, you have to test the object in relation to another set of parameters which aim to justify its existence. To begin with, the product must provide a new service, offer something more interesting than what is there already, establish a new skill... otherwise, you might just as well use an object that exists already. Next, it must perform its function completely, with as much honesty as possible. This honesty is difficult to identify, because often it is not what it seems. Objects serve other purposes than those for which they appear to be destined, so you have to know how to read between the lines, you have to know how to read in both our unconscious and in the objects' unconscious. ... Then, you have to try and perform the function purely, with as few preconceived ideas as possible, which means, as a rule, using the least possible quantity of matter. This is where I always mention the example of a client who asked for a boat, and he was very happy with the advice of his designer, who suggested he try swimming and in this way led him to rediscover the pleasures of swimming. Today, we have the means to redirect the efforts of research and industry to produce tools which would allow you, instead of having 20 per cent functionality against 80 per cent useless matter (which a a rule is only there to serve the greed of the producer), to invert the process and have 80 per cent functionality. To achieve this, designers have to stop thinking of their solutions in terms of matter. It is essential for designers, when faced with a question, to be extremely open and say: "the right answer is a biological answer, not an industrial answer; the right answer is a semantic answer, not a material answer..." Then the designer who stares at his paper and his pencil is no longer just the accomplice of systematic production, he is a conductor who has to bring certain skills to bear in relation to certain needs. This determination to get rid of what is useless and replace it with what is honest is based on a strong principle, which we can call "dematerialisation". The object, the non object of tomorrow, will be like a star in the sky which is in a state of perpetual implosion, that is, its volume is constantly decreasing, even as its mass increases – its mass of skills, its mass of honesty and its mass of emotion. The only way forward for the productive system is through dematerialisation ... Meanwhile, there is something essential that we must attend to provisionally, in parallel: we must reposition everything around us politically, socially, sexually and economically. This is easy. It doesn't require any substantial means, but just our awareness and determination.

On the political level, we must avoid making objects which represent aggression, violence, fascism, let's say, forms of darkness. ... This requires a great deal of reflection on the political meaning of what we do: we have to clean our objects of all these barbaric signs and load them instead with positive, constructive signs which can indicate another way forward...

The second parameter is social or financial, and is related to the first.

Objects should not serve as a means of representing money so that people can humiliate their neighbours. Much of today's production does nothing else. That is, its meaning is, "I've earned lots of money, mine is bigger than yours, and you can just fuck off." This is a big problem, because you cannot build a civilisation on such negativity. The third parameter is sex, which is again related to the first point, since everything has to do with politics. Today, 80 per cent of objects are unnecessarily macho. Yet it is plain:

The intelligence of a truly modern society must be feminine.

This is due to a series of structural differences, which are grounded in the protection of the species, the value of continuity, and in something which I find more difficult to explain – a sort of pragmatism which leads someone to do many different things simultaneously, rather than sacrificing everything to one big idea, which appropriates and perverts everything. So it is very interesting to ask these questions of every object we meet. Often, the answer is quite obvious and quite shocking, when you keep your eyes open. Apart from a machine pistol, I can't think of many objects which actually need to be extravagantly masculine!

The next point is economic, and concerns how affordable these products are.

It is absolutely essential to "dis-elitify" quality objects, so as to make the best things available to the greatest number of people. If an idea is right, and if it can be repeated over and over again, it would be an act of theft not to repeat it. This means we have to work on restoring dignity to the word "popular". We have to work on the power that comes from multiplication, on the increase in quality that comes from multiplication. And to this end – but this is already one of our hobbyhorses – we should not put our faith in craftsmanship, but in the moralisation of large businesses.

Is that what your role was at Thomson?

That was my main task when I was artistic director at Thomson for four years: to make the company virtuous. Not because there was a desire there to do evil, but because they had simply forgotten their purpose in life – to be of service, to use their skills to be of service. It is essential to try to play the role of a friendly "enemy within". That is, to catch the interest of these big companies so that they make money available, and research facilities, and distribution networks, for this return to what is the origin of all their activities – to serve others. It even means changing the words they use. One of the things I did at Thomson was to change their name. Thomson used to be called TCE, Thomson Consumer Electronic, and I asked them: who wants to be a "consumer of electronics?" At the time, I was lucky to work with an extraordinary managing director, Alain Prestat, who understood what I was getting at straightaway. We chose the name, Thomson Multimedia, because he was betting on the technological success of multimedia, and I wanted to talk about the multiple channels such a company must use to express itself, if it wants to act morally. For what's the use of making beautiful television sets if all you can watch on them is crap... The other important thing I did was that I outlawed the word "consumer" in all company meetings, and insisted it be replaced by the words "my friend", "my wife", "my daughter", "my mother", or "myself." It doesn't sound the same at all, if you say: "It doesn't matter, it's shit, but the consumers will make do with it," or if you start over again and say: "It's shit, but it doesn't matter, my daughter will make do with it." ... All of a sudden, you can't get away with it any more. So there is an enormous task to be done with this kind of symbolic repositioning, using just one word. The other thing I did at Thomson was to invent the slogan "Thomson: from technology to love," and again, that completely repositioned the problem. Because now we were saying that technology wasn't an end in itself, but just a means – and that the real goal, the final goal, was what had always been there, the original priority, humanity, whose fundamental criterion is love.

That connects back to your idea of the friendly object, the good object...

Yes, this takes us back more or less to the role of the designer. You're not designing the object for the sake of the object, you don't care whether it's beautiful or not. We have to replace beauty, which is a cultural concept, with goodness, which is a humanist concept. The object must be of good quality, it must satisfy one of the key modern parameters, which is to be long-lived, and we'll come

back to that. But above all it must be good for the person who is going to live with it – by which I mean, it mustn't hide the person behind logos, or oppress him or her by the admiration it provokes. Instead it must allow the person to blossom, to be him or herself, and to be happier with it than without it. Saying that an object must bring out the best in someone already eliminates 70 per cent of contemporary production, which turns people into clowns: fake Harley Davidsons which turn people into fake bikers, over-labelled sunglasses which turn people into coatstands for ridiculous brands... People disguise themselves so that they don't have to exist. And it is essential that people begin to exist again, otherwise, they will disappear. We have to fight against the way in which people are turned into an audience, into spectators, by working continually to restore them to their proper place, as actors.

After that, of course, there is ecology.

We have to talk to the big companies which are now moral actors, so that they make sure their production is not damaging to man, that the object is not a cause of harm in their lives.

This obviously means getting rid of recycling, which is just a marketing gimmick... Recycling was invented by the ecologists, but in the end, all it does is enable us to go on producing and consuming wastefully. A good product is a product which lasts. When it has lasted 10, 20, 30 years, then whether it is recyclable, whether it is actually recycled, in a sense is not important. But to recycle useless objects every year is a completely crazy waste of matter and energy. I am not against recycling, I am against its being used as a universal panacea. Recycling is a sticking plaster, a way of repairing a mistake, nothing more. It's a false solution, a false problem, a kind of ecological practical joke, of a kind that is proliferating nowadays: like electrically-powered cars, which are just a way of moving the exhaust pipe away from the car and towards the nuclear power plants. ...

You were talking a little earlier about the need to make products affordable. Is that why you are working on the Good Goods catalogue with Carrefour and La Redoute – because they are trying to democratise the best kind of product?

One of the few victories I've won in my career is to have succeeded in conferring a certain nobility on the idea of multiplication, that is, on the word "popular." I raised the status of contempt. Before, a toothbrush would be hidden in the bottom of a drawer. Then, overnight, people started giving toothbrushes for Christmas, they started showing them to their friends. The other thing I have achieved is to have brought prices down, and made them affordable. Over the space of ten years, I managed, despite all the resistance, to halve the price of my objects just about every year or two. One of my first successes, the Café Costes chair, started out at about 4,000 francs... Today, we make chairs for 300 francs, maybe even 200. ... We're even collaborating with Vitra to see if we can find a way to hire out furniture or buy it back again. We've been thinking about this idea for five or six years, and the problem is that today we don't know how to do it. We don't know how to oblige someone to bring back a chair in exchange for less than 50 francs, which very soon will be the price of the chair itself. ... This kind of scheme is necessarily for the super-mass market, but the people who make up that super-mass market aren't yet sufficiently educated for this. And there's also a problem of price. How much do you rent a chair for, when the chair's worth 50 francs? One franc a month? As you see, there are a number of real obstacles there. So it's better for us to use a style, a non-style, which will survive through time. Take the little Dr. No chair, for example: it's comfortable, you can stack it, it's more or less indestructible, with all the problems that represents, and you could keep it for 20 years... and in 20 years time, you'll find it at the bottom of the garden, someone will go and pick it up and melt it down. But for now, it's no use our trying to make a big push on this issue, we just don't have the means to do it. The supermarkets are a necessary part of what I do. Good Goods came out in 1998, and at the same time we were presenting our Seven Eleven operation in Japan. This was one of the biggest single operations in the history of design. Seven Eleven is a chain of convenience stores which are open 24 hours round the clock. They have 8,000 shops in Japan, 30,000 throughout Asia and I don't know how many in the US. They've given me more or less all their objects to design – yoghurt pots, razors, underpants, pencils, everything. They are the biggest buyer in the world, so this will really allow us to go to scale, to offer the best to everyone. We know already that 10 million copies of each object will be manufactured each year, and that means... I don't think any of these objects costs more than 10 or 12 francs. So that's really one in the face for the elitist notion of design. For me, this is something essential, it's almost like achieving my ultimate goal. After this, I don't know what more I can do, except keep going, and try to show that I can make better yoghurt pots, better underpants...

And Good Goods?

This is a project which has been close to my heart for many years. For two years I put an enormous amount of work into it, and for the first time in my life, I can even say that while I don't regret it, I wouldn't choose to do it again. It cost me a fortune in terms of lost earnings through all the time it consumed. I'm trying to move towards making objects which are honest, objects for non-consumers, for "modern rebels" who are fed up with marketing and advertising trying to make them believe that they absolutely have to change their R5 for an R6, their 4:3 television for one with a 16:9 screen... For me, these people represent a new unspoken political force. ... That's what interests me: these non-consumers, catalysed by the catalogue, will be establishing rules for what I call the "moral market," which is more or less what we've just described. People will get the catalogue, with a little message from me telling them something which is quite revolutionary in the world of commerce, that is, that it isn't worth buying these products, and that it's more important for them to read the catalogue, and read between the lines. In Good Goods, there are some interesting products, but they don't pretend to be the kind of non-product which I'm aiming for eventually, they're just there to kickstart the process. And what is important is that with each object there is a short explanation, not as long as I would have liked, because we didn't have space, but an attempt to explain why, and symmetrically, why not: why not other things, why we don't want these other things any more ...

Today, you can use your reputation to try and put these messages across... But in the Good Goods catalogue, you say that you're trying to "correct the course of a history in which I was doubtless an accomplice myself." Does that mean that, in relation to the criteria you've talked about, the Starck objects in this catalogue are those to which you now feel closest?

You know, I've always been the same, I've always pursued the same idea. Except in the beginning, because when you're young, you work for yourself in order to survive, and you do what you can. I'm 49 years old now, I have certain means at my disposition, and I'd be an idiot if I hadn't thought my strategy through, and I'd be dishonest if I didn't try to stick to it. So I admit that I've done what I could, that there have been high points and low points, but I have always proceeded honestly. Now, I can't say that everything is perfect, but I have the means to be more rigorous. You know, to begin with, what mattered was to assert myself, because I had to build up this power. When you're a French design-er... you must never forget that there's no such thing as a French designer!

...uszug aus einem Gespräch mit Elisabeth ...aville (im August 1998), veröffentlicht in ei-...er Sonderausgabe von *La Lettre d'Utopies* / ...Verantwortliches Design«

An die Stelle des wesentlich kulturellen Schönen muß das wesentlich humanistische Gute treten

...hilippe Starck beantwortete unsere Fragen ...n einem Samstagvormittag in der Stille sei-...es Hauses auf Formentera (Spanien): ein ...aus »irgendwo im Niemandsland, ohne ...Vasser und ohne Strom, mit Blick aufs Mit-...elmeer«, wo er »Gott auf ewig dafür dankt, ...aß es tragbare Geräte gibt« (Handy und ...aptop), die ihm ein genauso effizientes Ar-...eiten ermöglichen, als wäre er in seinen Pa-...ser Büros. Dank diesem »Management in ...bwesenheit« trifft er Entscheidungen krea-...v und mit kühlem Kopf und hält sich fern ...om »Fieber« und »Gebrodel« – darum ...ümmert sich sein kleines und »ungemein ...ompetentes« Team in Paris.

Welche Aufgabe hat für Sie ein Designer heute?

Einer der Pioniere des Designs, Raymond Loewy, hat in den fünfziger Jahren einen Slogan geprägt, der ihm persönlich und zum Teil auch der gesamten Designbewegung Erfolg gebracht hat: »Häßlichkeit verkauft sich schlecht.« Zu seiner Zeit hatte er damit vielleicht recht, doch lag im Kern der Aussage schon ein Fehler, den wir heute unbedingt abstellen müssen ... »Häßlichkeit verkauft sich schlecht« bedeutet ja im Grunde, daß das Design der Industrie und Produktion als bloßer Erfüllungsgehilfe dient, damit sich Waren besser verkaufen. Damit ist uns aber im Ansatz nicht mehr geholfen: Heute geht es nicht mehr darum, mehr zu produzieren, um mehr zu verkaufen. Vordringlich stellt sich vielmehr die grundsätzliche Frage, mit welchem Recht ein Produkt überhaupt existiert. Es ist das Recht und die Aufgabe des Designers, nach der Legitimität des Produktes zu fragen, darauf fußt seine wahre Existenz. Und je nachdem, wie die Antwort ausfällt, gehört zu den besten Dingen, die ein Designer tun kann, nein zu sagen – was aber nicht immer leichtfällt. Nein sagen, weil das Produkt bereits existiert und ganz ausgezeichnet funktioniert, so daß seine Wiederholung lediglich eine Frage der Verkäuflichkeit wäre. Und zwar mit schwerwiegenden Folgen, was sowohl die Plünderung der Bodenschätze als auch die Abstumpfung und Verarmung des menschlichen Intellekts anbelangt. Denn der Tätigkeit des Designers folgt die Arbeit derjenigen, die die Leute so lange verblöden, bis sie kaufen – ich spreche von der Werbung und ganz allgemein von der Presse ...

Wie läßt sich denn die Existenzberechtigung eines Objektes beurteilen?

Grundsätzlich muß es einen Katalog von mehr oder weniger strengen Kriterien erfüllen.

Das erste strenge Kriterium lautet, nichts zu tun, was den Menschen schaden kann. Das ist ein sehr schlichtes Gebot, aber man muß es trotzdem erst einmal einhalten, was manchmal herbe finanzielle Einbußen mit sich bringt: Es bedeutet, nicht für die Waffenindustrie zu arbeiten, nicht für harte Alkoholika, nicht für die Tabakindustrie, nicht für die Religion und für kein Projekt, das womöglich auf zweifelhafter Finanzierung beruht. Letzteres wird immer schwieriger. Schmutziges Geld, das durch irgendwelche Geschäfte gewaschen wurde, kann uns durchaus wiederbegegnen. Weil ich da meine Zweifel hatte, habe ich einmal ein überwältigendes Angebot aus Ostberlin abgelehnt. Übrigens enthalten unsere Verträge jetzt eine Klausel, die jeden Kunden verpflichtet, seine Geldquellen

offenzulegen – sollte sich herausstellen, daß er gelogen hat, wird der Vertrag automatisch nichtig. Soweit also die unmittelbaren Forderungen, die obligatorischen moralischen Regeln, die auf der Hand liegen.

Damit ein Objekt existieren darf, muß es aber noch weitere Kriterien erfüllen. Zunächst muß das Produkt etwas Neues bringen, es soll etwas Interessantes, bislang Unbekanntes leisten ... sonst kann man gleich auf schon Bestehendes zurückgreifen. Dann muß es seinen Zweck auch wirklich erfüllen, mit größtmöglicher Aufrichtigkeit, was schwer zu überprüfen ist, denn oft ist der Zweck ein anderer, als man glaubt. Etliche Produkte dienen in Wahrheit nicht dem Zweck, den man vordergründig zu erkennen meint. Deshalb kommt es darauf an, zwischen den Zeilen zu lesen, in unserem eigenen Unbewußten und in dem der Objekte. (...) Schließlich muß man den Zweck zu klären versuchen, und zwar mit möglichst wenig vorgefaßten Ideen, das heißt meistens, mit möglichst wenig Material. Hier führe ich immer mein kleines Beispiel von dem Kunden an, der ein Boot in Auftrag gibt. Als der Designer ihm rät, es doch mit Schwimmen zu versuchen, ist er hochzufrieden, weil er aufgrund dieser Empfehlung etwas wiederentdeckt, was ihm Spaß macht. Man könnte Forschung und Industrie so umstellen, daß das heutige Verhältnis von 20 Prozent Nutzen zu 80 Prozent Ballast (der meist nur der Profitmaximierung des Herstellers dient) umgekehrt würde zu 80 Prozent Nutzenanteil. Das setzt voraus, daß der Designer aufhört, die Lösung im Material zu suchen. Entscheidend ist, daß er unvoreingenommen an die Frage herangeht und etwa sagt: Hier hilft keine industrielle Lösung, sondern eine biologische, dort keine materielle, sondern eine semantische ... Dann nämlich ist der Designer nicht mehr der Komplize eines systematischen Produktionsbetriebs, der mit dem Bleistift vor einem Stück Papier sitzt, sondern jemand, der das Heft selbst in die Hand nimmt und bestimmten Bedürfnissen bestimmte Kompetenzen entgegenbringt. Man muß sich klarmachen, daß der Wunsch, unnützen Ballast abzuwerfen und ihn durch ehrliche Leistung zu ersetzen, auf einer wichtigen Entwicklungstendenz beruht, nämlich der zur Dematerialisation. Das Objekt oder, besser gesagt, das Nicht-Objekt von morgen befindet sich wie ein Stern am Himmel in dauernder Implosion: So stetig sein Volumen abnimmt, so stetig nimmt seine Masse zu – die Masse an Leistung, Aufrichtigkeit und Gefühl. Die Produktion kann sich nur in Richtung Dematerialisierung entwickeln. (...) Bis dahin kommen wir um eine vorläufige, aber unausweichlich mit diesem Prozeß verknüpfte Aufgabe nicht herum: unsere Umwelt politisch, sozial, sexuell und ökonomisch neu zu positionieren. Diese Arbeit ist einfach und erfordert keinen großen Aufwand, bloß Bewußtwerdung und Stehvermögen.

Die politische Positionierung: vermeiden, daß die Objekte Aggressivität, Gewalt, Faschismus, sagen wir, finstere Tendenzen vermitteln. (...) Das bedeutet, eine umfassende Rechenschaft abzulegen über den politischen Zweck unseres Tuns: Wir müssen die Objekte von den barbarischen Zeichen befreien und sie mit positiven, konstruktiven Zeichen aufladen. Nur so können wir einen anderen Weg aufzeigen ...

Die zweite Maßgabe ist die gesellschaftliche oder finanzielle, und sie hängt mit der ersten zusammen: Die Objekte dürfen keine Selbstdarstellung des Geldes werden, mit dem Ziel, die Mitmenschen zu demütigen. Ein Großteil der heutigen Produkte ist auf nichts anderes angelegt, als zu symbolisieren: »Ich habe Geld verdient, meiner ist dicker als deiner, und du kannst mich mal.« Dies ist sehr bedenklich, denn keine Zivilisation läßt sich auf Negativem aufbauen.

Der dritte Parameter ist die Sexualität. Auch sie hat mit dem ersten Punkt zu tun, denn mit der Politik hängt alles zusammen: Heute sind 80 Prozent aller Produkte völlig überflüssigerweise machistisch. Dabei steht fest:

Die moderne Intelligenz ist weiblich.

Und zwar deshalb, weil das Verhalten der Frauen in vieler Hinsicht strukturell anders ist, basierend auf dem Schutz der Gattung, der Sicherung des Fortbestands und auch auf etwas, das ich noch nicht richtig erklären kann: einer Art Pragmatismus, der verschiedene Handlungsweisen gleichzeitig zuläßt und großen Ideen, die sich vereinnahmen und pervertieren lassen, aus dem Weg geht. Deshalb ist es sehr wichtig, sich zu jedem Objekt Fragen zu stellen. Bei unverstelltem Blick ist die Antwort oft klar und schockierend: Von einer Maschinenpistole abgesehen, wüßte ich kaum einen Gegenstand, der unbedingt überwältigend männlich sein müßte!

Der nächste Punkt ist der ökonomische, er betrifft die Erschwinglichkeit der Produkte: Die Qualitätsprodukte müssen dringend »ent-elitisiert« werden, um möglichst viele mit dem Besten zu versorgen.

Wenn eine Idee richtig und vervielfältigbar ist, ist es Diebstahl, sie nicht zu vervielfältigen. Es bedarf also einer Aufwertung des Be-

griffs »populär«, einer Verbesserung der Vervielfältigungsmöglichkeiten und der Qualität, die Vervielfältigung liefern kann. Und dafür – aber für diese These haben Sie ja schon vehement gestritten – darf man nicht allzusehr auf das Handwerk bauen, sondern eher auf das Einsetzen eines moralischen Verantwortungsgefühls bei den Großunternehmen.

Und diese Rolle haben Sie bei Thomson übernommen?

Das war meine Haupttätigkeit während meiner vierjährigen Arbeit als Art-Direktor bei Thomson: das Unternehmen, das nicht willentlich Böses im Schilde führte, aber ganz einfach den Grund seines Daseins vergessen hatte, zu bestimmten Tugenden zu bekehren – sich nützlich zu machen und die eigenen Kompetenzen für eine Dienstleistung einzusetzen. Man muß dann so etwas wie einen freundlichen inneren Feind spielen, damit man die großen Firmen dafür gewinnt, ihr Fachwissen, ihre finanziellen Mittel, Forschungs- und Vertriebsmöglichkeiten verfügbar zu machen und zum Ausgangspunkt aller Dinge zurückzukehren, zur Dienstleistung. Das beinhaltet auch einen anderen Sprachgebrauch, weshalb ich übrigens bei Thomson unter anderem auf eine Namensänderung gedrungen habe. Thomson nannte sich TCE, Thomson Consumer Electronic. Ich habe gefragt: Wer will ein »Elektronik-Konsument« sein? Damals hatte ich das Glück, einen außergewöhnlichen Vorstand zu haben, Alain Prestat, dem dies sofort einleuchtete. Wir entschieden uns für den Namen Thomson Multimedia, weil Prestat auf den Erfolg der Multimedia-Techniken setzte und ich deutlich machen wollte, daß eine moralisch verfaßte Gesellschaft mehrere Ausdrucksträger benötigt. Schließlich ist es nicht der Mühe wert, schöne Fernsehapparate zu bauen, wenn darin nur Mist läuft ... Darüber hinaus haben wir das Wort »Verbraucher« aus den Besprechungen verbannt und verlangt, es durch »mein Freund«, »meine Frau«, »meine Tochter«, »meine Mutter« oder »ich« zu ersetzen. Es ergibt nämlich einen ganz anderen Sinn, wenn man, statt zu erklären: »Nicht schlimm, das Ding ist zwar Dreck, aber die Verbraucher werden sich damit schon zufriedengeben«, neu ansetzt und sagt: »Nicht schlimm, das Ding ist zwar Dreck, aber meine Tochter wird sich damit zufriedengeben.« Plötzlich kommt das gar nicht mehr so gut an. Mit einem Wort läßt sich also ungeheuer viel bewirken, und seien es auch nur symbolische Verschiebungen. Außerdem habe ich den Thomson-Slogan geprägt. Er lautet: »Thomson: von der Technologie zur Liebe« und verlagerte das Problem ebenfalls auf eine völlig andere Ebene, weil er klarstellte, daß Techno-

logie kein Selbstzweck, sondern ein Mittel ist, und daß es schließlich seit jeher in erster Linie auf das Menschliche ankommt, das einer so fundamentalen Empfindung wie der Liebe fähig ist.

Das führt uns wieder zu Ihrer Idee von einem freundschaftlichen, einem guten Objekt ...

Richtig, wir kehren damit praktisch zur Rolle des Designers zurück. Man entwirft das Objekt nicht um des Objektes willen, man pfeift darauf, ob es schön ist. Daß es gut ist, das ist das Entscheidende. An die Stelle des wesentlich kulturellen Schönen muß das wesentlich humanistische Gute treten. Selbstverständlich soll das Objekt von guter Qualität sein und eines der zeitgemäßesten Merkmale überhaupt, nämlich Langlebigkeit aufweisen (dazu kommen wir noch). Vor allem aber soll es gut für diejenigen sein, die mit ihm leben: Das heißt, es soll sie nicht hinter Logos verstecken und sie nicht dem Druck des Bewundernmüssens aussetzen, den Objekte ausüben können. Das Produkt soll dem Menschen erlauben, sich zu entfalten, er selbst zu sein und glücklicher zu werden. Unter der Voraussetzung, daß ein Produkt dem Menschen zu seiner Entfaltung verhelfen soll, kann man schon einmal 70 Prozent der derzeitigen Produktion wegwerfen, weil sie nämlich die Leute zu Kaspern macht. Falsche Harley Davidsons verwandeln die Leute in falsche Biker, mit Labels aufgemotzte Brillen verwandeln sie in Reklameschilder für Marken, die einem egal sind ... Die Menschen verkleiden sich, um nicht zu existieren. Es kommt aber darauf an, daß die Menschen wieder existieren, weil sie sonst verschwinden werden. Wir müssen fortwährend gegen eine Vorstellung ankämpfen, die Menschen zu Publikum, zu Zuschauern machen will, und sie wieder an ihren Platz als Handelnde stellen.

Dann gibt es natürlich noch das Problem der Ökologie.

Die moralisch gewordenen Großunternehmen müssen davon überzeugt werden, daß die Produktion den Menschen nicht schädigen, das Objekt sein Leben nicht beeinträchtigen darf.

Der Marketing-Gimmick Recycling hat dabei natürlich nichts zu suchen. Von den Ökologen erfunden, sorgt Recycling letzten Endes dafür, daß wir heute nutzlos weiterproduzieren und -konsumieren können. Ein gutes Produkt ist ein haltbares Produkt: Wenn es zehn, zwanzig, dreißig Jahre gehalten hat, darf es einem im Zweifelsfall egal sein, ob es wiederverwertbar ist und wiederverwertet wird. Aber jahraus, jahrein nutzlose Dinge zu recyceln, ist eine wahnsinnige Vergeudung von Material und Energie. Ich bin nicht gegen Recycling, aber gegen den Versuch, es zum Allheilmittel zu stilisieren. Recycling ist ein Notbehelf, das nachträgliche Ausbügeln eines Fehlers, und sonst nichts. Es ist eine Scheinlösung, ein falsches Problem, ein ökologischer Schmus, wie es ihn heute überall gibt: etwa der Elektroantrieb bei Autos, der bloß den Auspuff in die Atomkraftwerke verlegt. (...)

Sie sprachen vorhin von der Erschwinglichkeit der Produkte: Ist das der Grund, warum Sie an Ihrem Katalog Good Goods arbeiten und mit den Kaufhausketten Carrefour und La Redoute kooperieren, die sich die Demokratisierung der besten Produkte zum Ziel gesetzt haben?

Einer der wenigen Erfolge, die ich in meiner Laufbahn errungen habe, war die Aufwertung der Vervielfältigung, mit anderen Worten des Begriffs »populär«, die Nobilitierung des Verachteten. Früher wurde eine Zahnbürste im hintersten Eck einer Schublade versteckt, und von einem Tag auf den anderen schenkte man sie sich plötzlich zu Weihnachten. Sie wurde vorzeigbar. Mein zweiter Erfolg war es, die Preise zu brechen und Dinge erschwinglich zu machen: Im Verlauf eines Jahrzehnts habe ich es gegen alle und jeden durchgesetzt, die Preise meiner Objekte alle ein bis zwei Jahre praktisch zu halbieren. Einer meiner ersten Erfolge, der Stuhl für das Café Costes, kostete damals 4000 Francs ... Heute arbeiten wir an Stühlen für 300, vielleicht sogar 200 Francs. (...) Mit Vitra überlegen wir sogar, wie man Möbel vermieten oder zurücknehmen könnte. Daran arbeiten wir jetzt seit mindestens fünf bis sechs Jahren, das Problem ist nur, daß das derzeit nicht machbar ist. Wir wissen nicht, wie wir jemanden verpflichten können, gegen ein Entgelt von weniger als 50 Francs einen Stuhl zurückzubringen, was in Kürze der Preis sein wird, den er dafür bezahlt hat. (...) Diese Überlegung bezieht sich zwangsläufig auf den absoluten Massenmarkt, aber die Zielgruppe dieses Marktes ist dafür noch nicht aufgeklärt genug. Auch gibt es das Gebührenproblem: Für wieviel vermieten Sie einen Stuhl, der 50 Francs kostet? Einen Franc im Monat? Da tun sich einige Sackgassen auf. Besser also einen Stil bzw. Nicht-Stil entwickeln, der zeitresistent ist. Nehmen Sie zum Beispiel den kleinen Stuhl Dr. No: Er ist bequem, stapelbar, praktisch unverwüstlich, was wiederum das Problem mit sich bringt, daß man ihn zwanzig Jahre lang behält. Nach zwanzig Jahren findet man ihn in einer Ecke des Gartens wieder, jemand sammelt ihn auf, und er wird eingeschmolzen. Aber vorerst brauchen wir keine großen Geschütze aufzufahren, denn uns fehlen die Mittel, das oben erwähnte Projekt durchzuführen.

Großdistribution ist für mich unumgänglich. Der Katalog Good Goods kam 1998 heraus, und gleichzeitig präsentierten wir in Japan Seven Eleven, eine der größten Aktionen in der Geschichte des Designs. Seven Eleven, eine Kette durchgehend geöffneter *convenient stores* (8 000 in Japan, 30 000 in Asien und ich weiß nicht mehr wie viele in den USA), hat mir im Grunde die Gestaltung sämtlicher Artikel übertragen: Joghurts, Rasierer, Slips, Buntstifte, alles was Sie wollen. Sie ist der größte Auftraggeber der Welt, mit dem man wirklich Großes in Bewegung setzen kann, und zwar zum Besten aller. Wir wissen schon jetzt, daß jedes Objekt eine Auflage von 10 Millionen Stück pro Jahr haben wird. Ich glaube nicht, daß eines davon mehr als zehn oder zwölf Francs kostet – eine Ohrfeige für das elitäre Design. Das ist für mich das Wesentliche, fast ein Endziel. Was mir danach zu tun bleibt, weiß ich noch nicht so recht. Höchstens, weiterzuarbeiten und zu beweisen, daß man noch bessere Joghurts, noch bessere Slips machen kann ...

Und Good Goods?

Das ist ein Projekt, das mir seit Jahren am Herzen liegt und in das ich zwei Jahre lang enorm viel Mühe investiert habe. Ich würde sogar zum ersten Mal in meinem Leben behaupten, daß ich es nicht bereue, aber stünde es mir erneut bevor, ich würde es nicht noch einmal machen. Die Zeit, die ich in dieses Projekt gesteckt habe, hat mich ein Vermögen an Verdienstausfall gekostet. Ich versuche, eine Bresche für aufrichtige Objekte zu schlagen, Objekte für Nicht-Konsumenten, für »moderne Rebellen«, die es leid sind, daß Marketing und Werbung ihnen weismachen wollen, sie müßten unbedingt ihren R 5 gegen einen R 6 eintauschen, oder ihren 4/3-Fernseher gegen einen 16/9-Fernseher ... Diese Leute stellen für mich eine neue, bislang unbekannte politische Kraft dar. (...) Deshalb liegt mir daran, daß sie den Katalog als Katalysator benutzen, um Regeln aufzustellen, die ich die des *moral market* nenne, also in etwa das, was ich gerade beschrieben habe. Die Menschen werden den Katalog mit einer kleinen Notiz von mir bekommen, die ihnen etwas in der Geschäftswelt ziemlich Revolutionäres mitteilt, nämlich, daß sie die Produkte gar nicht kaufen müssen, sondern daß es wichtiger ist, im Katalog zwischen den Zeilen zu lesen. Im Good-Goods-Katalog gibt es interessante Produkte, die aber nicht den Anspruch erheben, Anti-Produkte in dem von mir angestrebten Sinn zu sein. Sie sind nur dazu da, die Sache ins Rollen zu bringen. Wichtig ist, daß jedes Produkt ein klein wenig erklärt wird – aus Platzmangel leider nicht so ausführlich, wie ich es wollte: Wir versuchen ver-

ständlich zu machen, warum, und umgekehrt, warum nicht; warum so und nicht anders, und warum wir dieses andere nicht mehr wollen. (...)

Heute benutzen Sie Ihren Ruf dazu, diese Botschaften unter die Leute zu bringen ... Trotzdem sagen Sie im Good-Goods-Katalog, Sie wollten »ein Unrecht wiedergutmachen, daß ich wahrscheinlich selbst mitverschuldet habe«. Heißt das, daß Sie hinsichtlich des Kriterienkatalogs, von dem wir sprachen, hinter den Starck-Objekten aus diesem Katalog stärker stehen als hinter anderen?

Wissen Sie, ich bin immer derselbe geblieben, mit derselben Idee im Kopf. Nur daß man anfangs, wenn man jung ist, arbeitet um zu überleben und jeden Auftrag annimmt. Jetzt bin ich 49 und habe gewisse Mittel zur Verfügung. Hätte ich meine Strategie nicht erst einmal in Konzepte gefaßt, wäre ich ein Trottel, und hielte ich mich nicht an sie, wäre ich ein Schwindler. Ich gebe also zu, daß ich getan habe, was ich tun konnte, mit Höhen und Tiefen, aber immer mit einer gewissen Aufrichtigkeit. Nicht, daß jetzt alles perfekt wäre, aber ich kann mir strengere Maßstäbe leisten. Wissen Sie, es kam ja zunächst darauf an, meinen Unterhalt zu bestreiten, und diese Fähigkeit mußte ich entwickeln. Wenn man ein französischer Designer ist ... ach was – lassen Sie uns nicht vergessen: Einen französischen Designer gibt es gar nicht!

Extrait d'une conversation avec Elisabeth Laville (en août 1998), initialement publiée dans *La Lettre d'Utopies* / Spécial « Design Responsable »

Il faut remplacer le beau d'essence culturelle par le bon d'essence humaniste

Philippe Starck a répondu à nos questions, un samedi matin, au calme dans sa maison de Formentera (Espagne) : une maison « au milieu de nulle part, sans eau ni électricité, face à la Méditerranée », et d'où il « remercie Dieu jusqu'à la fin des jours pour les portables » (téléphone et ordinateur) qui lui permettent de travailler aussi efficacement que s'il était dans ses bureaux parisiens – un « management par l'absence » qui, selon lui, permet d'être complètement froid et créatif pour les décisions en restant détaché des problèmes de « fièvre » et de « cuisine » que sa petite équipe « extraordinairement compétente » gère à Paris.

Quel est selon vous le rôle du designer, aujourd'hui ?

Un des pères du design, Raymond Lœwy, dans les années 50, a inventé un slogan qui a fait son succès et une partie du succès du design : « La laideur se vend mal .» A son époque, il avait peut-être raison mais hélas, déjà, ça portait un vice structurel dont il faut absolument sortir aujourd'hui en tuant la parole du père... Il faut bien comprendre que « la laideur se vend mal » signifie que le design n'est qu'un complice de l'industrie et de la production afin que les choses se vendent mieux. Structurellement, ce n'est plus le propos : aujourd'hui le problème n'est pas de produire plus pour vendre plus, la question fondamentale est d'abord celle de la légitimité des produits à exister. L'acte légitime du designer est d'abord la question sur la légitimité du produit, c'est ça qui lui donne sa vraie existence. Et suivant la réponse qu'il donnera à cette question, l'un des actes les plus positifs que le designer puisse faire, c'est le refus – ce qui n'est pas toujours facile. Refus parce que l'objet existe déjà et fonctionne extrêmement bien – le répéter ne serait qu'un acte vénal porteur de conséquences graves en termes d'appauvrissement des richesses de la Terre, en termes d'abrutissement et d'appauvrissement des gens puisqu'après c'est relayé par des services qui abrutissent les gens jusqu'à temps qu'ils achètent – je parle de la publicité, de la presse en général ...

Comment statuer, alors, sur cette légitimité de l'objet à exister ?

Il est fondamental de le faire passer à travers plusieurs grilles d'exigence, strictes ou plus malléables. La première grille stricte est de ne rien faire qui puisse aider à des choses néfastes pour l'homme. Cette grille-là est simpliste, mais il faut quand même la respecter et quelquefois cela représente de grosses pertes financières : c'est ne pas travailler pour l'armement, ne pas travailler pour les alcools durs, ne pas travailler pour le tabac, ne pas travailler pour la religion et ne pas travailler pour tout ce qui peut provenir de financement douteux, ce qui devient de plus en plus compliqué. L'argent sale qui est blanchi dans des affaires peut tout à fait nous rejoindre : je me suis vu refuser un marché sidérant à Berlin-Est pour une raison de doute et d'ailleurs, maintenant, nous avons dans nos contrats une clause selon laquelle tous nos clients doivent dire quelle est leur source de financement – et s'il s'avérait que ces gens avaient menti, le contrat serait automatiquement cassé. Donc ça, c'est les grilles d'exigence immédiates, les règles morales obligatoires, qui tombent sous le sens. Après, on doit faire passer l'objet à travers

une autre grille de paramètres qui vont en excuser l'existence. Le produit doit d'abord amener un service nouveau, apporter quelque chose de plus intéressant, une compétence nouvelle ... sinon, autant se retourner vers des objets déjà existants. Ensuite, il doit rendre profondément son service, avec le plus d'honnêteté possible : l'honnêteté du service est difficile à déchiffrer, car souvent ce n'est pas celui qu'on croit. Des objets servent à autre chose, réellement, que l'aspect qu'ils représentent, donc il faut savoir lire entre les lignes, il faut savoir lire à la fois dans notre inconscient et dans l'inconscient des objets. (...) Après, il va falloir essayer de rendre le service pur, avec le minimum d'idées préconçues c'est-à-dire en général le minimum de matière – c'est là que je cite toujours mon petit exemple du client qui a demandé un bateau et se trouve très satisfait des conseils du designer qui lui recommande d'essayer la nage et lui en fait redécouvrir les plaisirs. Il est possible désormais d'orienter la recherche et l'industrie vers des outils qui permettraient, au lieu d'avoir comme aujourd'hui 20 pour cent de service pour 80 pour cent de matière inutile (qui en général ne sert qu'à la vénalité du producteur), d'inverser le processus pour avoir 80 pour cent de service. Pour cela, il est fondamental que le designer cesse de penser la réponse à travers la matière. Il est fondamental que, devant une question, il soit extrêmement ouvert et qu'il puisse dire : la réponse est une réponse biologique et non pas industrielle, la réponse est une réponse sémantique et non pas matérielle... Dans ce cas-là, le designer n'est plus, en face d'un papier et d'un crayon, le complice d'une production systématique mais se retrouve en chef d'orchestre, mettant en face de certains besoins certaines compétences. Il faut comprendre que cette volonté de faire disparaître l'inutilité au profit de l'honnêteté est basée sur un axe fort qui s'appelle la dématérialisation. L'objet, le non-objet de demain matin, est, à l'exemple d'une étoile dans le ciel, en perpétuelle implosion, c'est-à-dire que son volume décroît en permanence au profit de sa masse – de sa masse de compétences, de sa masse d'honnêteté et de sa masse d'affectivité. Le seul axe possible de la production est la dématérialisation. (...) En attendant, il y a un travail provisoire mais parallèle dont on ne peut faire l'économie : le repositionnement politique, social, sexuel et économique de ce qui nous entoure. C'est un travail facile, qui ne demande pas de gros moyens mais simplement une prise de conscience et de la ténacité.

Le positionnement politique : éviter que les objets soient représentatifs de l'agressivité,

a violence, le fascisme... on va dire d'obscu-
rités. (...) C'est tout un travail sur le sens politique de ce que l'on fait : il est fondamental
de nettoyer les objets des signes barbares et
de les charger de signes positifs, construc-
tifs, pour montrer une autre voie... Le deuxième paramètre est le paramètre social ou
financier, qui est en rapport avec le premier :
les objets n'ont pas à devenir des moyens
de représentation de l'argent afin d'humilier
son voisin. Une grande part de la production
ne sert qu'à ça, c'est-à-dire « j'ai gagné de
l'argent, j'en ai une plus grosse que toi et je
t'emmerde ». C'est très grave, car on ne bâtit
pas une civilisation sur du négatif. Le troi-
sième paramètre est le sexe, qui a encore un
rapport avec le premier point puisque tout
a rapport avec la politique : aujourd'hui 80
pour cent des objets sont inutilement
machistes. Il est clair :

L'intelligence
moderne est
féminine,

à cause d'une série de fonctionnements
structurels différents, basés sur la protection
de l'espèce, sur le continuum, et sur quelque
chose que j'ai plus de mal à expliquer
encore : une sorte de pragmatisme qui
donne une simultanéité d'actions et évite la
grande idée, celle qui se récupère et qui se
pervertit. Donc il est très intéressant de se
poser des questions sur chaque objet. La réponse est assez souvent claire et choquante
quand on a l'œil ouvert là-dessus : excepté
un pistolet mitrailleur, je vois peu d'objets
qui ont besoin d'être outrageusement virils !
Le point suivant est le point économique,
qui touche à l'abordabilité des produits :
il est fondamental de « dés-élitiser » les objets de qualité pour donner ce qu'il y a de
mieux au maximum de gens.
Si l'idée est juste et multipliable, ne pas la
multiplier est un vol. D'où un travail sur
l'anoblissement du mot populaire, sur le
pouvoir que donne la multiplication, sur
l'augmentation de qualité que donne la
multiplication. Et pour cela – mais ça c'est
déjà un cheval de bataille pour vous – il ne
faut pas trop croire dans l'artisanat mais
dans la moralisation des grandes entreprises.
*C'est le rôle que vous avez joué chez Thom-
son ?*
Cela a été mon principal travail de directeur
artistique pendant 4 ans chez Thomson,
pour rendre vertueuses des sociétés qui n'a-
vaient pas de volonté de méchanceté, mais
qui avaient simplement oublié leur raison
d'être : rendre service, mettre leurs compé-
ences au profit d'un service. Il est fondamental de jouer une sorte d'ennemi intérieur

amical, c'est-à-dire d'arriver à intéresser les
grandes sociétés afin qu'elles donnent les
savoir-faire, les moyens financiers, la recherche, la distribution... en revenant à l'origine
des choses qui est le service. Cela implique
même un autre vocabulaire, et d'ailleurs une
des choses que j'avais faite chez Thomson
était de changer le nom. Thomson s'appelait
TCE, Thomson Consumer Electronic, et j'a-
vais posé la question : qui veut être un « consommateur d'électronique » ? A l'époque j'a-
vais eu la chance d'avoir un président
extraordinaire, Alain Prestat, qui avait com-
pris à la seconde. On avait choisi le mot
Thomson Multimédia, parce que lui pariait
sur le succès des technologies du multimédia et moi je voulais parler des multiples vec-
teurs d'expression qu'une société morale
doit avoir. Car ce n'est pas la peine de faire
des beaux téléviseurs si on y voit de la
merde... L'autre point important, c'est d'a-
voir interdit le mot « consommateur » dans
les réunions et d'avoir exigé qu'il soit remplacé par « mon ami », « ma femme », « ma
fille », « ma mère » ou « moi-même » . La
phrase n'est plus du tout la même quand on
dit : « C'est pas grave, c'est une merde, mais
les consommateurs s'en contenteront » et si
on recommence en disant : « C'est une
merde, mais c'est pas grave, ma fille s'en
contentera »... Tout d'un coup ça passe mal.
Il y a donc un travail gigantesque à faire, ne
serait-ce que sur des repositionnements
symboliques, avec un mot. L'autre chose que
j'ai faite chez Thomson, c'était le slogan, qui
était « Thomson : de la technologie à
l'amour », et qui là encore repositionnait
complètement le problème en disant que la
technologie n'est pas une fin en soi, c'est un
moyen – et que le but réel et final, c'est ce
qui a toujours été, c'est la priorité, c'est l'humain, avec un paramètre fondamental qui
est l'amour.
*On rejoint ici votre idée d'un objet ami, d'un
objet bon...*
Oui, là on en revient quasiment au rôle du
designer, on ne dessine pas l'objet pour l'objet, on se fout qu'il soit beau, il est fondamental qu'il soit bon ; il faut remplacer le
beau d'essence culturelle par le bon d'essence humaniste. L'objet doit être bon quali-
tativement évidemment, avec un des paramètres les plus modernes qui est la
longévité, on y reviendra, mais surtout il doit
être bon pour la personne qui va vivre avec –
ça veut dire qu'il ne doit pas la cacher par
des logos, ni l'opprimer par l'admiration que
l'on peut porter aux objets, il doit permettre
à la personne de s'épanouir, d'être elle-
même et d'être plus heureuse avec. Dire
qu'un produit doit épanouir la personne,
cela enlève déjà 70 pour cent de la produc-

tion actuelle qui transforme les gens en
clowns : les fausses Harley Davidson transforment les gens en faux *bikers*, les lunettes
griffées énormément transforment les gens
en des portemanteaux de marques dont on
se moque... Les gens se déguisent pour ne
pas exister. Et il est fondamental que les
gens ré-existent parce que sinon ils dispa-
raîtront. Il faut combattre l'idée de la transformation des gens en public, en specta-
teurs, par un travail continuel pour les
remettre à leur place d'acteurs.
Après, évidemment, il y a l'écologie.
On doit parler aux grandes sociétés devenues morales afin que l'élaboration n'ait pas
de nuisance pour l'homme, que l'objet ne
soit pas une nuisance dans sa vie, en enle-
vant évidemment le gimmick marketing du
recyclage... Le recyclage, inventé par les éco-
logistes, est finalement ce qui permet de
continuer aujourd'hui à produire et à con-
sommer inutilement. Un bon produit est un
produit qui dure : quand il a duré dix, vingt,
trente ans, qu'il soit recyclable, recyclé, à la
limite on s'en fout un petit peu. Mais recy-
cler tous les ans des objets inutiles est une
dépense de matière et d'énergie folle. Je ne
suis pas contre le recyclage, je suis contre
l'idée d'en faire une panacée universelle : le
recyclage est un pansement, la réparation
d'une erreur, pas autre chose. C'est une
fausse solution, un faux problème, une tarte
à la crème écologique comme il en existe
beaucoup aujourd'hui – comme l'énergie
électrique pour les voitures, qui n'est qu'un
déplacement du tuyau d'échappement vers
les centrales nucléaires. (...)
*Vous parliez d'accessibilité des produits tout
à l'heure : est-ce que c'est pour ça que vous
travaillez, sur le catalogue Good Goods, avec
Carrefour et La Redoute, parce qu'ils ont
cette volonté de démocratiser les meilleurs
produits ?*
L'une des rares victoires de ma carrière est
d'avoir anobli la multiplication, autrement
dit d'avoir anobli le mot « populaire », anobli
le mépris. Avant, une brosse à dents se ca-
chait au fond d'un tiroir, et du jour au lende-
main les gens se sont offert ça pour Noël et
tout d'un coup on se le montrait. L'autre
chose, c'est d'avoir rendu abordable, d'avoir
cassé les prix : en une décennie, j'ai réussi,
envers et contre tous, à presque casser le
prix de mes objets par deux tous les ans ou
tous les deux ans. L'un de mes premiers objets à succès, le siège du Café Costes, valait à
l'époque dans les 4000 francs... Aujourd'hui
on est sur des chaises à 300, peut-être même
200 francs. (...) On est même sur des réflexi-
ons, avec Vitra, sur la location ou sur la re-
prise du mobilier. Cela fait au moins 5–6 ans
qu'on est dessus, le problème c'est qu'au-

jourd'hui on ne sait pas le faire. On ne sait pas comment obliger quelqu'un à ramener une chaise contre moins de 50 francs, qui sera bientôt le prix qu'il l'aura payée. (...) Ce propos-là est forcément du super mass-market, or les populations du super mass-market ne sont pas encore assez éduquées pour ça. Et il y a le problème du prix : combien vous louez une chaise qui vaut 50 francs ? Un franc par mois ? On s'aperçoit qu'on est dans quelques impasses. Donc il vaut mieux adopter un style, un non-style à l'épreuve du temps : prenez la petite chaise Dr No, qui est confortable, qui s'empile, qui est quasiment indestructible, avec justement le problème que cela représente, eh bien on va la garder vingt ans... et dans vingt ans, on va la retrouver au bout d'un jardin, quelqu'un va la ramasser et on ira la faire fondre. Mais c'est pas la peine de sortir une grosse machine de guerre pour l'instant, on n'a pas les moyens de le faire. La grande distribution, pour moi, est obligatoire. Good Goods est sorti en 1998 et, à la même époque, on a présenté au Japon l'opération Seven Eleven, qui a été l'une des plus grosses opérations de l'histoire du design, puisque cette chaîne de *convenient stores* ouverts 24h/24 (8000 au Japon, 30 000 sur l'Asie et je ne sais plus combien sur les USA) m'a en gros donné tous les objets de la boutique – yaourts, rasoirs, culottes, crayons, tout ce que vous voulez : c'est le plus gros donneur d'ordres du monde, alors ça permet de passer réellement, en vraie grandeur, au mieux pour tout le monde. On sait déjà que chaque objet va être édité à 10 millions de pièces chacun dans l'année, et ça permet... je ne crois pas qu'il y ait d'objet qui coûte plus que dix ou douze francs. C'est une claque définitive au design élitiste. Pour moi, c'est fondamental, c'est presque une finalité : après je ne vois pas ce que je vais pouvoir faire, sauf continuer, montrer qu'on peut faire des yaourts mieux, des culottes mieux...

Et Good Goods ?

C'est un projet qui me tient à cœur depuis des années, qui a été un travail gigantesque pendant deux ans, pour la première fois de ma vie je dirais même que je ne le regrette pas mais que, si c'était à faire je ne le referais pas, ça m'a coûté des fortunes de manque à gagner par le temps que ça m'a pris. J'essaie d'ouvrir une voie vers des objets honnêtes, des objets pour des non-consommateurs, des «rebelles modernes» qui en ont marre que le marketing et la pub essaient de leur faire croire qu'il faut absolument changer leur R5 pour une R6, leur télévision 4/3 pour une 16/9... Ces gens-là pour moi représentent une nouvelle force politique non-dite. (...) C'est ça qui

m'intéresse : ces non-consommateurs installant, à travers ce catalyseur qui est le catalogue, des règles que j'appelle le *moral market*, qui est à peu près ce qu'on vient de décrire. Les gens vont recevoir le catalogue, avec un petit mot de moi qui leur dit quelque chose d'assez révolutionnaire dans le monde du commerce, à savoir que ce n'est pas la peine qu'ils achètent les produits et qu'il est plus important de lire le catalogue entre les lignes. Dans Good Goods, il y a des produits qui sont intéressants, mais qui n'ont en aucun cas la prétention d'être des non-produits comme j'en ai l'ambition, ils sont simplement là pour amorcer la pompe. Et c'est important, chaque objet est un petit peu expliqué, hélas pas autant que je le voulais par manque de place : on essaie de faire comprendre pourquoi, et symétriquement de faire comprendre pourquoi pas, pourquoi pas l'autre, pourquoi on ne veut plus de l'autre.

Aujourd'hui vous utilisez votre notoriété pour faire passer ces messages-là... Pourtant dans le catalogue Good Goods, vous dites vouloir «corriger une histoire dont j'ai sûrement été moi-même complice». Est-ce que cela veut dire que les objets Starck du catalogue sont, par rapport à ces grilles de critères dont on a parlé, ceux que vous revendiquez plus que d'autres ?

Vous savez, j'ai toujours été le même, sur la même idée. Sauf qu'au début, quand on est jeune, on travaille pour soi, pour survivre, et on fait ce qu'on peut. Moi j'ai 49 ans aujourd'hui, j'ai les moyens, si je n'avais pas d'abord conceptualisé ma stratégie je serais un imbécile et si je ne la respectais pas je serais un malhonnête. Donc je reconnais que j'ai fait ce que j'ai pu, qu'il y a des hauts et des bas mais que j'ai toujours fait avec une certaine honnêteté ; maintenant je ne dis pas que c'est parfait, mais j'ai les moyens d'avoir plus de rigueur. Vous savez, l'important c'était d'abord d'exister, parce qu'il a fallu construire ce pouvoir. Quand on est un designer français... n'oublions pas que ça n'existe pas, un designer français !

12   Architecture

74   Interiors

190   Furniture

296   Industrial Design

510   Magma

518   Words

542   Overview

574   A – Z

"I must be photographed with the chair..." | »Man muß mich mit dem Stuhl fotografieren,...« | « Il faut me photographier avec la chaise...»
Photo: Malick Sidibé

"...with my radio..." | »...mit meinem Radio...« | « ...avec mon poste radio... »
Photo: Malick Sidibé

Starck & Nori Starck

"...doing the twist." | »...Twist tanzend.« | « ...en position de twist. »
Photo: Malick Sidibé

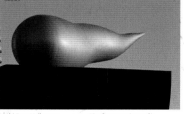

Larousse
Page | Seite 1636

Architecture
Architektur

Starck House (3 Suisses) 1994
Timber House | Holzhaus |
Maison en bois
Mail order sale | Versandhausverkauf | Vente par correspondance
3 Suisses
Photo: Jacques Dirand

Philippe Starck and inflatable structure | und aufblasbares Objekt | et structure gonflable
1969

Asahi Beer Hall 1990
Azumabashi 1-25-4-79, Sunida-Ku, Tokyo 150, Japan

Asahi breweries | Asahi Brauerei | Brasserie Asahi

The flame on the roof |
Die Flamme auf dem Dach |
La flamme sur le toit

Asahi Beer Hall 1990
Detail of the flame | Detail der Flamme | Détail de la flamme

View of the building at night |
Außenansicht bei Nacht | Vue d'ensemble la nuit
Geisha in front of the building |
Geisha vor dem Gebäude |
Geisha devant le bâtiment
Detail of a column | Detail einer Säule | Détail d'un pilier
White marble staircase | Treppe aus weißem Marmor | Escalier en marbre blanc
Photos: Alberto Venzago/ Nacása & Partners Inc.

Le Baron Vert 1992
Tanimachi 9-5-1, Chuo-Ku, Osaka, Japan

Office building | Bürogebäude | Immeuble de bureaux

View of the building (rear) |
Gebäudeansicht (Rückseite) |
Vue du bâtiment (face arrière)
Detail of the building | Gebäudedetail | Détail du bâtiment
View of the building (front) |
Gebäudeansicht (Vorderseite) |
Vue du bâtiment (face avant)
Photos: Hiroyuki Hirai/ Nacása & Partners Inc.

Nani Nani 1989
Shirokane Dai 4-273-42, Minato-Ku, Tokyo, Japan

Biomorphic building with a floor area of 959 m², including restaurant, showroom and offices in the centre of Tokyo, for the Rikugo group of companies | Biomorphes Gebäude von 959 m² Grundfläche mit Restaurant, Aus-

stellungsraum und Büros im Zentrum von Tokio im Auftrag des Rikugo-Konzerns | Immeuble biomorphique d'une surface-plancher de 959 m² comprenant un restaurant, un show-room et des bureaux dans le centre de Tokyo pour le compte du groupe Rikugo
Photos: T. Waki, Shokokusha Ou/Shigro Ogawa, Shinkenchi

Starck & Oa Starck

Formentera House 1995
Formentera, Spain

Private house | Privathaus |
Maison particulière

Formentera House 1995

Private house | Privathaus |
Maison particulière

Starck House (3 Suisses) 1994
Timber House | Holzhaus |
Maison en bois
Mail order sale | Versand-
hausverkauf | Vente par cor-
respondance
Starck House kit | Bausatz für
das Starck-Haus | Le coffret
de la maison Starck

The wooden box contains the
general plan of the house and
its components on a scale of
1:50, with and without canopy,
with additional 150 m² floor
space (ground floor, first
floor, roof, two sections and
all four façades), detailed
plans on a scale of 1:50 for the
ground woodwork, principles
of woodworking (beams and
joists, insulation, flooring and
parquet), roofing woodwork,
exterior construction work
(windows on the four façades
and plans for electrical wiring,
heating and plumbing), a site
checklist, a video showing the
various stages of construction, commented by Philippe
Starck, a step-by-step site

management notebook, a
blank notebook for the client's own comments, a hammer to symbolize the labour
of building a house and a
French flag for the topping
out ceremony.
The plans for the house,
which can be customized,
were drawn up by designer
Patrick Bouchain and archi-
tects L. Juliene and J. M. Mandon. Needless to say, imple-
mentation of the project calls
for skilled workers, official
planning permission and
adaptation to the site and
local conditions |
Der Holzkoffer enthält die
Konstruktionspläne und Bau-
teile im Maßstab 1:50, mit
oder ohne zusätzlicher 150 m²
großer überdachter Veranda
(Erdgeschoß, erster Stock,
Dach; zwei Schnitte und vier
Fassaden), die detaillierten
Pläne im Maßstab 1:50 für die
Gerüstverankerung im Boden,
die wichtigsten Holzarbeiten
(Wand- und Deckenbalken,
Isolierung, Fußböden und Par-

kett), Dachdeckerarbeiten,
äußere Konstruktionsarbeiten
(Fenster an den vier Fassaden, Schaltpläne für Strom,
Heizungs- und Wasserrohre),
eine Baumappe, eine Videokassette, auf der Philippe Starck die einzelnen Bauab-
schnitte des Hauses kom-
mentiert, ein Notizheft, in
dem die Entstehung und Ent-
wicklung des Projekts, die
Wahl des Ortes und die kleinen Schikanen der Behörden
festgehalten sind, ein leeres
Notizbuch für die Nieder-
schrift der eigenen Erfahrun-
gen, einen Hammer als Sym-
bol für den persönlichen Ein-
satz beim Hausbau und eine
französische Nationalflagge
für den Dachfirst. Die Pläne
für das Haus, die noch indivi-
duell geändert werden können, wurden von dem Desi-
gner Patrick Bouchain und
den Architekten L. Juliene und
J. M. Mandon ausgearbeitet.
Natürlich müssen Fachleute
mit der Verwirklichung des
Projekts, der Einholung be-

hördlicher Genehmigungen
und seiner Anpassung an die
örtlichen Voraussetzungen
und die landschaftliche Um-
gebung beauftragt werden |
Ce coffret en bois contient les
plans généraux au 1/50 de la
maison dans les formules,
avec ou sans auvent, d'une
surface de 150 m² supplé-
mentaire (rez-de-chaussée,
étage, toiture, 2 coupes et élé-
vation des 4 façades), les
plans spécifiques au 1/50 de
l'implantation de la charpente
au sol, les principes de charpente (poutres, solivages, iso-
lants, plancher et parquet), la
charpente toiture-couverture,
les menuiseries extérieures
(fenêtres des 4 façades et les
schémas de principe pour
l'électricité, le chauffage et la
plomberie), un classeur de
chantier, une vidéo montrant
les étapes de la construction
de la maison commentée par
Philippe Starck, le carnet de
notes qui explique les étapes
de la gestation du projet, le
choix de l'endroit et les pe-

tites tracasseries administratives, un carnet de notes
vierge pour noter ses propres
expériences, un marteau,
symbole de l'intervention personnelle dans la maison, un
drapeau français pour le faîte
de la maison. Les plans de la
maison, qui peuvent être per-
sonnalisés, ont été réalisés
par Patrick Bouchain, concep-
teur et par L. Juliene et J. M.

Mandon, architectes. Il faut
bien évidemment faire appel
à des spécialistes pour con-
crétiser le projet, obtenir les
autorisations administratives
et adapter le projet au terrain
et à l'environnement régional.
3 Suisses
Photos: Jacques Dirand

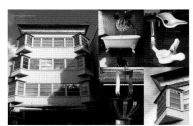 

Placido Arango Jr. House 1996
Madrid, Spain

Private house | Privathaus |
Maison particulière
Exterior | Außenansicht |
Extérieur

Staircase | Treppenhaus |
Escalier
Swimming pool | Swimming-
pool | Piscine
Photos: Cuauhtli Gutierrez

Le Moult House 1985–1987
29, rue Pierre Poli, 92130 Issy-
les-Moulineaux, France

Private house | Privathaus |
Maison particulière
On a Parisian island in the
Seine, not Saint-Louis but
Saint-Germain, near the for-
mer Renault factory, Philippe
Starck has undertaken the de-
sign of a house of remarkable
proportions: 5.6 m wide and
70 m long | Auf einer Pariser
Seine-Insel – nicht Saint-
Louis, sondern Saint-Germain

– unweit der früheren
Renault-Werke hat Philippe
Starck ein Haus von unge-
wöhnlichen Dimensionen ge-
baut: 5,60 m breit und 70 m
lang | Sur une île parisienne
de la Seine, non pas Saint-
Louis mais Saint-Germain,
près de l'ancienne usine
Renault, Philippe Starck a
aménagé une maison aux
dimensions surprenantes :
5,6 m de large x 70 m long
View of the house | Ansicht
des Hauses | Vue de la mai-
son

Le Moult House 1985–1987

View at night | Ansicht bei
Nacht | Vue de nuit

Pamela and | und | et Bruno
Le Moult
Staircase | Treppe | Escalier
Office | Büro | Bureau

Starck House 1991
27, rue Pierre Poli, 92130
Issy-les-Moulineaux, France

Facade on Seine river | Fas-
sade zur Seine | Façade sur la
Seine

Bathroom | Badezimmer |
Salle de bains
Lounge | Gesellschaftsraum |
Salon
Livingroom, detail | Wohnzim-
mer-Detail | Détail du séjour
Facade details | Fassaden-
details | Détails de la façade
Photos: Eric Morin

Citizenship is avant-garde

Zivilcourage ist avantgardistisch

Le civisme est d'avant-garde

⸍roningen Museum 1993
⸍useumeiland 1, Postbus 90,
⸍00 ME Groningen, The
⸍etherlands

⸍useum of Modern Art |
⸍useum für Moderne Kunst |
⸍usée d'art moderne
⸍chitects | Architekten | Ar-
⸍itectes : P. Starck, A. Men-
⸍i, Coop Himmelblau,
⸍ De Lucchi

Exterior | Außenansicht | Ex-
térieur
Exhibition room | Austel-
lungsraum | Salle d'exposi-
tion
*Photos: Ralph Richter/Archi-
tekturphoto*

**Manifesto by | Manifest von |
Manifeste de Philippe Starck**
1982

Groningen Museum 1993
Exhibition room with globe |
Austellungsraum mit Weltku-
gel | Salle d'exposition avec
globe terrestre
*Photo: Ralph Richter/Archi-
tekturphoto*

Laguiole factory 1987
Z.A. Route d' Aubrac,
12210 Laguiole, France

Cutlery factory at Laguiole |
Messerfabrik in Laguiole |
Coutellerie à Laguiole

Star's Door 1992
Parc de Bercy, Paris, France
Drawings | Entwurfszeichnun-
gen | Dessins de projet

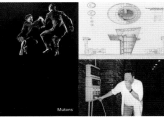

⸍e **must mutate**

⸍ir **müssen mutieren**

⸍utons

contrôle de l'aéroport de
Bordeaux-Mérignac
Competition entry in cooper-
ation with Luc Arsène-Henry Jr. |
Wettbewerbsentwurf mit Luc
Arsène-Henry Jr. | Projet de
concours en collaboration avec
Luc Arsène-Henry Jr.
Layouts, sections, elevations |
Grundrisse, Schnitte, Aufrisse |
Plans, coupes, vues

⸍ur de Contrôle 1993
⸍ntrol tower for the Bor-
⸍aux-Mérignac airport | Kon-
⸍llturm für den Flughafen
⸍rdeaux-Mérignac | Tour de

Moondog (project) 1990
Apartment building design
for the Rikugo group of com-
panies, Tokyo | Entwurf eines
Wohngebäudes für den
Rikugo-Konzern, Tokio | Ma-
quette pour un immeuble
d'habitation pour le compte
du groupe Rikugo, Tokyo

Computer graphics | Compu-
tergrafiken | Infographies

Maison de France, Venice 1990
Design for the French pavilion
at the Venice Biennale | Ent-
wurf für den Pavillon Frank-
reichs auf der Biennale in Ve-
nedig | Maquette du pavillon de
France à la Biennale de Venise
Model, east façade with open
door | Modell, Ostfassade mit
geöffneter Tür | Maquette, vue
façade est porte ouverte
Model, west and north façades

with open doors | Modell,
West- und Nordfassade mit ge-
öffneten Türen | Maquette, vue
façade ouest et nord portes
ouvertes
Bronze model | Bronzemodell |
Maquette en bronze

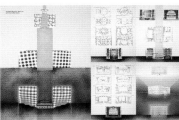

⸍ry 2001
⸍cineration plant | Müllver-
⸍ennungsanlage | Usine
⸍ncinération des déchets
⸍awings | Entwurfszeichnun-
⸍n | Dessins de projet
⸍productions: Hervé Ternisien

Ecole des Beaux-Arts 1991
Competition entry for the de-
sign of the Ecole des Beaux-
Arts of Paris city in cooperation
with Luc Arsène-Henry Jr. |
Wettbewerb für den Bau der
Hochschule für bildende Kün-
ste der Stadt Paris in Zusam-
menarbeit mit Luc Arsène-
Henry Jr. | Concours pour la
construction de l'Ecole des
Beaux-Arts de la ville de Paris
en collaboration avec Luc
Arsène-Henry Jr.
Façade design | Entwurf der
Fassade | Dessin de la façade

Floor plans and section of the
second building | Grundrisse
und Schnitt des zweiten Ge-
bäudes | Plans et coupe du
second bâtiment
Façades, ground floor plan
and section | Fassaden,
Grundriß des Erdgeschosses
und Schnitt | Façades, plan du
rez-de-chaussée et coupe
Floor plan and section of the
first building | Grundrisse und
Schnitt des ersten Gebäudes |
Plans et coupe du premier
bâtiment
Perspective view and façades |
Perspektivische Gesamtan-
sicht und Fassaden | Vue de
l'ensemble et des façades en
perspective

**ENSAD
(Ecole Nationale Supérieure
des Arts décoratifs)** 1993
rue d'Ulm, Paris, France

Competition entry for rede-
signing the school in cooperation with Luc Arsène-Henry
Jr. | Wettbewerbsentwurf für
die Neugestaltung der Hochschule in Zusammenarbeit mit
Luc Arsène-Henry Jr. | Con-

cours pour redessiner l'école en
collaboration avec Luc Arsène-
Henry Jr.
*Computer graphics | Computer-
grafiken | Infographies: DEIS*

Darkness grows

Die Dunkelheit verdichtet sich

L'obscurité s'épaissit

⸍NSAD 1998
⸍çade in the evening |
⸍ssade am Abend | Façade le
⸍ir
⸍oto: Jean-Marie Monthiers

ENSAD 1998
Façade in the daytime |
Fassade bei Tag | Façade le jour

Washbasin | Waschbecken |
Lavabo
Corridor | Korridor | Couloir
Studio | Werkstatt | Atelier
Staircase | Treppenhaus |
Escalier
Photos: Jean-Marie Monthiers

Rue Starck (project) 1991
rue Pierre Poli, 92130 Issy-les-
Moulineaux, France
Drawing | Zeichnung | Dessin

Starck House (project) 1991
Drawing | Zeichnung | Dessin

**Condominiums (project), Los
Angeles** 1992
Drawing | Zeichnung | Dessin

**Condominiums (project), Los
Angeles** 1992
Drawing | Zeichnung | Dessin

Angle (project), Antwerp 1991
Façade design | Fassadenent-
wurf | Projet de façade
Reproductions: Hervé Ternisien

Duravit Headquarters 2002
Werderstraße 36, 78132 Horn-
berg, Germany
Ill.: DEIS

Bond Street Hotel 2001
15 Bond Street, New York,
USA

Main elevation | Vorderan-
sicht | Façade

**Jean-Baptiste Mondino &
Philippe Starck**

Details, day view | Details be
Tag | Vue de jour, détails
Details, night view | Details
bei Nacht | Vue de nuit,
détails
Ian Schrager Hotels
Ill.: DEIS

Be a Citoyen

Sei ein Bürger

Soyez citoyen

**Interiors
Innenarchitektur
Intérieurs**

Café Costes 1984 (closed |
geschlossen | fermé en 1994)
4-6, rue Berger, place des
Innocents, Paris, France
Photo: Jacques Dirand

Les Bains-Douches 1978
7, rue du Bourg-l'Abbé, Paris,
France

Nightclub | Nachtklub |
Night-club
Photo: Anthony Oliver

La Main Bleue 1976
Centre Commercial de la
Mairie de Montreuil,
93100 Montreuil

Nightclub | Nachtklub |
Night-club

François Mitterrand 1991
Photo: Leo Erken/Agence Vu

Palais de l'Elysée 1983–1984
55-56, rue du Faubourg-
St-Honoré, Paris, France

President's apartment | Präsi-
dentenwohnung | Apparte-
ment présidentiel

Starck & Ara Starck

Café Costes 1984 (closed |
geschlossen | fermé en 1994)
4-6, rue Berger, place des Innocents, Paris, France

View of the stairs | Blick auf
die Treppe | Vue sur l'escalier
Photo: Stéphane Couturier

Row of chairs | Stuhlreihe |
Rangée de chaises
Photo: Guy Bouchet

Waiter | Ober | Garçon
Gallery | Galerie
Photos: Jacques Dirand

Café Costes 1984
Outside the café | Vor dem
Café | Devant le café
Detail | Détail
Costes Logo | Logo des Café
Costes | Logo du Café Costes

First floor | Erster Stock |
Premier étage
Photos: Jacques Dirand

Royalton Hotel 1988
44 West 44th Street,
New York 10036, NY, USA

Candleholder | Kerzenhalter |
Chandelier
Ian Schrager Hotels

Royalton Hotel 1988
Corridor | Korridor | Couloir
Lobby | Eingangshalle | Hall
d'entrée

Candleholder | Kerzenhalter |
Chandelier
Washbasin in a hotel bath-
room | Waschbecken im Bad
eines Hotelzimmers | Lavabo
dans la salle de bains d'une
chambre de l'hôtel
Entrance | Eingang | Entrée
Ian Schrager Hotels
Photos: Tom Vack

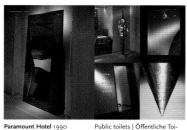

oyalton Hotel 1988
obby | Eingangshalle | Hall
'entrée
Restaurant
Lobby | Eingangshalle | Hall
d'entrée
Ian Schrager Hotels
Photos: Tom Vack

Vase in the lobby | Vase in der
Eingangshalle | Vase dans le
hall d'entrée

Paramount Hotel 1990
235 West 46th Street,
New York 10036, NY, USA

Entrance (detail) | Eingangsbe-
reich (Detail) | Entrée (détail)
Cladding (detail) | Eckschoner
(Detail) | Protège-coin (détail)
Staircase in the lobby | Treppe
in der Eingangshalle | Escaliers
dans le hall d'entrée
Lounge chair in the lobby by

Marc Newson | Stuhl in der
Eingangshalle von Marc New-
son | Chaise dans le hall d'en-
trée, par Marc Newson
Protective cladding, matt-finish
cast aluminium | Eckschoner,
mattiertes Gußaluminium |
Protège-coin, aluminium coulé
dépoli
Ian Schrager Hotels
Photos: Tom Vack

Paramount Hotel 1990
Distorting mirror in the lobby |
Vexierspiegel in der Eingangs-
halle | Miroir déformant dans
le hall d'entrée
Mahogany postcard display in
the lobby | Postkartenständer
aus Mahagoni in der Ein-
gangshalle | Présentoir de
cartes postales en acajou
dans le hall d'entrée

Public toilets | Öffentliche Toi-
letten | Toilettes publiques
Weather forecast in the lift
lobby | Wettervorhersage in
der Fahrstuhlhalle | Prévisions
météorologiques dans l'as-
censeur
Washbasin | Waschbecken |
Lavabo
Ian Schrager Hotels
Photos: Tom Vack

ra 1997

**Fax from Ara to Philippe
Starck | Fax von Ara an
Phliippe Starck | Fax d'Ara
pour Philippe Starck** 1999

Hotel Mondrian 1996
8440 Sunset Boulevard, West
Hollywood CA 90069, USA

Lobby | Eingangshalle | Hall
d'entrée
Ian Schrager Hotels
Photo: Todd Eberle

Drawing: Jean-Baptiste Mondino

Hotel Mondrian 1996
Photo: Todd Eberle

Lift lobby | Blick auf die
Fahrstühle | Ascenseurs

Philippe & Nori Starck

Terrace | Terrasse
Room | Zimmer | Chambre
Cocopazzo
Ian Schrager Hotels
Photos: Todd Eberle

lotel St Martins Lane 1999
5 St Martins Lane, London
'C2N 4HX, Great Britain

obby | Eingangshalle | Hall
d'entrée
ight Bar | Licht-Bar | Bar lu-
nière

Philippe Starck & Ian Schrager
Photo: Jean-Baptiste Mondino

Fish Bar | Fisch-Bar | Bar à
poissons
Asia de Cuba restaurant | Asia
de Cuba-Restaurant | Restau-
rant Asia de Cuba
Ian Schrager Hotels

Photos: Richard Davies

Starck Club 1982
703 McKinney, Dallas,
Texas 75202, USA

Nightclub | Nachtklub |
Night-club
Photo: Anthony Oliver

Photo: André Kertész

**Love is an endangered
species**

**Die Liebe ist eine vom
Aussterben bedrohte Art**

**L'amour est une espèce
en voie de disparition**

estaurant Manin 1987
22-12 Jingudae, Shibuya-Ku,
okyo, Japan

ntrance (detail) | Eingang
Detail) | Entrée (détail)
ashroom (detail) | Wasch-
um (Detail) | Lavabo (détail)
able in the restaurant | Tisch
n Restaurant | Table dans le
staurant

Detail of the ceiling: anti-earth-
quake system | Deckendetail:
Sicherheitskonstruktion gegen
Erdbebenerschütterung | Détail
du plafond : Dispositif de sécurité contre les secousses
sismiques
Bridge to the underground res-
taurant | Brücke zu dem unter-
irdisch gelegenen Restaurant |
Passerelle conduisant au restaurant souterrain

Boutique Hugo Boss 1991
2, place des Victoires, Paris,
France

Drawer handle | Schubladen-
griff | Poignée de tiroir
Photo: Jacques Dirand

Boutique Hugo Boss 1991
Staircase | Treppe | Escalier

Table in the shop | Tisch im
Laden | Table dans la boutique
Shop Interior | Inneneinrich-
tung | Intérieur
Staircase | Treppe | Escalier
Photos: Jacques Dirand

Puzzle 1987
rue Princesse et rue Balzac,
Paris, France

General store, snack bar and
nightclub | Lebensmittella-
den, Imbiß und Nachtklub |
Epicerie, snack-bar et night-
club

Interiors (details) | Innen-
raumdetails | Intérieurs
(détails)
Wire flower holder | Blumen-
halter aus Draht | Porte-fleurs
en fil de fer

Salon Coppola 1992
Corso Garibaldi 110, Milan,
Italy

Hairdressing salon | Friseur-
salon | Salon de coiffure
Entrance stairs | Eingangs-
treppe | Escalier d'entrée

Interior | Innenraum | Intérieur
Detail | Détail
Entrance | Eingang | Entrée

Philippe Starck

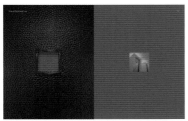

Restaurant Teatriz 1990
Hermosilla 15, Madrid, Spain

WC door (details) | WC-Tür
(Details) | Porte des W.C.
(détails)

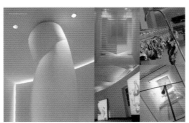

Restaurant Teatriz 1990
Pillar in the entrance hall |
Säule in der Eingangshalle |
Pilier dans le hall d'entrée

Corridor leading to toilets |
Gang zu den Toiletten | Cou-
loir menant aux toilettes
Washbasin | Waschbecken |
Lavabo
Corridor with illuminated wall
panelling | Korridor mit be-
leuchteten Wandtafeln | Cou-
loir avec tableaux muraux
éclairés
Interior | Innenraum | Intérieur
Photos: Jordi Sarra

Restaurant Teatriz 1990
Bar (detail | Detail | détail)
Ceiling decoration | Decken-
gestaltung | Décoration du
plafond
Floor design, based on a pain-
ting by Giorgio de Chirico |
Fußbodengestaltung nach einem Gemälde von Giorgio de
Chirico | Décoration du plan-
cher d'après un tableau de
Giorgio de Chirico

View of the restaurant | Blick
in das Restaurant | Vue du
restaurant
View of the bar, luminous ony
before a large mirror | Blick
auf die Bar mit beleuchtetem
Onyx vor einem großem Spie
gel | Vue du bar, avec onyx il-
luminé de l'intérieur et placé
devant une grande glace

Restaurant Teatriz 1990
View from the restaurant into
the bar | Blick vom Restaurant
auf die Bar | Vue du restaurant
sur le bar

Floor in the basement (detail) |
Fußboden im Untergeschoß
(Detail) | Plancher du salon au
sous-sol (détail)
Detail | Détail

Drawing: Jean-Baptiste Mondino

Café Mystique 1988
6-27-8 Jingumae, Shibuya-Ku,
Tokyo, Japan

Detail | Détail
View of the restaurant | Blick
in das Restaurant | Vue du
restaurant

Detail of the wall | Wanddetail |
Détail du mur
Entrance | Eingang | Entrée

La Cigale 1988
120, bd. Rochechouart,
75018 Paris, France

Concert Hall | Konzertsaal |
Salle de concert
Entrance | Eingang | Entrée
Seating (detail) | Sitze (De-
tail) | Sièges (détail)

Ceiling in the Concert Hall
(detail) | Decke im Konzert-
saal (Detail) | Plafond de la
salle de concert (détail)
Entrance | Eingang | Entrée

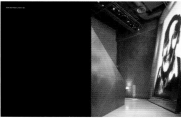

Restaurant Theatron 1985
Paseo de la Reforma, 50 Calle
Bosques de Chapultepec,
11560 Mexico City DF, Mexico

Entrance | Eingang | Entrée
Photo: Stéphane Couturier

Restaurant Theatron 1985
Staircase | Treppe | Escalier
Entrance | Eingang | Entrée
Washbasin in the toilets |
Waschbecken in den Toiletten |
Lavabo dans les toilettes

Staircase | Treppe | Escalier
Disco 'Crazy Box'
View of the restaurant | Blick
in das Restaurant | Vue du
restaurant
Photos: Stéphane Couturier

Restaurant Theatron 1985
Entrance | Eingang | Entrée
Photo: Stéphane Couturier

Delano Hotel 1995
1685 Collins Avenue, 33139
Miami Beach, Florida, USA

Lobby | Eingangshalle | Hall
d'entrée
Ian Schrager Hotels

Delano Hotel 1995
Public phone | Öffentlicher
Fernsprecher | Cabine télé-
phonique

Fitness centre | Fitneßcenter |
Centre de mise en forme
View of the exterior | Außen-
ansicht | Vue de l'extérieur
Bungalows in front of the
swimming pool | Bungalows
vor dem Swimming-pool |
Bungalows devant la piscine
Ian Schrager Hotels

Delano Hotel 1995
Lobby | Eingangshalle | Hall
d'entrée

Lobby with furniture by Ray
and Charles Eames | Eingangs-
halle mit Möbeln von Ray und
Charles Eames | Hall d'entrée
avec meubles par Ray et
Charles Eames
Lobby (detail) | Eingangshalle
(Detail) | Hall d'entrée (détail)
View of the restaurant | Blick
in das Restaurant | Vue du
restaurant
Ian Schrager Hotels

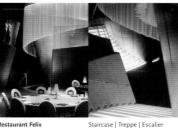

Delano Hotel 1995
View of the exterior | Außen-
ansicht | Vue de l'extérieur
Garden | Garten | Jardin
Dinner table | Eßtisch | Table
dressée
Entrance | Eingang | Entrée
Eat-in kitchen | Eßküche |
Cuisine-salle à manger

Bathroom | Badezimmer |
Salle de bains
Photo: Michael Mundy

Detail apple holder | Detail
Apfelhalter | Détail porte-
pomme
Restaurant
Ian Schrager Hotels

Photos: Todd Eberle

**Restaurant Felix
in the Peninsula Hotel** 1994
Salisbury Road, Kowloon,
Hong Kong

View of the restaurant | Blick
in das Restaurant | Vue du
restaurant

Staircase | Treppe | Escalier

**Restaurant Felix
in the Peninsula Hotel** 1994
View of the restaurant | Blick
in das Restaurant | Vue du
restaurant

Peninsula Hotel 1994
Oyster Bar | Austernbar | Bar
à huîtres
Ian Schrager Hotels

Peninsula Hotel 1994
Public toilets | Öffentliche Toi-
letten | Toilettes publiques
View of the restaurant | Blick
in das Restaurant | Vue du
restaurant

Bar
W.W. Stool
Lift (detail) | Fahrstuhl (De-
tail) | Ascenseur (détail)
Staircase (detail) | Treppe
(Detail) | Escalier (détail)
Ian Schrager Hotels

Asia de Cuba Restaurant 1997
237, Madison Avenue, New
York, USA

View of the restaurant | Blick
in das Restaurant | Vue du
restaurant
First floor lounge | Salon im
Erdgeschoß | Salon du rez-de-
chaussée
Rum bar | Rum-Bar | Rum Bar
View of the restaurant | Blick

in das Restaurant | Vue du
restaurant
Ian Schrager Hotels
Photos: Todd Eberle

Drawing: Jean-Baptiste Mondino

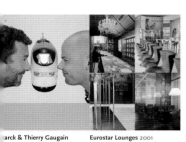

Starck & Thierry Gaugain
Photo: Jean-Baptiste Mondino

Eurostar Lounges 2001
First Class Lounges at the
Gare du Nord, Paris, and Wa-
terloo Station, London | Erste-
Klasse-Lounges im Gare du
Nord, Paris, und in der Wa-
terloo Station, London | First
Class Lounges en gare du
Nord, Paris, et Waterloo Sta-
tion, Londres
Photos: Matthew Winrib

We just need Love

Wir brauchen nur Liebe

On a juste besoin d'amour

Restaurant Kong 2002
15, rue du Pont-Neuf,
75002 Paris, France
Graphic Conception: Cake
Design/Thibaut Mathieu

Restaurant Bon 1 2000
25, rue de la Pompe,
75016 Paris, France

Starck & Laurent Taïeb
Photo: Jean-Baptiste Mondino

Grocery shop | Shop | Epicerie
Cross table detail | Kreuztisch-
Detail | Détail de la table en croix
Restaurant, details | Restau-
rant-Details | Détails du restau-
rant

Outside garden | Garten im
Außenbereich | Jardin extérieur
Cross table room | Raum mit
Kreuztisch | Salle de la table en
croix
Sushi Bar, details | Sushi-Bar-
Details | Détails du Sushi Bar
Restaurant details | Restaurant-
Details | Détails du restaurant
Sushi Bar
Photos: Patricia Bailer

Restaurant Bon 2 2001
2, rue du 4 septembre,
75002 Paris, France

Rhinoceros | Rhinozeros |
Rhinocéros
Details
Photos: Patricia Bailer

Starck's Wedding 2000
Starcks Hochzeit | Mariage de
Starck

Hudson Hotel 1998
356 West 58th Street,
New York, USA

Main facade, entrance |
Hauptfassade, Eingangs-
bereich | Façade principale,
entrée

Library | Bibliothek | Biblio-
thèque
Restaurant
Ground Floor, escalators | Erd-
geschoss, Rolltreppen | Rez-de-
chaussée, escalator
Bar
Ian Schrager Hotels
Photos: Michael Mundy

Hudson Hotel 1998
Front desk | Empfang | Récep-
tion
Outside terrace | Außenter-
rasse | Terrasse extérieure
Bar, details | Bar-Details |
Détails du bar

Public toilets | Öffentliche Toi-
letten | Toilettes
Ian Schrager Hotels
*Photos: Michael Mundy, Daniel
Pouzet*

**El Porteño Apartments and
Hotel** 1999
Juana Manso 1290 Dique,
Puerto Madero Este,
1107 Buenos Aires, Argentine

Interior | Innenansicht des
Gebäudes | Intérieur du bâti-
ment
Alan Faena
Show flat | Beispielwohnung |
Appartement-témoin
Facade detail | Fassaden-
Detail | Détail de la façade
*Photos: Ricardo Labougle/
Cosmic Carrot Group*

Clift Hotel 1999
495 Geary Street,
San Francisco, USA

Entrance and main facade |
Eingang und Hauptfassade |
Entrée et façade principale
Restaurant

Lobby | Eingangshalle | Hall
d'entrée
Lounge
Lobby | Eingangshalle | Hall
d'entrée
Guest room | Zimmer |
Chambre
Ian Schrager Hotels
*Photos: Bruno Borrione/Agence
Starck, Nikolas Koenig*

Sanderson Hotel 1998
50 Berners Street, London,
Great Britain

Lobby | Eingangshalle | Hall
d'entrée

Long Bar
Guest Bathroom | Badezim-
mer | Salle de bains
Elevator | Aufzug | Ascenseur
Guest room | Zimmer |
Chambre
Ian Schrager Hotels
Photos: Todd Eberle

Mikli Shop 2001
Königsallee 21/23,
40212 Düsseldorf, Germany
Photo: Mikli

Mikli Shop 2002
G/F 28 Wellington Street,
Central, Hong Kong
Photo: Virgile Simon Bertrand

Mikli Shop 1999
74, rue des Saints-Pères,
75007 Paris, France
Photo: Mikli

Nori Starck

Jean Paul Gaultier
Photo: Jean-Baptiste Mondino

Gaultier Shops 2001

759 Madison Avenue, 65th
Street, New York, USA
Photo: Stephen Lovekin

6, rue Vivienne, 75002 Paris,
France
Photos: Eric Morin

TASCHEN Shop 2000
2, rue de Buci, 75006 Paris,
France

Graphic design | Graphisches
Gestaltungselement | Elé-
ment de décoration graphi-
que

Front facade, Show window |
Vordere Fassade, Schaufen-
ster | Façade et vitrine
Interior, details | Interieur-De-
tails | Détails intérieurs
TASCHEN France offices | Ge-
schäftsräume von TASCHEN
France | Bureaux de TASCHEN
France
Book ends | Buchstützen |
Presse-livres
Photos: Eric Laignel

TASCHEN Shop 2002
North Beverly Drive,
Beverly Hills, CA 90210, USA

Main facade | Hauptfassade |
Façade
Section view | Längsschnitt |
Vue en coupe
Ill.: Agence Starck

Yoo

o Apartments 2001
Hall Road, NW8 London,
eat Britain

John Hitchcox

Show flat | Beispielwohnung |
Appartement-témoin
Photos: Yoo

**Everything
has a Birth a Life a Death**

**Alles hat einen Anfang,
ein Sein, ein Ende**

**Tout a un début,
une existence, une fin**

Nori, K & Philippe Starck
Photo: Jeff Riedel

**Furniture
Möbeldesign
Meubles**

Ceci n'est pas une brouette 1996
Armchair | Lehnstuhl | Fauteuil
Ashwood frame. Seat and back in
pale pink satin | Rahmen aus
Eschenholz. Rücken- und
Sitzflächen mit blaßrosafarbe-
nem Satinbezug | Structure en
frêne naturel. Siège et dossier
garnis satin rose pâle
140 x 43 x 84 cm
XO
Photo: Tom Vack

W.W. Stool 1990
Stool | Hocker | Tabouret
Sand-blasted cast aluminium,
lacquered | Sandgestrahltes
Gußaluminium, lackiert | Alu-
minium moulé traité au jet de
sable, laqué
97 x 56 x 53 cm
Vitra
Photo: Andreas Sütterlin/Vitra

Louis XX 1992
Chair | Stuhl | Chaise
Polypropylene, aluminium |
Polypropylen, Aluminium |
Polypropylène, aluminium
84.5 x 59 x 60 cm
Vitra
Photo: Andreas Sütterlin/Vitra

Hula Hoop 1998
Castor-mounted operator's
chair, injection-moulded poly-
propylene shell | Arbeitssessel
auf Rollen, Schale aus Spritz-
guß-Polypropylen | Fauteuil
de travail à roulettes, coque
en polypropylène injecté
80 x 68 x 56 cm
Vitra
Photo: Vitra

**Starck on Hula Hoop | Starck
auf Hula Hoop | Starck sur la
Hula Hoop**
Photo: Christian Coigny

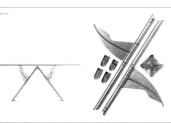

sident M. 1984
le designed for President
tterrand's private study at
e Elysée Palace | Tisch, ent-
rfen für Präsident Mitter-
ds privates Arbeitszimmer
Elysée-Palast | Table réalisée
ur le bureau du Président
tterrand à l'Elysée
uare table | Quadratischer
ch | Table carrée :
x 136 x 136 cm

Rectangular table | Rechteckiger
Tisch | Table rectangulaire :
73 x 170 x 120 cm
Round table | Runder Tisch | Table
ronde : H: 73.5 cm, ø: 150 cm
Baleri
Photo: Marco Schillaci

Pieces of the table | Einzelteile
des Tisches | Pièces détachées
Baleri
Photo: Carlo Orsi

Coque 1999
Computergraphics | Compu-
tergrafiken | Infographies

Richard III 1985
Armchair | Sessel | Fauteuil
Polyurethane, painted with
polyurethane enamel, cushion
in polyurethane and dacron,
woollen cloth or leather |
Polyurethan, Polyurethan-
Emailfarbe, Kissen aus Polyurethan und Dralon, Bezug
aus Wolle oder Leder | Po-
lyuréthane, peint à l'émail polyuréthane, coussin en po-

lyuréthane et dacron, garni-
ture laine ou cuir
92 x 93 x 82 cm
Baleri

We must share

Wir müssen teilen

Partageons

ss Trip 1996
e-apart chair | Zerlegbarer
hl | Chaise démontable
ypropylene, laminated
k, solid beechwood legs |
ypropylen, laminiertes
ckenteil, massive Buchen-
zbeine | Polypropylène,
ssier en multiplis de hêtre,
ds en hêtre tourné massif
x 42 x 85 cm
tell

Prince Aha 1996
Composite stool | Komposit-
Hocker | Tabouret composé
Coloured polypropylene | Far-
biges Polypropylen | Polypro-
pylène teinté
30 x 43 cm
Kartell

Photos: Fabrizio Bergamo

Dr. No 1996
Stackable chair | Stapelbarer
Stuhl | Chaise empilable
Coloured polypropylene, aluminium, epoxy polyester or
natural finish | Farbiges
Polypropylen, Aluminium, mit
oder ohne Polyesterbeschich-
tung | Polypropylène teinté,
aluminium, finition laquage
époxy ou naturel

54.5 x 51.5 x 80 cm
Kartell
Photos: Fabrizio Bergamo

We are mutants

Wir sind Mutanten

Nous sommes des mutants

**Saint Esprit, Napoléon and
Attila** 1999
Stools and table | Hocker und
Tisch | Tabourets et table
Polypropylene | Polypropylen |
Polypropylène
Stool: H: 46 cm, ø: 40 cm,
Table: H: 46 cm, ø: 35 cm
Kartell

La Marie 1998
Stackable monobloc chair |
Stapelbarer Monobloc-Stuhl |
Chaise monobloc, empilable
Transparent polycarbonate |
Transparentes Polycarbonat |
Polycarbonate transparent
50 x 52.5 x 87.5 cm
Kartell

Philippe Starck & La Marie
1999
*Photo: Karl Lagerfeld/
Deutsche Vogue*

Philippe Starck & Dr. Glob
1990
Stackable chair | Stapelbarer
Stuhl | Chaise empilable
Tubular steel, polypropylene |
Stahlrohr, Polypropylen | Tube
d'acier, polypropylène
48 x 47.5 x 73 cm
Kartell

Bubble Club 1998
Rotomolded polyethylene
garden sofa | Gartensofa aus
rotationsgeformtem Polyäthy-
len | Canapé de jardin en
polyéthylène rotomoulé
195 x 80 x 77 cm
Kartell

Bubble Club 1998
Rotomolded polyethylene gar-
den chair | Gartensessel aus
rotationsgeformtem Polyäthy-
len | Fauteuil de jardin en po-
lyéthylène rotomoulé
105 x 80 x 77 cm
Kartell

Ploof 1999
Rotomolded polyethylene
settee, structure in anodised
aluminium | Sofa aus rota-
tionsgeformtem Polyäthylen,
Gestell aus anodisiertem
Aluminium | Canapé en poly-
éthylène rotomoulé, structure
en aluminium anodisé
180 x 65 x 80 cm
Kartell

Ploof 1999
Rotomolded polyethylene
armchair, structure in anodise
aluminium | Sessel aus rota-
tionsgeformtem Polyäthylen,
Gestell aus anodisiertem Alu-
minium | Fauteuil en poly-
éthylène rotomoulé, structure
en aluminium anodisé
86 x 60 x 80 cm
Kartell

Zbork 2000
Rotomoulded polyethylene
armchair | Sessel aus rota-
tionsgeformtem Polyäthylen
Fauteuil en polyéthylène roto
moulé
100 x 88 x 60 cm
Kartell

*Photos: Kartell/Pesarini &
Michetti*

La Bohème 2000
Transparent polycarbonate
stools | Hocker aus durch-
sichtigem Polycarbonat | Ta-
bourets en polycarbonate
transparent
46 x 33 cm
Kartell
*Photo: Kartell/Pesarini &
Michetti*

Ero's 1999
Transparent polycarbonate
chair, injection-moulded aluminium or chromed steel
base | Stuhl aus durchsichti-
gem Polycarbonat. Fuß aus
Druckguß-Aluminium oder
verchromtem Stahl | Chaise
en polycarbonate transparent.
Piétement en aluminium injecté ou structure en acier
chromé

62 x 79 x 70 x 46 cm
Kartell
*Photo: Kartell/Pesarini &
Michetti*

Louis Ghost 2000
Transparent injection-moulded polycarbonate stacking
chair | Stapelbarer Stuhl aus
durchsichtigem Spritzguß-Po-
lycarbonat | Chaise empilable
en polycarbonate transparent
injecté
54 x 94 x 55 x 47 cm
Kartell
Photo: Studio Bleu

Jacqueline Starck

Lola Mundo 1988
Table-cum-chair | Tisch-Stuhl |
Table-chaise
Legs in polished cast aluminium. Tops in ashwood with
ebony finish. Hinge in black
coloured chromium-plated
steel. Studs in coloured rub-
ber | Beine aus poliertem
Gußaluminium. Holzflächen
aus ebenholzgetönter Esche.
Scharniere aus schwarzem
verchromten Stahl. Nägel-
köpfe aus farbigem Gummi |
Pieds en aluminium poli.
Dessus frêne, finition ébène.
Charnières en acier chromé
noir. Clous en caoutchouc
coloré
48.5 x 33.5 x 53 cm
Driade
Photo: Tom Vack

**We have to allow for the fall
of Western civilisation**

**Wir müssen den Verfall des
Westens einkalkulieren**

**Gérons la décadence de
l'Occident**

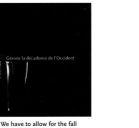

Lord Yo 1994
Stackable armchair | Stapel-
barer Lehnstuhl | Fauteuil
empilable
Body in polypropylene available in dark green, light green,
light yellow, ivory and pink.
Frame in aluminium: legs in
special anodised metal | Kor-
pus aus Polypropylen, erhältlich in Dunkelgrün, Hellgrün,
Hellgelb, Elfenbein und Rosa.

Aluminiumrahmen, Beine au
speziell anodisiertem Metall
Corps en polypropylène disponible dans les coloris : ver
foncé, vert clair, jaune clair,
ivoire et rose. Structure en
aluminium, pieds en métal
anodisé
94.5 x 64 x 66 cm
Driade
Photos: Tom Vack

Olly Tango 1994
Stackable chair | Stapelbarer
Stuhl | Chaise empilable
Body in curved plywood. Light
walnut wood or ebonized
finishing, or lacquered in the
following colours: grey, light
green, light yellow, ivory.
Chromium-plated metal legs |
Korpus aus geformten Sperr-
holz mit hell bzw. schwarz ge-
beiztem Walnußfurnier oder

lackiert in den Farben Grau,
Hellgrün, Hellgelb oder Elfenbein. Beine aus verchromtem
Metall | Corps en contre-plaqué.
Finition en bois de noyer clair
ou ébène, ou laquée dans les
couleurs : gris, vert pâle, jaune
pâle, ivoire. Pieds en métal
chromé
90 x 42 x 58 cm
Driade
Photos: Tom Vack

Asahy 1991
Armchair | Lehnstuhl | Fauteuil
Cherrywood and pearwood,
leather, polyurethane foam |
Kirsch- und Birnbaumholz,
Lederbezug, Schaumstoffpol-
sterung | Bois de cerisier et de
poirier, cuir, mousse de nylon
91.5 x 45 x 55.5 cm
Driade

Paramount 1991
Armchair | Lehnstuhl | Fauteuil
Cherrywood and pearwood,
leather, polyurethane foam |
Kirsch- und Birnbaumholz,
Lederbezug, Schaumstoffpol-
sterung | Bois de cerisier et de
poirier, cuir, mousse de nylon
95 x 67 x 71.5 cm
Driade

Vicieuse 1992
Height-adjustable table |
Höhenverstellbarer Tisch |
Table à hauteur réglable
Cast aluminium, polished
frame with central screw for
height adjustment. Top in
multilayered wood with diafos
laminate finish | Gestell aus
poliertem Gußaluminium mit
zentraler Schraube zur Höhen-
einstellung. Tischplatte aus
Schichtholz mit laminierter
Oberfläche | Aluminium coulé,
cadre poli avec vis de réglage
en hauteur. Dessus bois multiplis, finition lamellée
H: 50–73 cm, ø: 40 cm
Driade

Boom Rang 1992
Stackable chair | Stapelbarer
Stuhl | Chaise empilable
Frame in stiff polyurethane with
steel inserts. Available in the following versions: seat light grey
and back salmon pink, seat dark
grey and back light grey | Rah-
men aus gehärtetem Polyurethan
mit Stahleinlagen. Erhältlich in
den folgenden Versionen: hell-
grüner Sitz mit lachsfarbenem
Rücken oder dunkelgrauer Sitz
mit hellgrauem Rücken | Cadre
en polyuréthane rigide, inser-
tions acier. Disponible dans les
versions suivantes : siège gris
clair, dossier saumon ; siège gris
foncé, dossier gris clair
79 x 35.5 x 49 cm
Driade

Boom Rang 1992
Photo: Tom Vack

Asahy 1991

Paramount 1991

Royalton 1991
Chair and bench | Stuhl und
Bank | Chaise et banc
Cherrywood, pearwood, alu-
minium | Kirschholz, Birnbaum-
holz, Aluminium | Bois de
cerisier et de poirier, aluminium
Chair | Stuhl | Chaise :
69 x 46 x 42 cm
Bench | Bank | Banc :
69 x 138 x 42 cm
Driade
Photo: Tom Vack

Big Nothing 1997
High-backed two-seater sofa |
Hohes zweisitziges Sofa | Haut
canapé à deux places
Removable cover in cotton or
velvet | Abnehmbarer Bezug
aus Baumwolle oder Samt |
Housse amovible en coton ou
velours
170 x 84 x 93 cm
Driade
Photo: Emilio Tremolada

Cam El Eon 1999
Stackable chair | Stapelbarer
Stuhl | Chaise empilable
Aluminium frame, polypropylene seat. Available in ivory,
beige, orange and dark grey.
Also suitable for outdoor use |
Rahmen aus Aluminium, Sitz-
schale aus Polypropylen. Erhältlich in Elfenbein, Beige,
Orange und Dunkelgrau. Auch
für den Außenbereich geeignet |
Structure en aluminium, coque
en polypropylène. Existant dans
les tons : ivoire, beige, orange
et gris foncé. Utilisable aussi à
l'extérieur
55 x 59 x 76 cm
Driade
Photo: Tom Vack

Lola Mundo 1988

Titos Apostos 1985
Folding table | Klapptisch |
Table pliante
Epoxy, tubular steel, sheet
steel | Epoxyd, Stahlrohr,
Stahlblech | Epoxy, tube
d'acier, tôle d'acier
H: 71 cm, ø: 85 cm
Driade

J. (Série Lang) 1987
Armchair | Lehnstuhl | Fauteuil
Tubular steel, aluminium,
leather, padding | Stahlrohr,
Aluminium, Leder, Polsterung |
Tube d'acier, aluminium, cuir,
rembourrage
86 x 60 x 66 cm
Driade

Costes 1984
Armchair | Lehnstuhl | Fauteuil
Epoxy, tubular steel, padded
leather seat, mahogany |
Epoxyd, Stahlrohr, gepolsterter
Ledersitz, Mahagoni | Epoxy,
tube d'acier, siège en cuir
rembourré, acajou
80 x 47.5 x 55 cm
Driade

Costes Alluminio 1988
Armchair | Lehnstuhl | Fauteuil
Tubular aluminium, sheet
aluminium | Aluminiumrohr
und -blech | Tube d'alu-
minium, tôle d'aluminium
74.5 x 46.5 x 56.7 cm
Driade

Pratfall 1985
Armchair | Lehnstuhl | Fauteuil
Tubular steel, leather seat,
black laquered or mahogany
finish | Stahlrohr, Ledersitz,
Rückenlehne aus Holz,
schwarz lackiert oder mit Ma-
hagonifurnier | Tube d'acier,
siège cuir, finition laque noire
ou acajou
86 x 61.5 x 78 cm
Driade

J. (Série Lang) 1991
Table | Tisch
Cast aluminium, glass or
wood | Gußaluminium, Glas
oder Holz | Aluminium coulé,
verre ou bois
Square version | Quadra-
tische Version | Version
carrée : 72,5 x 135 x 135 cm
Rectangular version | Recht-
eckige Version | Version rec-
tangulaire : 72,5 x 90 x 210 cm
Round version | Runde Ver-
sion | Version ronde :
H: 72.5 cm, ø: 130 cm
Driade

Colucci 1986
Stool and container | Hocker-
Behälter | Tabouret-récipient
Aluminium, red or blue | Alu-
minium, rot oder blau | Alu-
minium, rouge ou bleu
H: 45 cm, ø: 38 cm
Driade

Tippy Jackson 1985
Folding table | Klapptisch |
Table pliante
Epoxy, tubular steel, sheet
steel | Epoxyd, Stahlrohr, Stahl-
blech | Epoxy, tube d'acier, tôle
d'acier
H: 71 cm, ø: 120 cm
Driade

Sarapis 1986
Stool | Hocker | Tabouret
Epoxy, tubular steel | Epoxyd,
Stahlrohr | Epoxy, tube d'acier
85.5/105 x 35 x 45.4 cm
Driade

Von Vogelsang 1985
Stackable chair | Stapelbarer
Stuhl | Chaise empilable
Tubular steel, sheet steel |
Stahlrohr, Stahlblech | Tube
d'acier, tôle d'acier
71.5 x 54 x 45.5 cm
Driade

Titos Apostos 1985

Romantica 1987
Stackable chair | Stapelbarer
Stuhl | Chaise empilable
Aluminium
85.4 x 42.7 x 62.5 cm
Driade

Dick Deck 1989
Chair | Stuhl | Chaise
Beechwood | Buchenholz |
Bois de hêtre
91 x 35.5 x 62 cm
Driade

Costes Alluminio 1988

Bob Dubois 1987
Chair | Stuhl | Chaise
Cherrywood, pearwood, wicker |
Kirsch- und Birnbaumholz,
Korbgeflecht | Bois de cerisier,
bois de poirier, assise cannée
91.5 x 39 x 54 cm
Driade

Tessa Nature 1989
Chair | Stuhl | Chaise
Beechwood, pearwood, wicker |
Buchen- und Birnbaumholz,
Korbgeflecht | Bois de hêtre,
bois de poirier, assise cannée
74 x 48 x 52.5 cm
Driade

Cameleon 1992
Table | Tisch
Multi-layered wood frame,
pearwood finish with connect-
ing parts in cast aluminium.
Glass top with sand-blasted
parts and bevelled edges |
Gestell aus Schichtholz, Bir-
nenholzfurnier. Verbindungs-
stücke aus Gußaluminium.
Glasplatte mit sandge-
strahlten Bereichen und ab-
geschrägten Kanten | Cadre en
bois multiplis, finition poirier.
liaisons en aluminium moulé.
Dessus verre avec parties
décapées au jet de sable et
coins biseautés
Square version | Quadra-
tische Version | Version
carrée : 723 x 130 x 130 cm
Rectangular version | Recht-
eckige Version | Version rec-
tangulaire : 73 x 100 x 210 cm
Round version | Runde Ver-
sion | Version ronde :
H: 73 cm, ø: 140 cm
Driade

Placide of the Wood 1989
Chair | Stuhl | Chaise
Cherrywood, pearwood |
Kirschbaum- und Birn-
baumholz | Bois de cerisier,
bois de poirier
91.5 x 44 x 56.5 cm
Driade

Photos: Tom Vack

Ara Starck & Brigitte Starck
Philippe Starck, 1989
Photos: Tom Vack

Royalton Couch 1991
Couch with one armrest | Sofa
mit einer Armlehne | Canapé
avec accoudoir unique
Steel, polyurethane foam, aluminium, pearwood, cotton
fabric, velvet | Stahl, Schaum-
stoff, Aluminium, Birnbaum-
holz, Baumwollstoff, Samt |
Acier, mousse de nylon,
aluminium, bois de poirier,
coton, velours
113 x 207 x 100 cm
Driade

Royalton Couch 1991
Couch with two armrests |
Sofa mit zwei Armlehnen |
Canapé avec deux accoudoirs
Steel, polyurethane foam, aluminium, pearwood, cotton
fabric, velvet | Stahl, Schaum-
stoff, Aluminium, Birnbaum-
holz, Baumwollstoff, Samt |
Acier, mousse de nylon,
aluminium, bois de poirier,
coton, velours
113 x 207 x 100 cm
Driade

Royalton Long Chair 1991
Long chair | Liegesofa | Divan
Steel, polyurethane foam, cast
aluminium | Stahl, Schaum-
stoff, Gußaluminium | Acier,
mousse de nylon, aluminium
coulé
93 x 89 x 173 cm
Driade

Royalton Armchair 1991
Armchair | Sessel | Fauteuil
Steel, cotton fabric, velvet,
polyurethane foam, pearwood,
aluminium | Stahl, Baumwoll-
stoff, Samt, Schaumstoff, Birn-
baumholz, Aluminium | Acier,
coton, velours, mousse de nylon, bois de poirier, aluminium
113 x 98 x 100 cm
Driade

Pouf | Hocker | Tabouret
Steel, cotton fabric, polyur-
ethane foam, aluminium |
Stahl, Baumwollstoff, Schaum-
stoff, Aluminium | Acier, coton,
mousse de nylon, aluminium
45 x 60 x 60 cm
Driade

Asahy 1991
Armchair | Lehnstuhl | Fauteuil
Cherrywood and pearwood,
leather, polyurethane foam |
Kirsch- und Birnbaumholz,
Lederbezug, Schaumstoffpol-
sterung | Bois de cerisier et de
poirier, cuir, mousse de nylon
91.5 x 45 x 55.5 cm
Driade

Paramount 1991
Armchair | Lehnstuhl | Fauteuil
Cherrywood and pearwood,
leather, polyurethane foam |
Kirsch- und Birnbaumholz,
Lederbezug, Schaumstoffpol-
sterung | Bois de cerisier et de
poirier, cuir, mousse de nylon
95 x 67 x 71.5 cm
Driade

Le paravent de l'autre 1992
Screen | Paravent
Pearwood, glass, polished cast
aluminium | Birnbaumholz,
Glas, Gußaluminium | Bois de
poirier, verre, aluminium coulé
190 x 150 x 3 cm
Driade

Royalton Bed 1992
Bed | Bett | Lit
Steel frame with board in laminar
wood. Cotton wool padding, removable cover in velvet. Head-
board with a removable cover in
white piqué. Front feet in cast
aluminium, back feet in black
plastic | Stahlrahmen, Preßholz-
platte, Baumwollpolsterung,
abziehbarer Samtbezug, abziehbarer Kopfbezug aus weißem Pi-
qué-Stoff. Vordere Beine aus
Gußaluminium, hintere Beine
aus schwarzem Plastik | Cadre
acier, panneau aggloméré. Rembourrage laine de coton, couver-
ture amovible en velours. Dosse-
ret amovible en piqué blanc.
Pieds avant en aluminium
moulé, pieds arrière en plastique
noir
49/175 x 175 x 210 cm
Driade

Royalton 1988
Chair | Stuhl | Chaise
Wooden seat with mahogany or
ebony finish. Back and armrests
in curved plywood. Front legs in
mahogany or ebony. Rear legs in
cast aluminium. Also with four
wooden legs | Sitzfläche aus
Holz mit Mahagoni- oder Eben-
holzfurnier. Rücken- und Arm-
lehnen aus gebogenem Sperr-
holz. Vordere Stuhlbeine aus
Mahagoni- oder Ebenholz. Hintere Stuhlbeine aus Gußaluminium. Auch erhältlich mit vier
Stuhlbeinen aus Holz | Siège en
bois, finition acajou ou ébène.
Dossier et accoudoirs en contre-
plaqué. Pieds avant en acajou ou
ébène. Pieds arrière aluminium
coulé. Existe également avec
quatre pieds en bois
87 x 55.6 x 54 cm
Driade

Photos: Tom Vack

Toy 1999
Stackable chair | Stapelbarer
Stuhl | Chaise empilable
Polypropylene; available in
ivory, yellow, orange and grey |
Polypropylen; erhältlich in
Elfenbein, Gelb, Orange und
Grau | Polypropylène ; existant
dans les tons : ivoire, jaune,
orange et gris
61.5 x 57.5 x 78 cm
Driade
Photos: Tom Vack

Neoz Kitchen 1999
Kitchen | Küche | Cuisine
Legs of solid, mahogany-coloured cherry wood with die-cast aluminium feet. Worktop of Carrara marble, two sinks of white stoneware and a gas cooker | Tischbeine aus massivem mahagonifarbenem Kirschholz mit Füßen aus Aluminium-Spritzguß. Arbeitsplatte aus Carrara-Marmor, zwei Spülbecken aus weißem Steingut und ein Gaskochfeld | Pieds en cerisier massif teinté acajou avec extrémités en moulage d'aluminium. Plan de travail en marbre de Carrare, deux cuvettes en grès blanc et une cuisinière à gaz
140 x 140 x 94 cm
Driade

Neoz Kitchen 1999
Kitchen | Küche | Cuisine
Cupboard in mahogany-coloured cherry with die-cast aluminium feet . Worktop and back edge of Carrara marble, two sinks of white stoneware and a gas cooker | Unterschrank aus mahagonifarbenem Kirschholz, mit Füßen aus Aluminium-Spritzguß. Arbeitsplatte und rückwärtiger Aufsatz aus Carrara-Marmor, zwei Spülbecken aus weißem Steingut und ein Gaskochfeld | Placard en cerisier teinté acajou, pieds en moulage d'aluminium. Plan de travail et plaque arrière en marbre de Carrare, deux cuvettes en grès blanc et une cuisinière à gaz
214 x 70 x 168 cm
Driade

Neoz 1997
Table at two different heights with chair | Tisch in zwei verschiedenen Höhen mit Stuhl | Table à deux niveaux avec chaise
Legs of mahogany-coloured cherry, on rollers of injection-moulded aluminium. Table top in wood with mahogany-coloured cherry veneer or Carrara marble | Beine aus mahagonifarbenem Kirschholz, auf Rollen aus Aluminium-Spritzguß. Tischplatte aus Holz mit mahagonifarbenem Kirschbaumfurnier oder aus Carrara-Marmor | Pieds en cerisier teinté acajou, roulettes en aluminium moulé par injection. Plan de travail en bois avec plaquage en cerisier teinté acajou ou marbre de Carrare
H: 73 cm, ø: 129 cm,
H: 102 cm, ø: 129 cm,
Driade

Neoz 1997
Two-seater sofa and high-backed sofa | Zweisitziges Sofa und Sofa mit hoher Rückenlehne | Canapé deux places et canapé à dossier haut
Mahogany-coloured cherry, on rollers of injection-moulded aluminium. Cover available in white fifty-per-cent linen and in white or sand-coloured cotton | Mahagonifarbenes Kirschholz, auf Rollen aus Aluminium-Spritzguß. Bezug erhältlich in weißem Halbleinen und in weißer oder sandfarbener Baumwolle | Cerisier teinté acajou, roulettes en aluminium moulé par injection. Housse disponible en toile métis de couleur blanche et en coton blanc ou beige
146 x 82 x 85 cm and
207 x 88 x 156 cm
Driade

Neoz 1997
Bed and bedside table | Bett und Beistelltisch | Lit et table
Legs in mahogany-coloured cherry, on rollers of injection-moulded aluminium | Beine aus mahagonifarbenem Kirschholz, auf Rollen aus Aluminium-Spritzguß | Pieds en cerisier teinté acajou, roulettes en aluminium moulé par injection
Bed: 199 x 205 x 165 cm,
Table: 30 x 30 x 50 cm
Driade

Neoz 1997
Tables | Tische
Legs in mahogany-coloured cherry, castors in die-cast aluminium. Table top in Carrara marble | Beine aus mahagonifarbenem Kirschholz, auf Rollen aus Aluminium-Spritzguß. Tischplatte aus Carrara-Marmor | Pieds en cerisier teinté acajou, roulettes en aluminium moulé par injection. Plateau en marbre de Carrare
Carrara
Driade

Neoz 1997
Three-seater sofa | Dreisitziges Sofa | Canapé trois places
Mahogany-coloured cherry, on rollers of injection-moulded aluminium. Cover available in white fifty-per-cent linen and in white or sand-coloured cotton | Mahagonifarbenes Kirschholz, auf Rollen aus Aluminium-Spritzguß. Bezug erhältlich in weißem Halbleinen und in weißer oder sandfarbener Baumwolle | Cerisier teinté acajou, roulettes en aluminium moulé par injection. Housse disponible en toile métis de couleur blanche et en coton blanc ou beige
206 x 152 x 85 cm
Driade

Photos: Tom Vack

Drawing: Jean-Baptiste Mondino

Soft Egg 1999
Injection-moulded polypropylene stacking chair | Stapelbarer Stuhl aus Spritzguß-Polypropylen | Chaise empilable en polypropylène injecté
60.5 x 57.5 x 74 x 43.5 cm
Driade
Photo: Driade/Tom Vack

Bo 2000
Injection-moulded polypropylene stacking chair | Stapelbarer Stuhl aus Spritzguß-Polypropylen | Chaise empilable en polypropylène injecté
50 x 53 x 81 x 45 cm
Driade
Photo: Driade/Tom Vack

Hairdressing furniture for L'Oréal | Friseursalonmöbel für L'Oréal | Meubles de salons de coiffure pour L'Oréal 1989

Adjustable wash unit | Verstellbarer Sessel mit Waschbecken | Fauteuil de lavage réglable 1989
Hydraulic system incorporated in the legs. Shaped shower, wash basin in polished fibreglass, arm rest. Plastic | In den Fuß eingelassene Hydraulik. Gestylte Handdusche. Waschschüssel aus poliertem Glas. Armstütze mit Ablage. Kunststoff | Installation hydraulique intégrée dans les piétements. Douchette façonnée. Cuvette en verre poli. Accoudoir avec tablette. Plastique
95 x 53 x 105 cm
Maletti/L'Oréal

Basic 1989
Swivel work chair, assembled on star base | Arbeitsdrehstuhl mit sternförmigem Fuß | Fauteuil de travail pivotant, monté sur piétement en étoile
Metal, plastic, cast aluminium | Metall, Kunststoff, Gußaluminium | Métal, plastique, aluminium coulé
80 x 50 x 50 cm
Maletti/L'Oréal

Stool 1989
Multi-purpose stool on castors, adjustable height. Pump and castors incorporated. Pump lever under the seat | Vielzweckhocker auf Rollen, Höhe verstellbar. Pumpe und Rollen integriert. Pumphebel unter dem Sitz | Tabouret emplois multiples sur roues, hauteur réglable. Pompe et roues intégrées. Levier de la pompe sous le siège
Plastic | Kunststoff | Plastique
H: 40 cm, ø: 40 cm
Maletti/L'Oréal

Techno 1989
Swivel work chair assembled on star base with hydraulic pump | Arbeitsdrehstuhl mit sternförmigem Fuß und hydraulischer Pumpe | Fauteuil de travail pivotant, monté sur piétement en étoile avec pompe hydraulique
Plastic, cast aluminium | Kunststoff, Gußaluminium | Plastique, aluminium coulé
95 x 53 x 105 cm
Maletti/L'Oréal

Starck with toque | Starck mit Pelzmütze | Starck avec toque
Photo: Jean-Baptiste Mondino

Ara with toque | Ara mit Pelzmütze | Ara avec toque

Ara 1985
Stool | Hocker | Tabouret
Plastic | Kunststoff | Plastique
42 x 30 x 30 cm
VIA

Ray Menta (project) 1984
Lamp | Lampe
XO

Ara & Yanara
Photo: Malick Sibidé

Heritage 1998
Polished or brushed aluminium | Poliertes oder gebürstetes Aluminium | Aluminium poli ou brossé

Collection of chairs, armchairs, stools, bar stools and office chairs | Kollektion von Stühlen, Sesseln, Hockern, Barhockern und Bürostühlen | Collection de chaises, fau-

teuils, tabourets, chaises de bar et fauteuils de travaux
Polished or brushed aluminium | Poliertes oder gebürstetes Aluminium | Aluminium poli ou brossé
Different sizes
Emeco
Photos: Studio Bleu

Dole Melipone 1981
Folding table | Klapptisch | Table pliante
Epoxy, tubular steel, glass | Epoxyd, Stahlrohr, Glas | Epoxy, tube d'acier, verre
H: 73 cm, ø: 120 cm
XO

Dr. Sonderbar 1983
Chair | Stuhl | Chaise
Nickel-plated metal | Metall, vernickelt | Métal, nickelé
63 x 90 x 47 cm
XO
Photo: Tom Vack

Philippe Starck 1999
Photo: Helmut Newton

Helmut Newton and Benedikt Taschen 1999
Photo: Alice Springs

SUMO table 1999
Folding table, designed exclusively for Helmut Newton's SUMO book | Klappbarer Tisch, exclusiv entworfen für Helmut Newtons SUMO | Table pliante, dessinée exclusivement pour le livre SUMO de Helmut Newton

M.T Minimum Table 1998
Table | Tisch
Glass, wood, steel | Glas, Holz, Stahl | Verre, bois, acier
210 x 85 cm, H: 71.5-73 cm
Cassina
Photo: Matthew Donaldson

M.T Minimum Table 1998
Table | Tisch
Glass, wood, steel | Glas, Holz, Stahl | Verre, bois, acier
211 x 85 cm, H: 71.5–73 cm
Cassina
Photos: Matthew Donaldson

Nori & Philippe Starck

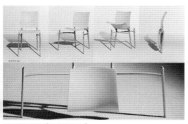

Miss C.O.C.O (five pictures of how to use it) 1998
Folding chair | Klappstuhl | Chaise pliante
Aluminium, polypropylene | Aluminium, Polypropylen | Aluminium, polypropylène
41 x 46 x 80 cm
Cassina
Photos: Matthew Donaldson

L.W.S Lazy Working Sofa 1998
Sofa | Sofa | Canapé
Polyurethane and polyester wadding, cloth, aluminium, wood. The sofa can be fitted with side tables and electrical wiring for lamps, computers etc. | Polyurethanschaumstoff, Stoff, Aluminium, Holz. Das Sofa kann mit seitlichen Ablageflächen ausgestattet und verkabelt geliefert werden, so daß Strom für Lampen, Computer usw. zur Verfügung steht | Polyuréthane, tissu, aluminium, bois. Le canapé peut être munis de plans d'appui latéraux et équipés de systèmes intégrés d'alimentation électrique pour lampes, ordinateurs, etc.
218 x 97 x 83 cm
Cassina
Photo: Matthew Donaldson

L.W.S Lazy Working Sofa (two people relaxing over 16 photos) 1998
Cassina
Photos: Matthew Donaldson

Strange Thing 1999
2-seater settee. Resin shell and cloth-covered foam cushion | Zweisitziges Sofa. Schale aus Kunstharz und Polsterung aus stoffbezogenem Schaumstoff | Canapé 2 places. Coque en résine laquée et garniture en mousse recouverte de tissu
181 x 82 x 81 cm
Cassina
Photo: Cassina

Strange Thing 1999
Armchair. Resin shell and cloth-covered foam cushion | Sessel. Schale aus Kunstharz und Polsterung aus stoffbezogenem Schaumstoff | Fauteuil. Coque en résine laquée et garniture en mousse recouverte de tissu
98 x 79 x 76 cm
Photo: Cassina

Drawing: Jean-Baptiste Mondino

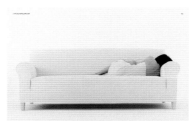

M.I.S.S. 1999
Settee with integral video projector, DVD player and audiosystem | Sofa mit integriertem Videoprojektor, DVD-Spieler und Audiosystem | Canapé avec projecteur vidéo, lecteur de DVD, et système acoustique intégré
250 x 110 x 85 cm
Cassina with Sony
Ill.: DEIS

Bubu 1er 1991
Stool | Hocker | Tabouret
Injection-moulded polypropylene | Polypropylen-Spritzguß | Polypropylène injecté
H: 43.5 cm, ø: 33 cm
up to | bis | jusqu'à 1995 OWO
from | ab | depuis 1996 XO

Bubu 1er 1991
in four colours | in vier Farben | en quatre couleurs

Photos: Tom Vack

Bo Boolo 1995
Table, console and bench | Tisch, Konsole und Bank | Table, console et banc
Mahogany-stained beechwood, natural birch trunk | Mahagonifarben gebeiztes Buchenholz mit naturbelassenem Birkenstamm | Hêtre teinté acajou, tronc en bouleau naturel

190 x 90 x 73 cm;
190 x 40 x 82 cm;
170 x 27 x 42 cm
up to | bis | jusqu'à 1995
3 Suisses/O.N.F.
from | ab | depuis 1996 XO
Photo: Jean-Philippe Piter

Slick Slick 1999
Stackable chair | Stapelbarer Stuhl | Chaise empilable
Coloured polypropylene | Farbiges Polypropylen | Polypropylène teinté
44 x 52 x 80 cm
XO
Photo: Tom Vack

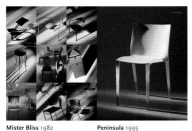

Mister Bliss 1982
Stool | Kniehocker | Agenouilloir
Epoxy, tubular steel, material, padding | Epoxyd, Stahlrohr, Stoff, Polsterung | Epoxy, tube d'acier, tissu, rembourrage
50 x 40 x 58 cm
XO

Dr. Sonderbar 1983
Chair | Lehnstuhl | Chaise
Nickel-plated metal | Metall, vernickelt | Métal, nickelé
63 x 90 x 47 cm
XO

Pat Conley II 1986
Armchair | Lehnstuhl | Fauteuil
Frame and seat of epoxy-lacquered sheet metal, in silver or anthracite finish | Rahmen und Sitzfläche aus Metall, mit silber- oder anthrazitfarbenem Epoxydlack überzogen | Structure et assise en tôle laquée époxy, argent ou anthracite
105 x 44 cm
XO

Royalton Bar Stool 1988
Bar stool | Barhocker | Tabouret de bar
Cast aluminium, velvet, padding | Gußaluminium, Samt, Polsterung | Aluminium coulé, velours, rembourrage
H: 77 cm, ø: 37 cm
XO

Peninsula 1995
Chair | Stuhl | Chaise
Mahogany-stained beechwood. Upholstered seat and back with removable cotton covering | Rahmen aus mahagonifarben gebeiztem Buchenholz. Sitz und Rückenlehne gepolstert und mit abziehbarem Baumwollstoff bezogen | Structure en hêtre teinte acajou. Siège et dossier rembourrés. Housse de coton amovible
89 x 46 x 46 cm
XO

Théâtre du Monde 1984
Secretaire | Sekretär | Secrétaire
Polyester, lacquer or anthracite finish, with four shelves and castors | Polyester, klar- oder anthrazitfarben lackiert, ausgestattet mit vier Fächern und Rollen | Polyester laqué ou anthracite équipé de quatre étagères et roulettes
198 x 55 x 55 cm
XO

Lundi Ravioli 1995
Chair | Stuhl | Chaise
Chrome-plated tubular steel frame. White skai seat. Armrest in laminated wood. Wooden back in various finishes | Rahmen aus verchromten Stahlrohr. Gepolsterter Sitz mit weißem Skai-

Bezug. Lehne aus laminiertem Holz in verschiedenen Farbtönen | Structure en tube d'acier chromé. Siège rembourré en skaï blanc. Dossier bois lamellé collé en plusieurs finitions.
81 x 50 x 46 cm
XO

Lila Hunter 1988
Stackable chair | Stapelbarer Stuhl | Chaise empilable
Metal, wood, leather | Metall, Holz, Leder | Métal, bois, cuir
75 x 51 x 56 cm
XO

Lio Comun 1991
Chair | Stuhl | Chaise
Welded pale grey tubular steel frame and varnished wooden seat and back with crocodile pattern, or welded dark grey tubular frame and pearwood or mahogany seat and back | Rahmen aus verschweißtem hellgrauen Stahlrohr mit lackiertem Sitz und Rückenlehne aus Holz mit »Krokodil«-Muster oder Rahmen aus verschweißtem anthrazitfarbenem Stahlrohr mit lackiertem Sitz und Rückenlehne aus Birnbaumholz oder Mahagoni | Structure en tube acier soudé gris clair avec siège et dossier en bois impression « crocodile » laqué ou structure en tube acier soudé anthracite avec siège et dossier en poirier

ou acajou
88 x 49 x 56 cm
XO

Slick Slick 1999
Stackable chair | Stapelbarer Stuhl | Chaise empilable
Coloured polypropylene | Farbiges Polypropylen | Polypropylène teinté
44 x 52 x 80 cm
XO

Photos: Tom Vack

Monsieur X Rocking 1996
Folding rocking chair | Klapp-Schaukelstuhl | Fauteuil pliant
Beech, seat and back in coloured cotton canvas | Buche, Sitzfläche und Rückenlehne aus farbiger Baumwolle | Hêtre clair, assise et dossier en toile de coton
55 x 59 x 88 cm
XO

Os Library 1998
Shelf | Regal | Etagère
Wenge, supporting elements in china | Wenge, Stützelemente aus weißem Porzellan | Wenge, éléments de support en porcelaine blanche
L: 180 cm
XO

Popopo 1993
Vase
Polyester resin, aluminium base | Polyester, Fuß aus Aluminium | Résine de polyester, base en aluminium
H: 158 cm, ø: 40 cm
XO

Monsieur X Chaise longue 1996
Folding chair | Klappsessel | Fauteuil pliant
Beech, seat and back in coloured cotton canvas | Buche, Sitzfläche und Rückenlehne aus farbiger Baumwolle | Hêtre clair, assise et dossier en toile de coton
55 x 115 x 84 cm
XO

Cheap Chic Table 1998
Table | Tisch
Base in epoxy-laquered steel, top in polypropylene | Sockel aus epoxid-harz-lackiertem Stahl, Tischplatte aus Polypropylen | Piétement acier laqué, époxy, plateau en polypropylène
H: 72 cm, ø: 60 cm
XO

Cheap Chic 1997
Stackable chair | Stapelbarer Stuhl | Chaise empilable
Laquered tubular aluminium frame, epoxy resin. Polypropylene shell | Rahmen aus epoxidharz-lackiertem Aluminiumroh Sitzschale aus Polypropylen | Structure en tube d'aluminium laqué, époxy. Coque polypropylène
45 x 49 x 80 cm
XO

Cheap Chic Armchair 1997
Stackable armchair | Stapelbare Lehnstuhl | Fauteuil empilable
Frame and arms in laquered tubular aluminium, epoxy resir Polypropylene shell | Rahmen aus epoxid-harz-lackiertem Alu miniumrohr, Sitzschale aus Polypropylen | Structure et bras en tube d'aluminium laqué, époxy. Coque polypropylène
58 x 49 x 80 cm
XO

Photos: Tom Vack

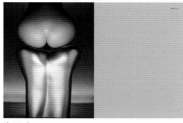

You are God

Ihr seid Gott

Vous êtes Dieu

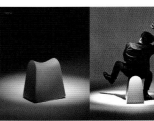

Poaa 1999
Dumb-bells | Hantel | Haltère
Polished die-cast aluminium, filled with steel | Polierter Aluminium-Spritzguß mit Stahlkern | Fonte d'aluminium, noyau en acier
L: 20 cm
XO
Photo: Tom Vack

Dadada 1993
Stool | Hocker | Tabouret
Injection-moulded polypropylene stacking chair | Stapelhocker aus Polypropylen-Spritzguß | Siège empilable en polypropylène injecté
51.8 x 46.5 x 31.2 cm
up to | bis | jusqu'à 1995 OWO
from | ab | depuis 1996 XO

Philippe Starck on Dadada

Photos: Tom Vack

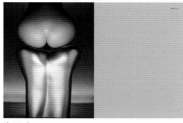

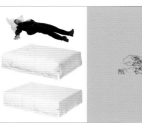

The Tooth 2002
Moulded polypropylene stool | Hocker aus rotationsgeformtem Polypropylen | Tabouret en polypropylène rotomoulé
40 x 44 cm
XO
Photo: Fabrice Bouquet/Elle

The Club 1999
Injection-moulded polypropylene stacking chair | Stapelbarer Sessel aus Spritzguß-Polypropylen | Fauteuil empilable en polypropylène injecté
54 x 56 x 86 cm
XO
Photo: XO

Night and Day 2000
Descamps
Ill.: DEIS

Drawing: Jean-Baptiste Mondino

Night and Day 2000
Bedhead, bedside table and
tray | Kopfteil des Bettes,
Nachttisch und Tablett | Tête
de lit, table de chevet et
plateau
Descamps
Ill.: DEIS

Trimmings
Details: Bed linen, buttons,
towel | Details: Bettwäsche,
Knöpfe, Handtuch | Détails:
Linge de lit, boutons, serviette
Descamps
Photo: Studio Bleu/DEIS

Bathwear
Bathwear | Bademodenkollek-
tion | Collection éponge
Descamps
Photo: Jean-Baptiste Mondino

Bedding
Bed linen | Bettwäsche | Linge
de lit
Descamps
Photo: Studio Bleu/DEIS

Pax Now

Frieden jetzt

La paix maintenant

Industrial Design
Industriedesign
Design industriel

Faitoo 1996
Diverse kitchen utensils |
Diverse Küchenzubehör |
Divers ustensiles de cuisine
Alessi
Photo: Jean-Baptiste Mondino

Plywood car (project) 1996
Plywood | Sperrholz | Bois
contre-plaqué
Ill.: DEIS

Drawing: Jean-Baptiste Mondino

Toto la toto car (project) 1996
Photo: Jean-Baptiste Mondino

TeddyBearBand 1998
Children's soft toy | Plüschtier |
Animal en peluche
Bear's head, 3 limbs with
heads of a dog, a goat, and a
rabbit, and one leg with a nor-
mal paw. Cotton covering |
Bärenkopf, drei Gliedmaßen
laufen in verschiedenen Köpfen
aus: Hund, Ziege und Kanin-
chen, die vierte ist als Pfote
gestaltet. Bezug aus Baum-
wolle | Tête d'ours, 3 membres
sont terminés par des têtes
différentes, chien, chèvre,
lapin, membre inférieur droit
en forne d'une patte. Dessus
coton
H: 37 cm
Moulin Roty
Photos: Michel Lelièvre/Studio
Bleu for GOOD GOODS/
La Redoute

Drawing: Jean-Baptiste Mondino

Dr. Life 1991
Floor lamp giving direct light |
Bodenleuchte mit direktem
Licht | Lampadaire à lumière
directe
Cast iron and aluminium base,
aluminium stem, 'Bright eye'
made of moulded etched
glass with continuous colour
change. May be adapted to
wall or ceiling use. Dr. Life's
300-watt halogen beam may
be tinted in many hues thanks
to a multi-coloured filter and
an auxiliary low-voltage halo-
gen bulb | Sockel aus Guß-
eisen und Aluminium, Fuß aus
Aluminium. »Großes Auge«
aus mattglänzendem Relief-
glas mit variierenden Farben.
In Wand- oder Deckenleuchte
umwandelbar. Dank eines
Farbfilters und einer zusätz-
lichen Halogenbirne mit Nied-
rigspannung kann der 300-
Watt-Halogenstrahl von Dr.
Life in den verschiedensten
Farbtönen leuchten | Socle en
fer forgé et aluminium, pied
aluminium, « œil large » en
verre gaufré satiné aux couleurs variables. Adaptable au
mur et au plafond. Le rayon
halogène de 300 watts de Dr.
Life peut être teinté dans de
nombreuses nuances grâce
à un filtre aux couleurs multiples et un bulbe halogène
auxiliaire à bas-voltage
40 x 197 cm
Flos

Rosy Angelis 1994
Floor lamp giving diffused light |
Bodenlampe mit indirektem
Licht | Lampadaire à lumière
diffuse
Carbon fibre legs, special shade
of lightweight fabric. Technopo-
lymer structural support, elec-
tronic dimmer | Beine aus Kar-
bonfaser. Schirm aus besonders
leichtem Stoff. Technopolymer-
Struktur. Elektronischer Dim-
mer | Pieds en fibre de carbone.
Diffuseur en tissu spécial extra
léger. Structure en technopo-
lymère. Variateur d'intensité
électronique
H: 185 cm, ø: 50 cm
Flos

Miss Sissi 1990
Table and wall lamp | Tisch- und
Wandleuchte | Lampe de table
et suspension murale
H: 28.4 cm, ø: 14.3 cm
Flos

Romeo Moon 1995
Pendant lamp | Deckenleuchte |
Plafonnier
Pendant lamp giving diffused
light, supported by three steel
wires. White satin-finished glass
inside, moulded glass outside |
Indirektes Licht spendende, an
drei Stahldrähten aufgehängte
Deckenlampe. Innerer Schirm
aus weißsatiniertem Glas, äuße-
rer Schirm aus Reliefglas | Sus-
pension à lumière diffuse, re-
tenue par trois fils d'acier. Abat-

jour intérieur en verre blanc satiné, abat-jour extérieur en
verre gaufré
Crown height | Höhe des
Schirms | Hauteur de la cou-
ronne: 22.5 cm
Flos

Light Lite 1992
Lamp | Lampe
Energy-saving lamp of a special plastic material that has
been thermoformed in a vac-
uum and serigraphed, either
hanging from the ceiling or
plugged into the wall socket
and hung from a hook. Available in four metallized colours
with six coloured interchange-
able inserts | Energiesparende
Lampe aus in einem Vakuum
thermogeformten und serigra-
phierten Kunststoff; kann an
der Decke befestigt, an eine
Wandsteckdose angeschlossen
oder an einen Haken gehängt
werden. In vier Metallicfarben
mit sechs auswechselbaren
Farbfiltern erhältlich | Lampe
économisant l'énergie, elle est
faite de plastique thermoformé
au vide et sérigraphié, et peut
être suspendue au plafond,
branchée dans une prise de
courant au mur ou pendue à
un crochet. Elle existe en quatre couleurs métallisées avec
six filtres colorés interchangeables
H: 24 cm, ø: 43 cm
Flos

Walla Walla 1994
Wall fitting providing diffused
light | Wandleuchte mit indirek-
tem Licht | Lampe murale à lu-
mière diffuse
Thermopolymer plastic (clear/
green, grey, terracotta) with an
opaline plastic diffuser and a
set of cloroured filters for
different lighting effects | Ther-
mopolymer-Kunststoff (Trans-
parent/Grün, Grün, terrakottafarben) mit opalem Lichtdiffu-
sor mit Plastik und vier Farb-
filtern für unterschiedliche
Lichteffekte | Plastique thermo-
polymère (transparent/ vert,
gris, terre cuite) avec diffuseur
en plastique opalin et quatres
filtres colorés pour divers effets
de lumière
30 x 37 x 10 cm
Flos

Ara 1988
Table lamp | Tischlampe |
Lampe de table
Chrome-plated metal, halogen |
Verchromtes Metall, Halogen |
Métal chromé, halogène
H: 56.5 cm
Flos

Photos: Jean-Baptiste Mondino

Jean-Baptiste Mondino
Photo: Philippe Starck

Romeo Moon Soft T2 1998
Table lamp | Tischlampe |
Lampe de table
Base in metallic grey, cast alu-
minium. Double lampshade:
white satin-finished glass in-
side, fabric outside | Lampen-
fuß aus metallic-grauem
Gußaluminium. Doppelter
Lampenschirm: innerer
Schirm aus weiß-satiniertem
Glas, äußerer Schirm aus
Stoff | Pied en aluminium
coulé gris métallique. Abat-
jour double : abat-jour in-
térieur en verre blanc satiné,
abat-jour extérieur en tissu
H: 73 cm, ø: 50 cm
Flos

Romeo Moon T2 1998
Table lamp | Tischlampe |
Lampe de table
Base in metallic grey, cast aluminium. Double lampshade:
white satin-finished glass in-
side, moulded glass outside |
Lampenfuß aus metallic-
grauem Gußaluminium. Dop-
pelter Lampenschirm: innerer
Schirm aus weiß-satiniertem
Glas, äußerer Schirm aus Re-
liefglas | Pied en aluminium
coulé gris métallique. Abat-
jour double : abat-jour intérieur en verre blanc satiné,
abat-jour extérieur en verre
gaufré
H: 73 cm, ø: 50 cm
Flos

Photos: Piero Fasanotto

ArchiMoon Tech 1998
An almost dematerialized
version with a halogen bulb |
Eine beinahe entmateriali-
sierte Version mit einer Halo-
genlampe | Une version
presque dématérialisée, avec
ampoule halogène
Low wattage lamp, 35 watt,
grey metallic aluminium body,
yellow polycarbonate filter |
Niedervoltleuchte, 35 Watt,
Korpus Aluminium metallic-
grau, Lampenschirm Polycar-
bonat | Lampe basse tension,
35 watts, corps aluminium
gris métal, diffuseur polycarbonate jaune
H: 44 cm
Flos

ArchiMoon Eco 1998
Low wattage lamp | Nieder-
voltleuchte | Lampe basse
tension
Max 18 watt, grey metallic aluminium body, polycarbonate
filter | Max. 18 Watt, Korpus
Aluminium metallic-grau,
Lampenschirm Polycarbonat |
18 watts maxi, corps alu-
minium gris métal, diffuseur
polycarbonate
H: 56.6 cm
Flos

ArchiMoon Classic 1998
Interpretation of a great clas-
sic, the architect's lamp |
Interpretation eines großen
Klassikers: der Architekten-
lampe | Interprétation du
grand classique de la lampe
d'architecte
Max 60 watt bulb, metallic
grey aluminium body, polycar-
bonate lampshade | Glüh-
birne max. 60 Watt, Korpus
Aluminium metallic-grau,
Lampenschirm Polycarbonat |
Lampe puissance 60 watts
maxi, corps aluminium gris
métal, abat-jour en polycar-
bonate
H: 56.6 cm
Flos

ArchiMoon Soft 1998
A work light fitted with a
pleated shade | Ein gefalteter
Schirm über einer Arbeits-
leuchte | Un abat-jour plissé
sur une lampe de travail
Low wattage lamp, 35 watt,
body of metallic grey var-
nished aluminium. Taffeta
and glass shade, white filter |
Niedervoltleuchte, 35 Watt,
Korpus metallic-grau lack-
iertes Aluminium. Lampen-
schirm aus Glas und Taft mit
weißem Filter | Lampe basse
tension, 35 watts, corps gris
metal aluminium verni. Abat-
jour taffetas et verre diffuseur
blanc
H: 44 cm
Flos

*Photos: Michel Lelièvre/Studio
Bleu for GOOD GOODS/
La Redoute*

SuperArchimoon 1999
Giant lamp, silver-finished
steel structure and cloth
shade | Riesige Wohnzimmer-
lampe, Gestell aus versilber-
tem Stahl, Schirm aus Stoff |
Lampadaire de salon geante
structure en acier finition argent et diffuseur en tissu
345 x 320 cm, ø: 79 cm
Flos

Magic Slabe 2000
Table lamp, injection-moulded
polycarbonate | Tischleuchte,
Spritzguß-Polycarbonat | lampe
de table en polycarbonate injecté
20 x 27 x 30 cm
Flos

Photos: Flos

Cicatrices de Luxe 1999
Lighting system: hand-moul-
ded blown crystal, structure
in nickel-plated steel | Leuch-
ten aus geblasenem und
handgeschliffenen Glas, Ge-
stell aus vernickeltem Stahl |
Luminaires en cristal soufflé
et gravé à la main, structure
en acier nickelé

Different sizes
Flos
Photos: Jean-Baptiste Mondino

Miss Yee 1987
Drawing | Zeichnung | Dessin

Miss Yee 1987
Shelf | Regal | Etagère
Chrome-plated sheet steel,
silk cording | Verchromtes
Stahlblech, Seilaufhängung
aus Seide | Tôle d'acier
chromée, cordons en soie
4.3 x 90 x 30 cm
Idée

Oa Starck
Photo: Patricia Bailer

Target 2000
Baby monitors | Babyphone |
Babyphones
14 x 9 x 4 cm
Target
Photo: Target/Studio Bleu

Target 2000
Baby bottle | Babyflasche |
Biberon
19 x 5.5 cm
Photo: Target/Studio Bleu

**Starck and Target objects |
Starck mit Target-Produkten |
Starck et objets Target**
Photo: Jean-Baptiste Mondino

Target 2000
Baby fork/spoon | Babygabel
und -löffel | Fourchette et
cuillère pour bébé
11 x 2 cm

Toilet training set | Toilettentrai-
ner | Kit toilettes pour bébé
33.5 x 30 x 17 cm
Scale | Waage | Pèse-personne
29 x 29 x 4.5 cm
Sippy cup | Trinkbecher | Tasse
à bec
14.5 x 13 cm
Photos: Target/Studio Bleu

Target 2000
Toy car | Spielzeugauto |
Voiture pour bébé
55 x 80 x 40 cm
Short pop-up playhouse | Klei-
nes Stoff-Spielhaus | Tente en
toile
106 x 101 cm
Cozy chair | Kindersessel |
Chaise pliante en toile
84 x 58 x 55 cm

Ethno plastic stool/table/con-
tainer | Ethno-Plastik-Hocker/
Tisch/Behälter | Ethno tabouret/
table/rangement en plastique
43 x 36 cm
Photos: Target/Studio Bleu

K Starck
Photo: Nori Starck

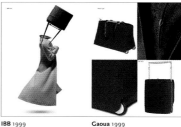

Target 2000
Stapler | Tacker | Agrafeuse
15.5 x 6.5 x 7.5 cm
Tape dispenser | Klebefilmroller | Dévidoir de ruban adhésif
8 x 6 x 3 cm
Magazine rack | Zeitschriftenständer | Porte-revues
32 x 32 x 35 cm
Book ends | Buchstützen | Presse-livres
10 x 3 x 18 cm
Pencil cup | Stiftebecher | Pot à crayons
11 x 14 cm
Mechanical pencil | Druckbleistift | Porte-mine
Letter opener | Brieföffner | Coupe-papier
23 x 2 cm
Scissors | Schere | Ciseaux
19 x 7.5 cm
Letter tray | Briefablage | Boîte à courrier
32 x 24 x 6 cm
Letter sorter | Briefständer | Porte-lettres
17.5 x 22.5 x 15.5 cm
Mail center/Bulletin board | Schwarzes Brett/Info-Board | Panneau d'affichage
24.5 x 37 x 13 cm
Calculator | Rechner | Calculatrice
10.3 x 5.5 x 0.8 cm
Wet tunes | Duschradio | Radio étanche
5.8 x 5.8 x 19 cm

Light table | Tisch mit eingebautem Licht | Table lumineuse
57 x 39 x 39 cm
Table lamp | Tischleuchte | Lampe de table
31 x 18 cm
Tissue box | Papiertuchspender | Boîte pour mouchoirs en papier
15.5 x 12.5 x 12.5 cm
CD storage box | CD-Aufbewahrung | Boîte à CD
16 x 27 x 16 cm
Project file | Projektablage | Classeur à dossiers suspendus
16 x 25 x 35 cm
Wastebasket | Abfalleimer | Corbeille à papier
31.5 x 25.5 cm
Plastic food storage | Plastikvorratsbehälter | Boîte alimentaire en plastique
Severals sizes
Soap dish/nail brush | Seifenhalter/Nagelbürste | Portesavon/Brosse à ongles
8.5 x 12.5 x 1 cm
Lotion dispenser | Seifenspender | Flacon-pompe
20 x 7.5 cm
Beard trimmer | Bartschneider | Taille-barbe
19 x 6 x 6 cm
Men's foils shaver | Elektrorasierer | Rasoir électrique pour homme
17 x 6 x 6 cm
Hair dryer | Haartrockner | Sèche-cheveux
23 x 27 x 8 cm

Curling iron set | Lockenstab | Kit fer à friser
22 x 9 x 39 cm
Bath towels | Badehandtücher | Serviettes de bain
Severals sizes
Tumbler | Becher | Gobelet
13 x 8 cm
Adult sonic pick | Ultraschall-Zahnstocher für Erwachsene | Appareil anti-tartre aux ultra-sons pour adulte
28 x 6 x 6 cm
Juvenile sonic pick | Ultraschall-Zahnstocher für Jugendliche | Appareil anti-tartre aux ultra-sons pour enfant
23 x 6 x 6 cm
Juvenile ultrasenex toothbrush | Elektrozahnbürste für Kinder | Brosse à dents électrique pour enfant
24 x 6 x 6 cm
Tooth brush and holder | Zahnbürste mit Halter | Brosse à dents et socle
4.5 x 4.5 x 19 cm
Baby bowl | Babyteller | Bol pour enfant
16 x 8 cm
Baby soft carrier | Babytrage | Porte-bébé en tissu
21 x 30 x 40 cm
Tall pop-up playhouse | Großes Stoff-Spielhaus | Grande tente en toile
172 x 99 cm
Pop-up playhouse tunnel | Stofftunnel für Kinder | Tunnel de jeu
121 x 45 cm

Baby bottle brush | Babyflaschenbürste | Brosse à biberon
29 x 11.5 cm
Bottle warmer | Flaschenwärmer | Chauffe-biberon
20 x 23 x 32 cm
Diaper backpack | Wickelrucksack | Sac à dos change-bébé
40 x 13 x 35 cm
Diaper weekend bag | Wochenend-Wickeltasche | Grand sac change-bébé
38 x 13 x 35 cm

Photos: Target/Studio Bleu

IBB 1999
Bag in polyester, handles in injection-moulded plastic | Tasche aus Polyesterstoff, Halterungen aus Spritzguß-Kunststoff | Serviette en tissu polyester, poignées en plastique injecté
42 x 37 x 13 cm
Samsonite

Gaoua 1999
Polyester and injection-moulded plastic travelling bag with rollers and aluminium handles | Rollreisetasche aus Polyesterstoff, Griffe aus Aluminium und Spritzguß-Kunststoff | Sac de voyage à roulettes en tissu polyester, poignées en aluminium et plastique injecté
67 x 40 x 26 cm
Samsonite

Yeza 1999
Polyester and injection-moulded plastic suitcase with rollers and aluminium handles | Rollkoffer aus Polyesterstoff, Griffe aus Aluminium und Spritzguß-Kunststoff | Valise à roulettes en tissu polyester, poignées en aluminium et plastique injecté
40 x 55 x 20 cm
Samsonite

Photos: Air

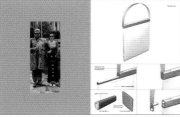

Philippe & Nori Starck
Photo: Malick Sibidé

Soft Safe for computers 2000
'Spectra' canvas bag, woven steel and overmoulded plastic strap | Tasche aus »Spectra«-Stoff, Gurt aus geflochtenem Stahl mit Kunststofüberzug | Sac en toile « spectra », bride en acier tissé et plastique surmoulé
28 x 40 cm
Project
Photo: Agence Starck

Shoe (prototype) 1996
Schuh | Chaussure
Della Valle

God is dangerous

Gott ist gefährlich

Dieu est dangereux

Male model wearing a Starck mask | Männermodell mit Starck-Maske | Modèle masculin portant un masque de Starck
Photo: Jean-Baptiste Mondino

Starck Masks by Ingo Maurer | Starck-Masken von Ingo Maurer | Masques de Starck par Ingo Maurer
Cologne 1998

We must share

Wir müssen teilen

Partageons

Mandala 1987
Pasta | Nudel | Pâtes
ø: 5 mm
Panzani
Photo: Hervé Ternisien

Ti Tang 1992
Teapot | Teekanne | Théière
White porcelain, with aluminium coat coloured with epoxy
resins | Weißes Porzellan, Alu-
miniummantel mit farbiger
Epoxydharzbeschichtung | Por-
celaine blanche, gaine résine
époxy
22 x 14 x 18 cm
Alessi

Su Mi Tang 1992
Cream jug | Sahnespender |
Pot à crème
White porcelain | Weißes
Porzellan | Porcelaine blanche
H: 14 cm, ø: 7.5 cm
Alessi

Mister Meumeu 1992
Cheese grater | Käsedose mit
Reibe | Fromagère avec râpe
Stainless steel, polyamide |

Edelstahl, Polyamid | Acier
inoxydable, polyamide
13.5 x 8.5 x 20.5 cm
Alessi

**Toothbrush and toothbrush
holder | Zahnbürste und
Behälter | Brosse à dents et
base** 1989
H: 19.5 cm
Fluocaril

Starck Wars

**Toothpaste dispenser | Zahn-
pastaspender | Doseur à den-
tifrice** 1989
Fluocaril

**Toothbrush | Zahnbürste |
Brosse à dents** 1989
Fluocaril

**Toothbrush and toothbrush
holder | Zahnbürste und
Behälter | Brosse à dents et
base** 1989
Fluocaril

**Toothbrushes and toothbrush
holder | Zahnbürsten und
Behälter | Brosses à dents et
base** 1989
Fluocaril

Dr Skud 1998
Fly swat | Fliegenklatsche |
Tapette à mouches
Polyamide | Polyamid
L: 44 cm
Alessi

Nous n'avons pas
besoin de tuer pour survivre

**We do not have to kill to
survive**

**Wir müssen nicht töten,
um zu überleben**

**Nous n'avons pas besoin
de tuer pour survivre**

Washtub, pump, wash-bowl
(traditional form) | Zuber,
Pumpe, Waschschüssel (Ur-
formen) | Baquet, pompe,
bassine (formes traditionelles)

**Washbasin | Waschbecken |
Lavabo** 1994
Sanicryl
85 x 58 x 58 cm
Duravit/Axor/Hoesch

**Washbasin mixer | Einarmige
Mischbatterie | Mitigeur d'évier**
1994
Chrome | Chrom
Duravit/Axor/Hoesch

**Bathtub | Badewanne |
Baignoire** 1994
Sanicryl
180 x 90 x 59 cm
Duravit/Axor/Hoesch

Photos: Rudolf Schmutz

**Toilet and bidet | Toilette und
Bidet | Toilette et bidet** 1998
Ceramic | Keramik |
Céramique
Duravit

**Bathtub | Badewanne | Baig-
noire** 1998
Sanicryl
Hoesch

Photos: Rudolf Schmutz

**Two-handled mixing faucet |
Zweiarmige Mischbatterie |
Mélangeur à deux robinets**
1998
Chrome-plated brass | Mes-
sing, verchromt | Laiton
chromé
Axor
Photo: Rudolf Schmutz

*Drawing: Jean-Baptiste
Mondino*

Shower | Dusche | Douche 1998
Hoesch
Photo: Jean-Baptiste Mondino

Jelly Cube 2000
Bathroom storage unit in
translucent injection-moul-
ded polypropylene | Aufbe-
wahrungsmöbel für das Bade-
zimmer aus durchscheinen-
dem Spritzguß-Polypropylen |
Meuble de rangement pour
salle de bains en polypropylène translucide injecté
45 x 48 x 87 cm
Duravit
Photo: Nick Veasey

Mixing Faucets 2000
Chrome-plated brass | Messing,
verchromt | Laiton chromé
20 x 15 x 10 cm
Hansgrohe
Photo: Hansgrohe

Beneteau Collection « First S »
1988–1994

First 41 S5 Voilier L Coque 1989
L: 12.30 m
Beneteau

First 35,7 Voilier L Coque 1992
Interior | Innenausstattung |
Intérieur
L: 10.55 m
Beneteau

First 35 S5 Voilier L Coque 1988
Detail | Détail
L: 10.60 m
Beneteau

Photos: G. Martin Raget

Ara III
House boat | Hausboot |
Bateau aménagé
Various views | Verschiedene
Ansichten | Vues diverses

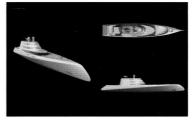

Ara III
House boat | Hausboot |
Bateau aménagé
Various views | Verschiedene
Ansichten | Vues diverses

Virtuelle 1997
Racing boat | Rennboot |
Bateau de régate
Sloop, carbon kevlar sand-
wich hull, carbon mast, milar
and carbon sails | Sloop,
Sandwichrumpf aus Kevlar-
Karbon, Karbonmast, Milar-
Karbonsegel | Sloop, coque
sandwich, carbone kevlar, mât
carbone, voile milar/carbone

L: 26 m
Ill.: DEIS

Under sail | Beim Segeln | En
mer
Cockpit | Cockpit | Cabine de
pilotage
Details | Détails
Interior | Interieur | Intérieur
*Photo: Guillaume de
Laubier/Elle Decoration*

120 m Powerboat 2002
Private powerboat | Privates
Powerboot | Super yacht
L: 120 m
Ill.: DEIS

**My friends | Meine Freunde |
Mes amis**

Wedge Too 1999
Yacht
L: 65 m
Photo: Feadship

Nori Starck

Detail, inside door | Detail
einer Innentür | Détail de la
porte intérieure
Ill.: DEIS

Upper deck with swimming
pool | Oberes Deck mit
Schwimmbad | Pont
supérieur avec piscine
Drawing: Daniel Pouzet

Urgency is back again

Rückkehr der Dringlichkeit

L'urgence est revenue

Motó 6,5 1995
Single-cylinder, four strokes,
with balancing countershaft,
light alloy cylinder, with Gilni-
sil coating. Liquid cooled, one
radiator with separate expan-
sion tank | Einzylinder, Vier-
takter, Vorgelegewelle,
Leichtmetallzylinder mit Gil-
nisil-Beschichtung, wasserge-
kühlt, Kühler mit separatem
Ausdehnungsgefäß | Monocy-

lindre 4 temps à transmission
intermédiaire, cylindre en al-
liage léger à revêtement Gilni-
sil. Refroidissement par liquide, radiateur à vase d'expansion séparé
213.3 x 80 x 106 cm
Aprilia
Photos: Tom Vack

Motó 6,5 & friends
Bigas Luna
Patricia Bailer
Ivano Beggio + Philippe Starck
Javier Mariscal
Peter Gabriel
Philippe Starck
Florent Pagny
Placido Arango
Jenna de Rosnay
Azucena Caamano

Thierry Gaugain
Jean-Louis Aubert
Photos: Jean-Philippe Piter

Motó 6,5 1995
Detail | Détail
Photo: Tom Vack

Motó 6,5 1995
*Photo: Michel Lelièvre/
Studio Bleu for GOOD GOODS/
La Redoute*

X-ray 1996
Motorbike | Motorrad | Motó
Aprilia

X3 2000
Motorbike | Motorrad | Motó
Aprilia
Ill.: Agence Starck

Drawing: Jean-Baptiste Mondino

Scooter Lama (prototype) 1992
Vehicle with two wheels for urban transport for one or two
persons with a large load capacity. Two-stroke combustion
engine with catalyser. Plastic
recyclable materials | Zweirad
für Stadtverkehr, Zweisitzer,
mit großer Ladekapazität.
Zweitaktmotor, Katalysator.
Recycelbare Kunststoffmate-
rialien | Un deux-roues pour

déplacements urbains, bi-
place, grande capacité de
chargement. Moteur deux
temps, pot catalytique. Matières plastiques recyclables
120 x 72 x 173 cm
Aprilia
Photo: Gianni Sabbadin

**Philippe Starck, Alberto
Capella, Thierry Gaugain** 1992

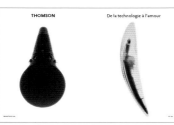

Remote control 1994
Remote control unit | Fernbedienung | Télécommande
ABS plastic | ABS-Kunststoff | Plastique ABS
2.5 x 6 cm, ø: 3 cm
Thomson
Photo: Tom Vack

Alo 1996
Voice command telephone | Durch Zuruf bedienbares Telefon | Téléphone à commande vocale
Soft case made of translucent polymer coloured with natural dyes, revealing an oblong aluminium core protecting the delicate technical components | Der weiche Korpus besteht aus durchsichtigem, mit Naturfarben gefärbtem Polymer-Kunststoff und enthüllt einen rechteckigen Aluminiumkern aus der das empfindliche technische Innenleben enthält | Son corps moelleux en polymère translucide coloré de pigments naturels révèle un noyau oblong en aluminium protégeant ses délicats composants techniques
14 x 6 cm
Thomson
Concept: Philippe Starck
Designer: Jérôme Olivet
Photo: Guido Mocafico

From technology to love

Von der Technologie zur Liebe

De la technologie à l'amour

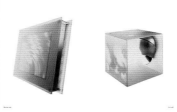

Plasmaa 1995
Ultra-flat Television set | Ultraflacher Fernseher | Téléviseur ultra-plat
Plasmaa is the result of a dream: an ultra-flat TV visible only as a screen. Plasmaa frees the image from its cathode ray tube: two glass walls, only a hundred or so microns apart, enclose a gaseous mixture that is activated by electrodes. The ultraviolet radiation from this plasma is then converted into the basic colours visible to the human eye. When the power is off, its front layer of glass looks like a mirror reflecting the first artificial image that marked mankind: his own reflection | Plasmaa ist das Ergebnis eines Traums: ein ultraflacher Fernseher, der äußerlich nur aus einem Bildschirm zu bestehen scheint. Plasmaa befreit das Bild von der Kathodenstrahlröhre: Zwei Glaswände, die nur wenige hundert Mikrone auseinanderliegen, enthalten ein Gasgemisch, das von den Elektroden aktiviert wird. Die von diesem Plasma ausgehende ultraviolette Strahlung wird dann umgewandelt in die Spektralfarben, die für das menschliche Auge sichtbar sind. Das Hochpräzisionsbild kommt von einer dünnen Oberfläche. Ausgeschaltet sieht die Vorderseite wie ein Spiegel aus: Sie reflektiert das erste künstliche Bild, das die Menschheit kennzeichnet: die eigene Spiegelung | Plasmaa concrétise un rêve : le téléviseur ultra plat uniquement incarné par la présence magistrale de son écran. Plasmaa libère de son tube cathodique : deux parois de verre distantes d'une centaine de microns renfermant un mélange gazeux activé par des électrodes. Le rayonnement ultraviolet de ce plasma est ensuite traduit en couleurs de base perceptibles par l'homme. Une image d'une grande finesse jaillit alors d'une surface mince. Mis en veille, il devient miroir par un jeu de surface de son verre frontal, proposant la première image artificielle qui ait marqué l'homme : son propre reflet
58 x 47 x 8.8 cm
Thomson
Concept: Philippe Starck
Designer: Bernard Guerrin
Photo: Guido Mocafico

Cub 1996
LCD projector – overhead projector | LCD Projektor – Overheadprojektor | Projecteur LCD – Rétroprojecteur
A diaphanous form containing a core of dense energy emitting a light ray carrying the image. Can be viewed on the opposite side of the cube made of a liquid crystal screen or freed for the projection of a larger image | Eine durchscheinende Form mit einem Energiezentrum, das einen hellen Strahl aussendet und so das Bild trägt: Dieses kann entweder auf die gegenüberliegende Seite des Würfels projiziert werden, der aus einer Kristallwand besteht, oder auch unabhängig davon größer projiziert werden | Une forme diaphane contenant un noyau d'énergie dense d'où s'échappe un rayon lumineux véhiculant l'image. Elle peut être lue sur la surface opposée du cube devenu écran à cristaux liquides ou peut être libérée pour une projection en plus grande dimension
22 x 22 x 22 cm
Thomson
Concept & Design: Matali Crasset
Photo: Didier Griffoullière/ Edelkoort Conseil

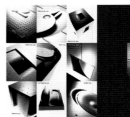

Radio 1995
ABS plastic | ABS-Kunststoff | Plastique ABS
5.7 x 19.8 x 16.6 cm
Thomson

Video recorder 1995
Video recorder | Videorekorder | Lecteur vidéo
ABS plastic | ABS-Kunststoff | Plastique ABS
9 x 39.4 x 43.9 cm
Thomson

Television 14" 1994
Television set | Fernseher | Téléviseur
ABS plastic | ABS-Kunststoff | Plastique ABS
33.7 x 34 x 37.8 cm
Thomson

Speaker 16.9 1995
Speaker | Lautsprecher | Haut-parleur
ABS plastic | ABS-Kunststoff | Plastique ABS
54 x 85.8 x 53.8 cm
Thomson

Don'O 1995
Clock | Uhr | Horloge
ABS plastic | ABS-Kunststoff | Plastique ABS
26 x 16 x 11.5 cm
Thomson

Television 14" 1994

Television 1994
Television set | Fernseher | Téléviseur
ABS plastic | ABS-Kunststoff | Plastique ABS
55.8 x 66.1 x 48.2 cm
Thomson

Aloo Telephone 1995
Voice command telephone | Durch Zuruf bedienbares Telefon | Téléphone à commande vocale
ABS plastic | ABS-Kunststoff | Plastique ABS
55 x 16.3 x 20.5 cm
Thomson

Speaker 1994
Speaker | Lautsprecher | Haut-parleur
ABS plastic | ABS-Kunststoff | Plastique ABS
54 x 95 x 63.8 cm
Thomson

Photos: Guido Mocafico

TV Bicolonne 1996
Television set | Fernseher | Téléviseur
70 cm
Saba

TV Bicolonne M5116F Screen 1995
Screen | Bildschirm | Ecran
51 cm
Saba

TV Bicolonne T7049SLT 1994
Television set | Fernseher | Téléviseur
70 cm
Saba

Photos: Edelkoort Conseil

Zéo TV 1994–1995
Television set | Fernseher | Téléviseur
36 x 36 x 36 cm
Thomson
Photo: Guido Mocafico

Lebanon 1975

Drawing: Jean-Baptiste Mondino

Oz 1994
Portable TV set | Tragbarer Fernseher | Téléviseur portable
Mahogany, tinted glass | Mahagoni, getöntes Glas | Acajou, vitre teintée
136 x 39 x 34.5 cm
Telefunken

Jim Nature 1994
Portable TV | Tragbarer Fernseher | Téléviseur portable
High-density wood, plastic | Preßholz, Kunststoff | Bois aggloméré, plastique
38.5 x 37 x 37.5 cm
Saba

Photos: Jean-François Aloisi

Starck's eyes | Starcks Augen | Yeux de Starck
Starck's hands | Starcks Hände | Mains de Starck
Photos: Francis Giacobetti/ Turner & Turner

Remote control unit (M 5107) 1994
Remote control unit | Fernbedienung | Télécommande
Saba

Remote control unit 1995
Remote control unit | Fernbedienung | Télécommande
24 x 3 x 3 cm
Thomson

Remote control unit 1995
Remote control unit | Fernbedienung | Télécommande
ABS plastic | ABS-Kunststoff | Plastique ABS
4 x 4 x 23 cm
Telefunken

Photos: Tom Vack

Drawing: Jean-Baptiste Mondino

Torche radio 1996
Radio
Thomson

Ola 1996
Monoblock telephone | Mono-
block-Telefon | Téléphone
monobloc
ABS plastic | ABS-Kunststoff |
plastique ABS
27.5 x 6 x 5.2 cm
Thomson

Moa Moa 1994
Radio
Bakelite | Bakelit | Bakélite
23.2 x 11.6 x 13.4 cm
Saba
Photo: Jean-François Aloïsi

PalaPala 1996
Digital telephone-answering
machine | Digitaler Anrufbeant-
worter | Répondeur télépho-
nique digital
17.5 x 17.5 x 3.2 cm
Thomson

*Photos: Michel Lelièvre/
Studio Bleu for GOOD GOODS/
La Redoute*

Hook 1996
Telephone | Telefon | Téléphone
ABS plastic | ABS-Kunststoff |
Plastique ABS
26 x 6 x 39 cm
Thomson/Alessi

CooCoo 1996
Radio alarm-clock | Radio-
wecker | Réveil-radio
Analog clock, quartz controlled, made in ABS plastic, terracotta coloured. Alarm on radio or melody, with adjustable
volume. Back lighting | Ana-
loge Quarzuhr aus ABS-
Kunststoff, terrakottafarben.
Alarm und Radiowecker mit
verstellbarer Lautstärke. Be-
leuchtetes Zifferblatt |
Horloge à quartz analogique,
produit en plastique ABS,
couleur terracotta. Réveil par
radio ou sonnerie avec volume réglable. Cadran de
l'horloge éclairable
22 x 10 x 10 cm
Alessi

To yoo 1996
Telephone | Telefon | Téléphone
ABS plastic | ABS-Kunststoff |
Plastique ABS
24 x 6.6 x 7.7 cm
Thomson/Alessi

Poe 1996
Radio
ABS plastic | ABS-Kunststoff |
Plastique ABS
25.5 x 19 cm
ø: 7.5 cm
Thomson/Alessi

Moosk 1996
Radio
ABS plastic | ABS-Kunststoff |
Plastique ABS
19 x 12 x 10 cm
Alessi
Designer: Jérome Olivet

Photos: Hervé Ternisien

Krazy Jacket 1996
Sound-emitting nylon jacket |
Klingende Nylonjacke | Blou-
son en nylon sonore
Saba/Adidas
Concept: Patrick Jouin
Designer: Michael Michalsky

Street Master 1996
FM Radio
17.5 x 20 x 8.2 cm
Saba
Concept: Philippe Starck
Designer: Claude Bressan

Vertigo 1996
TV and video projector | Fern-
seher und Videoprojektor |
Téléviseur et vidéoprojecteur
Projector used like a torch to
project images in phase with
the user's movements. Vertigo
can also be placed on one
of the branches of its bronze
support; the other holds a
glass screen that delivers a
small overhead image | Die-
ser Projektor wird wie eine
Taschenlampe benutzt, die die
Programme in Einklang mit
der Bewegung des Benutzers
bringt. Anschließend legt
man Vertigo auf einen Ast des
bronzenen Ständers; an dem
anderen Ast sitzt ein kleiner
Bildschirm aus Glas, der ein
kleines Overhead-Bild über-
mittelt | Ce projecteur s'utilise
comme une torche, projetant
ses programmes au gré des
mouvements de son manipu-

lateur. Ensuite Vertigo vient
se poser sur l'une des deux
branches d'un support de
bronze, l'autre extrémité
accueillant un petit écran de
verre qui livre une image
intime en rétroprojection
55 x 21 x 41 cm
Saba
Designer: Jean-Michel Policar

Boa 1996
Stereo FM Radio
96 x 9 x 3 cm
Saba
Concept: Philippe Starck
Designer: Claude Bressan

*Photos: Didier Griffouliere/
Edelkoort Conseil*

TV Partoo 1996
Portable TV with integrated
satellite antenna | Tragbarer
Fernseher mit integrierter Sa-
tellitenantenne | Téléviseur
portable avec récepteur satel-
lite
40.8 x 34.8 x 44 cm
Saba
Concept: Philippe Starck
Designer: Claude Bressan
Photo: Edelkoort Conseil

Icipari 1995
AM/FM radio with three mem-
ories and digital tuning | mit
drei Speichern und digitalem
Tuning | avec trois mémoires
et tuner digital
14 x 8 x 9.5 cm
Telefunken
Concept & Design: Matali
Crasset
Photo: Guido Mocafico

Comboo 1995
Combined TV and video disc
player | Kombinierter Fernse-
her und Videorecorder | Télé-
viseur et lecteur DVD com-
biné
Comboo combines the large
format of a 16:9 TV with the
visual and auditory precision
of a digital video disc (SD-
DVD) | Comboo kombiniert
das Großformat eines 16:9
Fernsehers mit der audiovisu-
ellen Präzision einer digitalen
Videokassette (SD-DVD) |
Avide d'images pures, Com-

boo unit le format spectacle
d'un téléviseur 16/9 à la préci-
sion visuelle et sonore d'un
lecteur de vidéo disque
numérique DVD
67.8 x 41 x 43.5 cm
Thomson
Concept: Philippe Starck
Designer: Gérard Vergneau
Photo: Guido Mocafico

Lux Lux 1996
16:9 Pal Plus television set |
Fernseher | Téléviseur
Telefunken
Concept: Philippe Starck
Designer: Mike Davison
Photo: Guido Mocafico

Toccata 1996
Front-loading CD-player. Inte-
grated touch-sensitive keys |
Von vorne bedienbarer CD-
Player. Tastenempfindliche
Bedienung | Lecteur CD à
chargement frontal. Touches
à effleurement intégrées.
Closed | Geschlossen | Fermé :
60 x 40 x 2.5 cm
Open | Geöffnet | Ouvert :
30 x 40 x 5 cm
Telefunken
Concept & Design: Manuela
Simonelli, Andréa Quaglio
Photo: Guido Mocafico

Ego 1996
Video recorder | Videorecor-
der | Lecteur vidéo
A collective work equipped
with a digital video disk (SD-
DVD) player and encyclopae-
dic memory, its sole page is a
glass screen controlled by a
bookmark across the left-hand
side. The leather case and
silky papers | Ausgestattet mit
einem digitalen Videorecor-
der (SD-DVD) und enzyklopä-
dischem Speicher ist die
einzige Seite dieser Kollektiv-
arbeit ein gläserner Bildschirm, der von einem Lese-
zeichen auf der linken Seite
kontrolliert wird. Kasten aus
feinem Leder und Seidenpa-
pieren | Ouvrage collectif
équipé d'un lecteur de vidéo
disque numérique SD à mé-
moire encyclopédique, sa
page unique est un écran de
verre sont commandé par un
signet. Ecrin de cuir fin et papier de soie
26.7 x 21 x 1.7 cm
Telefunken
Concept: Philippe Starck
Designer: Gérard Vergneau

Perso 1996
Portable visiophone in a Her-
mès leather case | Tragbares
Visiophon im Lederkasten
von Hermès | Visiophone
portable dans un coffret de
cuir Hermès
11.6 x 14.5 x 1.1 cm
Telefunken/Hermès
Concept: Philippe Starck
Designer: Matali Crasset

Fuga 1996
Portable CD player | Tragbarer
CD-Player | Lecteur CD
portable
Lining of silky fabric | Verklei-
dung aus Seidenstoff | Capi-
tonnage intérieur de tissu
soyeux
46 x 13.3 x 4.1 cm
Telefunken
Concept & Design: Elsa
Frances

Photos: Guido Mocafico

Rock'n'Rock 1996
Micro hi-fi system | Mikro Hi-
Fi-System | Micro chaîne hi-fi
Amplifier, wireless infrared
speakers and CD player,
which can also be used separately with headphones. When
not used, the units can be
stacked together to form a
pile of rocks | Verstärker,
kabellose Infrarot-Lautspre-
cher und CD-Player, der auch
einzeln als tragbares Gerät
mit Kopfhörern genutzt werden kann. Ungenutzt können
die einzelnen Teile aufeinan-
der gesteckt werden und bil-
den so einen Steinhaufen |
Amplificateur, haut-parleurs
infrarouges sans fil et lecteur
CD, qui peut aussi devenir
nomade en utilisant un
casque. Quand il n'est pas
utilisé, les éléments peuvent
s'encastrer pour former une
pile de pierres
Rocks | Steine | Pierres :
20.8 x 13.5 cm
Telefunken
Concept: Philippe Starck
Designer: Elsa Frances
Photo: Guido Mocafico

Babel 1996
Multimedia column | Multi-
mediaturm | Tour multimédia
vidéo
Satellite, cable, digital VCR,
digital video disc (SD-DVD),
CD-ROM, PC and CDs. Its
rectangular column can hold
up to 100 + 1 digital discs
(SD-DVD), CD-ROM and au-
dio CD) or the equivalent of a
home media centre | Satellit,
Kabel, digitales VCR, digitale
Videokassette (SD-DVD), CD-
ROM, PC und Audio-CDs. Die
rectangular Säule kann bis zu
100 und 1 digitale Disketten
(SD-DVD, CD-ROM und Au-
dio-CD) oder das Äquivalent
eines Heim-Mediencenters
aufnehmen | Satellite, réseaux
câblés, vidéo disque numérique DVD, CD-ROM, ordina-
teur personnel. Sa colonne
rectangulaire peut accueillir
jusqu'à 100 + 1 disques
numériques (DVD, CD-ROM,
CD Audio), l'équivalent d'une
médiathèque domestique
170 x 42 x 21 cm
Thomson
Concept: Philippe Starck
Designer: Bernard Guerrin
Photo: Edelkoort Conseil

Starck Eyes for Mikli

Starck Eyes Biocity 1998
Sunglasses | Sonnenbrille |
Lunettes de soleil
Black acetate, amber lenses |
Schwarzes Acetat, bernstein-
farbene Brillengläser | Acétate
noire, verres ambres
Mikli
Photo: Silver Azoulay

**Philippe Starck with Starck
Eyes**
Photo: Jean Larivière

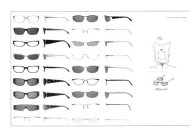

Glasses and sunglasses 1995-
2000
Sun and optical glasses, me-
tal and acetate | Sonnenbril-
len und Brillen mit Korrektur-
linsen, Metall und Acetat | Lu-
nettes de soleil et lunettes de
vue, métal et acétate

Biocity 3
Biocity 1P
Biocity 6
Biocity 2P
Biocity 5
Onabio
Onabio
Bioman
Alu-X
Biospeed
Bioop.T15
Bioop.T17
Biohalf 1
Biosun 1
Bioop.S2
Biospeed 2
Bioop.T5
Biolight 5
Mikli
Photos: Mikli

Drawing: Jean-Baptiste Mondino

Tomorrow will be less

Morgen wird es weniger sein

Demain sera moins

**Montre sous-cutanée
(project)** 1976
Watch | Armbanduhr | Montre

Montre digitale (project) 1996
Watch | Armbanduhr | Montre
Ill.: DEIS

Low Cost Watch 1998
Watch | Armbanduhr | Montre
Seven Eleven
Ill.: Michel Lelièvre/Studio Bleu

Starck Watches 1999
Range of watches with liquid
crystal display. Straps in rub-
ber or metal | Kollektion von
Uhren mit Flüssigkristallan-
zeige. Armbänder aus
Gummi oder Metall | Gamme
de montres avec affichage à
cristaux liquides. Bracelets en
caoutchouc ou métal
Fossil
Photos: Studio Bleu

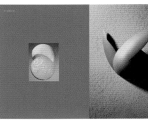

ECU (project) 1996
Photo: Hervé Ternisien

Walter Wayle 1989
Wall clock | Wanduhr | Hor-
loge murale
Thermoplastic resin, grey
coloured | Thermoplastisches
Harz, grau | Résine thermo-
plastique, colorée gris
H: 2 cm, ø: 28/11 cm
Alessi

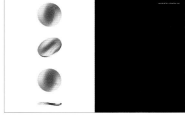

L'Ultime Franc 1999
Solid silver coin | Franc-Mün-
ze aus massivem Silber |
Pièce d'un franc français en
argent massif
ø 3.3 cm
Monnaie de Paris
Photo: Monnaie de Paris

**L'Ombre, Exposition Centre
Georges Pompidou, Paris**
2003
Shape in different sizes |
Form in verschiedenen
Größen | La Forme, différen-
tes dimensions
Project
Photo: Agence Starck

**Philippe Starck, Exposition
Centre Georges Pompidou,
Paris** 2003

Cosmic Vase Collection 2000
Universe Expansion: Representation of the three phases
of the universe: exponential
expansion, regular expansion
(our universe), contraction |
Universe Expansion: Darstellung der drei Ausdehnungs-

formen des Universums:
exponentielle Ausdehnung,
regelmäßige Ausdehnung
(unser Universum), abneh-
mende Ausdehnung durch
Kontraktion | Universe Expan-
sion: Représentation des trois
expansions de l'univers: expansion exponentielle, expansion régulière (notre univers),
expansion en contraction
Project

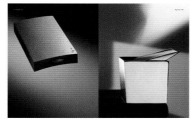

Patastarck 2000
Plastic toy, to be plugged into a potato | Plastikspielzeug, das man in eine Kartoffel stecken muss | Jouet en plastique avec une pomme de terre
21 x 13,7 x 0,4 cm
Project
Ill.: DEIS

K 1 1991
Hard disk | Festplatte | Disque dur
Plastic | Kunststoff | Plastique
4.4 x 14.5 x 25.4 cm
D2
Photo: Hervé Ternisien

Ray Hollis 1986
Ashtray | Aschenbecher | Cendrier
Polished aluminium | Poliertes Aluminium | Aluminium poli
7.5 x 11.5 x 10 cm
XO
Photo: Tom Vack

Snake (prototype) 1999
4 megapixel digital camera | 4 Megapixel Digitalkamera | Appareil numérique, 4 mega pixels
Aluminium body | Korpus Aluminium | Corps aluminium
Fujifilm

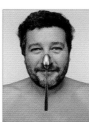

Stackable Plastic Knife 2000
Disposable injection-moulded polystyrene knife | Wegwerf-Messer aus Spritzguß-Polystyrol | Couteaux jetables en polystyrène injecté
L: 18 cm
IPI
Ill.: Agence Starck

Nori Starck

Philippe Starck
Photo: Jean-Baptiste Mondino

Miam Miam 2000
Table service in porcelain, glass and stainless steel. Plates in wood, nylon or marble. Cutlery in stainless steel | Geschirrkollektion aus Porzellan, Glas und rostfreiem Stahl. Teller aus Holz, Nylon oder Marmor. Besteck aus rostfreiem Stahl | Gamme de vaisselle en porcelaine, verre et acier inoxydable. Assiettes en bois, nylon ou marbre. Couverts en acier inoxydable
Driade
Photo: Driade

Pour la vie 1990
Vase with flowers | Vase mit Blumen | Vase avec fleurs
Marble and glass | Marmor und Glas | Marbre et verre
72 x 55 cm
up to | bis | jusqu'à 1995
OWO
from | ab | depuis 1996 Alessi

Moondog model 1987
Numbered scale model | Numeriertes Architekturmodell | Maquette d'architecture numérotée
Polished aluminium | Poliertes Aluminium | Aluminium poli
12 x 5.5 x 19 cm
up to | bis | jusqu'à 1995
OWO
from | ab | depuis 1996 Alessi

Pour la vie 1990

Laguiole model 1987
Numbered scale model | Numeriertes Architekturmodell | Maquette d'architecture numérotée
Polished aluminium | Poliertes Aluminium | Aluminium poli
15.3 x 10.5 x 6.5 cm
up to | bis | jusqu'à 1995
OWO
from | ab | depuis 1996 Alessi

Asahi model 1986
Numbered scale model | Numeriertes Architekturmodell | Maquette d'architecture numérotée
Polished aluminium | Poliertes Aluminium | Aluminium poli
14 x 18 x 19 cm
up to | bis | jusqu'à 1995
OWO
from | ab | depuis 1996 Alessi

Pour la vie 1990

Joe Raspoutine 1987
Wall candle-holder | Wandkerzenhalter | Bougeoir mural
Polished cast aluminium | Aluminium, Muschelguß, glänzend | Aluminium moulé en coquille, brillant
20 x 11 cm
up to | bis | jusqu'à 1995
OWO
from | ab | depuis 1996 Alessi

Photos: Tom Vack

Oa 1996
Table lamp providing diffused light | Tischleuchte mit indirektem Licht | Lampe de table à lumière diffuse
Vase and flower in handcrafted Murano glass. Touch dimmer | Vase und Blume aus mundgeblasenem Murano-Glas. Mit Dimmer | Vase et fleur en verre de Murano. Touche variateur de lumière
59 x 50 x 50 cm
Flos

Berta Youssouf 1987
Table card holder | Platzkartenhalter | Porte-carte
Polished aluminium | Poliertes Aluminium | Aluminium poli
H: 5.3 cm
up to | bis | jusqu'à 1995
OWO
from | ab | depuis 1996 Alessi

Teatriz 1988
Fire screen | Funkenschutz | Ecran de cheminée
Polished aluminium | Poliertes Aluminium | Aluminium poli
86 x 60 cm
up to | bis | jusqu'à 1995
OWO
from | ab | depuis 1996 Alessi

Nani Nani model 1986
Numbered scale model | Numeriertes Architekturmodell |

Maquette d'architecture numérotée
Polished aluminium | Poliertes Aluminium | Aluminium poli
15 x 10.5 x 6.5 cm
up to | bis | jusqu'à 1995
OWO
from | ab | depuis 1996 Alessi

Laguiole Set 1986
6 table knives | 6 Tafelmesser | 6 couteaux de table
Stainless steel | Edelstahl | Acier inoxydable
L: 21.5 cm
up to | bis | jusqu'à 1995
OWO
from | ab | depuis 1996 Alessi

O'Kelvin 1989
Table candlestick | Tischkerzenhalter | Bougeoir de table
Base in polished turned aluminium. Glass lampshade in four colour versions: green, blue, cognac and transparent | Fuß aus gedrechseltem Aluminium, glänzend. Glasschirm in vier Farbversionen: Grün, Blau, Cognac und Transparent | Pied en aluminium façonné au tour et poli. Abat-jour en quatre versions-couleur: vert, bleu, cognac et transparent
14 x 36 cm
up to | bis | jusqu'à 1995
OWO
from | ab | depuis 1996 Alessi

Paramount IV 1990
Mirror | Spiegel | Miroir
Nickel-plated brass | Vernickeltes Messing | Laiton nickelé
100 x 70 cm
up to | bis | jusqu'à 1995
OWO
from | ab | depuis 1996 Alessi

Miss Zenzen 1986
Numbered scale model | Numeriertes Architekturmodell | Maquette d'architecture numérotée
Polished aluminium | Poliertes Aluminium | Aluminium poli
H: 26 cm
up to | bis | jusqu'à 1995
OWO
from | ab | depuis 1996 Alessi

Paramount II 1990
Mirror | Spiegel | Miroir
Nickel-plated brass | Vernickeltes Messing | Laiton nickelé
205 x 66 cm
up to | bis | jusqu'à 1995
OWO
from | ab | depuis 1996 Alessi

Objets Pointus 1986
Tableware | Besteck | Couverts
Knife | Messer | Couteau: 25 cm
Fork | Gabel | Fourchette: 22.5 cm
Spoon | Löffel | Cuiller: 22 cm

Teaspoon | Teelöffel | Petite cuiller: 15.5 cm
Chopsticks | Eßstäbchen | Baguettes: 24.5 cm
up to | bis | jusqu'à 1995
OWO
from | ab | depuis 1996 Alessi

Photos: Tom Vack

Jojo Long Legs 1991
Cheese knife | Käsemesser | Couteau à fromage
Bakelite handle, blade in stainless steel. Available in yellow ocre, red, green and black | Griff aus Bakelit, Klinge aus rostfreiem Stahl. Erhältlich in Ockergelb, Rot, Grün und Schwarz | Manche en bakélite, lame en acier inoxydable. Exisatant dans les tons: ocre jaune, rouge, vert et noir
L: 29.5 cm
up to | bis | jusqu'à 1995
OWO
from | ab | depuis 1996 Alessi

Jojo Long Leg 1991

Laguiole knife 1986
Folding knife | Klappmesser | Couteau pliant
Handle in polished aluminium. Blade in stainless steel | Griff aus poliertem Aluminium. Klinge aus Edelstahl | Manche en aluminium poli. Lame en acier inoxydable
L: 21 cm
up to | bis | jusqu'à 1995
OWO
from | ab | depuis 1996 Alessi

Joe Cactus 1990
Ashtray | Aschenbecher |
Cendrier
Bakelite in three colour combinations: ochre and green,
red and green, black and
green | Bakelit in drei Farb-
kombinationen: Ocker und
Grün, Rot und Grün, Schwarz
und Grün | Bakélite en trois
versions couleur : ocre et vert,
rouge et vert, noir et vert
20.5 x 9 cm
up to | bis | jusqu'à 1995
OWO
from | ab | depuis 1996 Alessi

Miss Donna 1987
Mirror | Spiegel | Miroir
Polished aluminium | Polier-
tes Aluminium | Aluminium
poli
41 x 24 x 1.9 cm
up to | bis | jusqu'à 1995
OWO
from | ab | depuis 1996 Alessi

Luciana Fortyfour 1988
Lantern | Windlicht | Photo-
phore
Polished aluminium, frosted
pyrex glass | Poliertes Alumi-
nium, Mattglas | Aluminium
poli, pyrex dépoli
H: 25 cm
up to | bis | jusqu'à 1995
OWO
from | ab | depuis 1996 Alessi

Smoki Christiani 1986
Corkscrew | Korkenzieher |
Tire-bouchon
Polished cast aluminium.
Teflon-coated screw | Poliertes
Gußaluminium. Schraube
teflonbeschichtet | Alumi-
nium poli, moulé en coquille.
Vis revêtue de teflon
H: 27 cm
up to | bis | jusqu'à 1995
OWO
from | ab | depuis 1996 Alessi

Tito Lucifer 1986
Andirons | Kaminböcke |
Chenets
Cast iron | Gußeisen | Fonte
brute
28.5 x 38.5 x 8 cm
up to | bis | jusqu'à 1995
OWO
from | ab | depuis 1996 Alessi

Joe Cactus 1990
Three colour combinations |
Drei Farbkombinationen |
Trois versions-couleurs

Picfeu 1986
Poker | Schürhaken |
Tisonnier
Chrome steel | Verchromter
Stahl | Métal chromé
H: 59 cm
up to | bis | jusqu'à 1995
OWO
from | ab | depuis 1996 Alessi

Mimi Bayou 1987
Handle | Griff | Poignée de
placard
Polished aluminium | Polier-
tes Aluminium | Aluminium
poli
Depth | Tiefe | Profondeur :
5 cm
up to | bis | jusqu'à 1995
OWO
from | ab | depuis 1996 Alessi

Chab Wellington 1987
Coat hooks | Kleiderhaken |
Patères
Polished aluminium | Polier-
tes Aluminium | Aluminium
poli
20 x 5.3 cm
up to | bis | jusqu'à 1995
OWO
from | ab | depuis 1996 Alessi

Le Moult model 1987
Numbered scale model | Nu-
meriertes Architekturmodell |
Maquette d'architecture
numérotée
Polished aluminium | Polier-
tes Aluminium | Aluminium
poli
7.5 x 4.5 x 23.5 cm
up to | bis | jusqu'à 1995
OWO
from | ab | depuis 1996 Alessi

Photos: Tom Vack

Dr Kiss 1998
Toothbrush | Zahnbürste |
Brosse à dents
Available in orange, pink,
violet and yellow. Conical ABS
base | Erhältlich in Orange,
Rosa, Violett und Gelb. Kegel-
förmiger Ständer aus ABS-
Kunststoff | Existant dans les
tons : orange, rose, violet et
jaune. Base conique en ABS
H: 20 cm
Alessi

Dr Spoon 1998
Set of four small ear-cleaning
spatulas | Set vier kleiner
Ohrenreiniger | Lot de 4 pe-
tites spatules cure-oreilles
Heat-moulded plastic resin,
ABS base | Thermoplasti-
sches Kunstharz, kegelförmiger Ständer aus ABS-
Kunststoff | Résine thermo-
plastique avec base en ABS
Alessi

Dr Cheese 1998
Interdental toothbrush | Inter-
dentale Zahnbürste | Brosse
interdentaire
Resin, sold with 6 interchange-
able heads, conical ABS base |
Thermoplastisches Kunst-
harz, mit sechs Ersatzbürsten
und kegelförmigem Ständer
aus ABS-Kunststoff | Résine
thermoplastique livrée avec 6
brossettes interchangeables,
base conique en ABS
Alessi

Dr Kleen 1998
Set of six toothpicks | 6er-
Satz Zahnstocher | Lot de 6
cure-dents
Polyamide, conical ABS base |
Polyamid, kegelförmiger Stän-
der aus ABS-Kunststoff |
Polyamide, base conique en
ABS
Alessi

Photos: Michel Lelièvre/
Studio Bleu for GOOD
GOODS/
La Redoute

Curling Iron Set PS 603 2000
Curling iron set | Lockenstab |
Kit fer à friser
Salton

Tooth Brush PS 601 2000
Tooth brush | Zahnbürste |
Brosse à dents
Salton

Flosser PS 600 2000
Flosser | Zahnzwischenraum-
bürste | Hydropulseur den-
taire
Salton

Beard Trimmer PS 602 2000
Beard trimmer | Rasierappa-
rat | Taille-barbe
Salton

Hair Dryer PS 607 2000
Hair dryer | Haartrockner |
Sèche-cheveux
Salton

Photos: Salton

Juicy Salif 1990–1991
Drawings | Zeichnungen |
Dessins

Juicy Salif 1990–1991
Lemon squeezer | Zitronen-
presse | Presse-citron
Cast aluminium. Thermo plas-
tic rubber feet | Gußalumi-
nium. Füße aus thermoplasti-
schem Gummi | Fonte
d'aluminium. Pieds en
caoutchouc thermoplastique
H: 29/11.5 cm, ø: 14/5.5 cm
Alessi

**Philippe Starck and | und | et
Juicy Salif** 1990

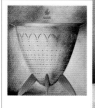

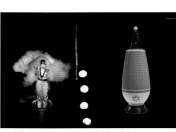

Max le Chinois 1990–1991
Design drawing | Entwurfs-
zeichnung | Dessin de con-
ception

Max le Chinois 1990–1991
Colander | Abtropfsieb |
Passoire
Stainless steel, brass | Edel-
stahl, Messing | Acier inoxy-
dable, laiton
H: 29 cm, ø: 30 cm
Alessi

Hot Bertaa 1990–1991
Design drawing | Entwurfs-
zeichnung | Dessin de con-
ception

Hot Bertaa 1990–1991
Kettle | Wasserkessel |
Bouilloire
Aluminium, plastic | Alumi-
nium, Kunststoff | Aluminium,
plastique
H: 25 cm
Alessi

Vase Mendini 1990
Vase with lid in white porcelain, and decorated with indeli-
ble transfer and fired at a
temperature of 850 °C |
Deckelvase aus weißem Por-
zellan mit bei 850 °C aufge-
branntem unverwüstlichem
Abziehbilddekor | Ce vase
avec couvercle en porcelaine
blanche décorée avec décal-
comanie appliquée de ma-

nière indélébile par cuisson à
850 °C
H: 38.5 cm, ø: 12.5 cm
Alessi

Olympic Flame for the Winter
Olympics at Albertville |
Olympisches Feuer für die
Winterspiele in Albertville |
Flambeau Olympique pour
les Jeux olympiques d'hiver
d'Albertville 1992
Stainless steel | Edelstahl |
Tôle d'inox
H: 41.4 cm, ø: 8 cm
Photo: Hervé Ternisien

**Computer image of a dustbin |
Computergraphik eines Müll-
eimers | Visualisation infor-
matisée d'une poubelle** 1992
Decaux
Ill.: Pascal Cagninacci/DEIS

**Dustbin | Mülleimer | Pou-
belle** 1992
Decaux

Bench | Bank | Banc 1992
Decaux

**Dustbin | Mülleimer | Pou-
belle** 1992
Decaux

Fence | Zaun | Clôture 1992
Decaux

Fence | Zaun | Clôture 1992
Decaux

Bench | Bank | Banc 1992
Decaux

**Dustbin | Mülleimer | Pou-
belle** 1992
Decaux

**Historic sign | Historisches
Schild | Panneau historique**
1992
Decaux

**Dustbin | Mülleimer | Pou-
belle** 1992
Decaux

Ill.: Marc Auger

Eau St Georges 1997
Mineral water bottle | Mineral-
wasserflasche | Bouteille d'eau
minérale
PET plastic | PET-Kunststoff |
plastique PET
Eau St Georges, Corse
Photo: Guido Mocafico

Eau St Georges
Photo: Select

Sesamo 1991
Door handle | Türgriff | Poi-
gnée de porte
Handle reduced to a small
metal wing, without any true
references: looks like a knob,
but works like a handle with-
out a catch mechanism | Der
Griff ist auf eine schmale Flü-
gelform reduziert, ohne ältere
Vorbilder: Er ähnelt einem
Knopf, funktioniert aber wie
ein Griff, ohne Verschlußme-
chanismus | La poignée est
réduite à une étroite aile de
métal, sans références vérita-
bles : elle ressemble à un bou-
ton mais fonctionne comme
une poignée, sans méca-
nisme de fermeture
Aluminium
Rds Kleis

**Door handle (prototype) | Tür-
griff (Prototyp) | Poignée de
porte (prototype)** 1991
Chrome-plated steel | Ver-
chromter Stahl | Acier chromé
14 x 5.5 cm
FSB

Apriti 1991
Door handle | Türgriff | Poi-
gnée de porte
It harks back to the traditional
curved metal handle but with
a special study of the mecha-
nism: one brushes the handle
to open rather than applying
pressure | Rückbezug auf die
traditionelle Grifform, aber

mit einem speziellen Mecha-
nismus: Zum Öffnen der Tür
reicht eine leichte Berührung
des Griffs | Un retour appa-
rent à la poignée en métal
traditionnelle, mais le méca-
nisme est spécialement
étudié : il suffit d'effleurer la
poignée pour ouvrir la porte
Aluminium
Rds Kleis

**PS 1 Door handle | Türgriff |
Poignée de porte** 1991
Matt silver backplate. Polish-
ed lever. Both in high-quality
aluminium | Matt-silberne
Rückenplatte. Polierter Griff.
Beides in hochwertigem Alu-
minium | Face arrière argentée
mate. Poignée polie. Les deux
éléments en aluminium de
haute qualité
FSB

Less 2001
Pylone for mobile phones |
Antennenmast für Mobiltele-
fone | Pylône pour reseaux
celluairs
12 x 40 m
Escom

Cap and lightning conductor |
Oberer Abschluß und Blitzab-
leiter | Chapeau de tête et par-
afoudre
Installing the antennae and

coaxial cables | Verankerung
der Antennen und der Koaxi-
alkabel | Implantation des an-
tennes et des câbles coaxiaux
Lift | Gondelaufzug | Nacelle
élevatrice
Exploded view and entry of
coaxial cables | Explosionsan-
sicht und Eingangsbuchse
der Koaxialkabel | Vue éclatée
et entrée des câbles coaxiaux
Escom
Ill.: DEIS

Intelligence is feminine

Intelligenz ist weiblich

L'intelligence est féminine

Visionnaire 1999
Plastic box for the magazine
Visionnaire | Kunststoffbox für
die Zeitschrift *Visionnaire* |
Boîtier en plastique pour le
magazine *Visionnaire*
Ill.: DEIS, Paris

Street Lamp 1992
Street lamp | Straßenlaterne |
Réverbère
Decaux
Ill.: Marc Auger/Decaux

Bus stop 1996
Bus shelter and bench |
Bushäuschen und Sitzbank |
Abribus et banc
Decaux
Ill.: DEIS, Paris

Beto-Vent 1992
Aeolian organ | Windorgel |
Orgue-éolienne
H: 26 m
Project
Photo: Agence Starck

**Mineral water bottle | Mine-
ralwasserflasche | Bouteille
d'eau minérale** 1991
Plastic | Kunststoff | Plastique
H: 19 cm, ø: 7 cm
Glacier
Photo: Hervé Ternisien

T-Book 1999
E-book | Elektronisches Buch |
Livre électronique
23 x 18 x 2.5 cm
Project
Ill.: DEIS

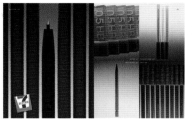

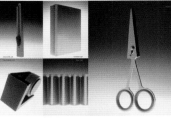

Ballpoint pen | Kugelschreiber | Stylo à bille 1998
Polypropylene | Polypropylen | Polypropylène
Seven Eleven

Lead refill, 0.5 HB | Bleistift-Ersatzminen, 0,5 HB | Recharge de mines, 0,5 HB 1998
Seven Eleven

Fluorescent marker pens | Fluoreszierende Marker | Marqueurs fluorescents 1998
Polypropylene | Polypropylen | Polypropylène
Seven Eleven

Retractable pencil | Druckbleistift | Porte-mines 1998
Polypropylene | Polypropylen | Polypropylène
Seven Eleven

Pencils | Bleistifte | Crayons à papier 1998
Polypropylene | Polypropylen | Polypropylène
Seven Eleven

Photos: Yukio Shimizu

Toothbrush | Zahnbürste | Brosse à dents 1998
Polycarbonate | Polycarbonat
Seven Eleven

Toothbrush for children | Kinderzahnbürste | Brosse à dents pour enfants 1998
Polycarbonate | Polycarbonat
Seven Eleven

Hairbrush Blow 1998
Hairbrush | Haarbürste | Brosse à cheveux
Polypropylene | Polypropylen | Polypropylène
Seven Eleven
Photos: Yukio Shimizu

X-Acto Knife 1998
Cutter
Stainless steel, polystyrene | Rostfreier Stahl, Polystyrol | Acier inoxydable, polystyrène
Seven Eleven

Note Book 1998
B5 Notebook, 40 pages | Heft, B5, 40 Seiten | Cahier B 5, 40 pages
Seven Eleven

Tape dispenser | Tesafilm-Abroller | Dévidoir de ruban adhésif 1998
Polystyrene | Polystyrol | Polystyrène
Seven Eleven

Eraser | Radiergummi | Gomme 1998
Seven Eleven

Scissors | Schere | Ciseaux 1998
Stainless steel | Rostfreier Stahl | Acier inoxydable
Seven Eleven

Photos: Yukio Shimizu

Low Cost Clock 1998
Clock | Wecker | Réveil
ABS plastic, polycarbonate | ABS-Kunststoff, Polycarbonat | Plastique ABS, polycarbonate
Seven Eleven

Lighter 1998
Refillable lighter | Nachfüllbares Feuerzeug | Briquet rechargeable
Seven Eleven

Photos: Michel Lelièvre/Studio Bleu

StarckNaked 1998
Seamless tubular garment with integrated pantihose | Nahtloses Schlauchkleid mit integrierter Strumpfhose | Collants intégrés à un tube, sans coutures
Wearable as a skirt, or short to medium-length dress. 80 denier, 92% polyamide and 8% elasthan | Mehrzweckkleidungsstück: Tragbar als

Rock und als kurzes oder mittellanges Kleid. 80-Denier-Strickstoff, 92% Polyamid, 8% Elastan | Vêtement susceptible d'être porté aussi bien comme une jupe, une robe courte ou moyenne. Maille 80 deniers, 92% polyamide et 8% élasthane
Wolford
Photos: Jean-Baptiste Mondino

Catalogue Good Goods – La Redoute
Photos: Michel Lelièvre/Studio Bleu

Starck as Shiva 1998
Catalogue Good Goods – La Redoute
Photo: Jean-Baptiste Mondino

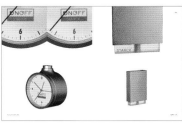

Le Devoir de Vision 2002
The Need for Vision | Pflicht zur Vision
Ill.: Cake Design/Thibaut Mathieu

La Conscience Globale 2002
Global Consciousness |
Globales Bewusstsein
*Ill.: Cake Design/Thibaut
Mathieu*

Nori Starck with K Starck
Photo: Jeff Riedel

Philippe Starck as Napoleon
Photo: Jeff Riedel

Starck Team 2002
Photos: Agence Starck

Anda Andrei
Catherine Bertrand
George Beylerian
Dorothée Boissier
Lorenzo Boni
Bruno Borrione
Maud Bury
Pascal Cagninacci
Michele Caniato
Leonardo De Carlo
Arturo Del Punta
Pierre Doze
Youlun Eon
Thierry Gaugain
Soraya Gonzalez-Mata
Jean Philippe Hazard
Sébastien Jupille
Céline Louf
Jérémy Magdalou
Milan
Nicolas Minvielle
Jean-Baptiste Mondino
Philippe Ouakrat
Eugeni Quitllet
Laurent Taïeb

Anda Andrei
ma sœur

Catherine Bertrand
mon ange

George Beylerian
mon entremetteur

Dorothée Boissier
mon chat

Lorenzo Bo
mon mâle

Bruno Borrione
mon ténébreux

Maud Bury
ma flamboyante

Pascal Cagninacci
ma virtualité

Michele Carliato
mon latin lover

Leonardo De C
mon prince

Arturo Del Punta
mon origine

Pierre Doze
mon pervers

Youlun Eon
ma joueuse de go

Thierry Gaugain
mon cerveau

Soraya Gonzales
mon air

Jean Philippe Hazard
mon magicien

Sébastien Jupille
mon nouveau

Céline Louf
l'ange de mon ange

Jérémy Magdalou
mon mousquetaire

Milan
mon fidèle

Nicolas Minvielle
mon net

Jean-Baptiste Mondino
mon frère

Philippe Ouakrat
mon élégance

Eugeni Quitllet
ma poésie

Laurent Taïe
mon gros né

Merci

Dadada 1993 **284/285, 556**
Decaux Bench | Bank | Banc 1992 **469, 567**
Decaux Bus stop | Bushaltestelle | Abribus 1996 **467, 567**
Decaux Dustbin | Mülleimer | Poubelle 1992 **468, 469, 567**
Decaux Fence | Zaun | Clôture 1992 **469, 567**
Decaux Historic sign | Historisches Schild | Panneau historique 1992 **469, 567**
Decaux Street lamp | Straßenlampe | Réverbère 1992 **466, 567**
Delano Hotel 1995 **138-145, 549**
Dick Deck 1989 **231, 553**
Dole Melipone 1981 **252/253, 554**
Don'O 1995 **384, 562**
Dr Spoon 1998 **449, 566**
Dr. Cheese 1998 **449, 566**
Dr. Glob 1990 **212, 552**
Dr. Kiss 1998 **449, 566**
Dr. Kleen 1998 **449, 566**
Dr. No 1996 **206/207, 551**
Dr. Skud 1998 **346, 560**
Dr. Sonderbar 1983 **276, 556**
Duravit Headquarters 2002 **68/69, 546**
Duravit Toilet and bidet 1998 **350, 560**
Duravit/Axor/Hoesch Bathtub | Badewanne | Baignoire 1994 **349, 560**
Duravit/Axor/Hoesch Washbasin | Waschbecken | Lavabo 1994 **348, 560**
Duravit/Axor/Hoesch Washbasin mixer | Mischbatterie | Mitigeur monocommande 1994 **349, 560**

Babel 1996 **409, 563**
Basic 1989 **245, 554**
Berta Youssouf 1987 **445, 565**
Beto-Vent 2000 **471, 567**
Big Nothing 1997 **234, 553**
Biocity **414/415, 564**
Biohalf **414/415, 564**
Biolight **414/415, 564**
Bioman **414/415, 564**
Bioop **414/415, 564**
Biospeed **414/415, 564**
Biosun **414/415, 564**
Bo 2000 **242/243, 554**
Bo Boolo 1995 **272/273, 555**
Boa 1996 **403, 563**
Bob Dubois 1987 **231, 553**
Bon 1 Restaurant 2000 **162/163, 550**
Bon 2 Restaurant 2001 **164/165, 550**
Bond Street Hotel 2001 **70/71, 546**
Boom Rang 1992 **228, 229, 553**
Bubble Club Chair 1998 **215, 552**
Bubble Club Sofa 1998 **214, 552**
Bubu 1er 1991 **270/271, 555**

Café Costes 1984 **75, 82-85, 546**
Café Mystique 1988 **128/129, 548**
Cam El Eon 1999 **235, 553**
Cameleon 1992 **231, 553**
Catalogue Good Goods – La Redoute **492-509, 568**
Ceci n'est pas une brouette 1996 **191, 551**
Chab Wellington 1987 **447, 566**
Chaussure (prototype) 1996 **332/333, 559**
Cheap Chic Armchair 1997 **279, 556**
Cheap Chic Chair 1997 **279, 556**
Cheap Chic Table 1998 **279, 556**
Cicatrices de Luxe 1999 **312/313, 558**
Clift Hotel 1999 **174/175, 550**
Colucci 1986 **230, 553**
Comboo 1995 **404, 563**
Condominiums (project) 1992 **67, 546**
CooCoo 1996 **401, 563**
Coppola Salon 1992 **116/117, 548**
Coque 1999 **200, 551**
Cosmic Vase Collection 2003 **431, 564**
Costes 1984 **230, 553**
Costes Alluminio 1988 **230, 231, 553**
Cub 1996 **387, 562**

Faitoo 1996 **297, 557**
Felix Restaurant in the Peninsula Hotel 1994 **146-149, 549**
First 35 S5 Voilier L Coque 1988 **359/560**
First 35,7 Voilier L Coque 1992 **359, 560**
First 41 S5 Voilier L Coque 1989 **358, 560**
Fluocaril Toothbrush and toothbrush holders | Zahnbürsten und Behälter | Brosses à dents et récipients 1989 **342-345, 560**
Formentera House 1995 **25-27, 543**
FSB Door handle | Türgriff | Poignée de porte 1991 **464, 567**
Fuga 1996 **407, 563**

Hansgrohe Mixing Faucets | Mischbatterie | Mélangeur 2000 **357, 560**
Heritage 1998 **250, 554**
Hoesch Bathtub | Badewanne | Baignoire 1998 **350, 560**
Hoesch Shower | Dusche | Douche 1998 **355, 560**
Hook 1996 **400, 563**
Hot Bertaa 1990-1991 **458/459, 566**
Hotel Bond Street 2001 **70/71, 546**
Hotel Clift 1999 **174/175, 550**
Hotel Delano 1995 **138-145, 549**
Hotel Hudson 1998 **168/171, 550**
Hotel Mondrian 1996 **98-101, 547**
Hotel Paramount 1990 **92-95, 547**
Hotel Peninsula 1994 **150-153, 549**
Hotel Royalton 1988 **87-91, 547**
Hotel Sanderson 1998, **176/177, 550**
Hotel St. Martins Lane 1999 **102/103, 547**
Hudson Hotel 1998 **168/171, 550**
Hugo Boss Shop 1991 **110-113, 547**
Hula Hoop 1998 **196/197, 551**

J. (Série Lang) Armchair | Lehnstuhl | Fauteuil 1987 **230, 553**
J. (Série Lang) Table | Tisch 1991 **230, 553**
Jelly Cube 2000 **356, 560**
Jim Nature TV 1994 **394, 562**
Joe Cactus 1990 **446, 447, 566**
Joe Raspoutine 1987 **443, 565**
Jojo Long Legs 1991 **443, 565**
Juicy Salif 1990-1991 **452-455, 566**

IBB 1999 **328, 559**
Icipari 1995 **404, 563**
IPI Stackable Plastic Knife 2000 **438, 565**

K 1 Hard disk | Festplatte | Disque dur 1991 **434, 565**
Kong Restaurant 2002 **160/161, 549**
Krazy Jacket 1996 **402, 563**

L.W.S Lazy Working Sofa 1998 **262-265, 555**
L'Ombre 2003 **428/429, 564**
L'Oréal Hairdressing Furniture 1989 **244, 245, 554**
L'Ultime Franc 1999 **426, 564**
La Bohème 2000 **217, 552**
La Cigale 1988 **130/131, 548**
La Main Bleue 1976 **78/79, 54**
La Marie 1998 **210/211, 552**
Laguiole factory 1987 **48, 545**
Laguiole knife 1986 **443, 565**
Laguiole model 1987 **443, 565**
Laguiole set 1986 **445, 565**
Lama Scooter (prototype) 1998 **382, 561**
Le Baron Vert 1992 **20/21, 543**
Le Moult House 1985-1987 **36 39, 544**
Le Moult model 1987 **447, 566**
Le Paravent de l'Autre 1992 **32 553**
Les Bains-Douches 1978 **76/7 546**
Less 2001 **275, 555**
Light Lite 1992 **305, 557**
Lila Hunter 1988 **276, 556**
Lio Comun 1991 **276, 556**
Lola Mundo 1988 **222/223, 25 552, 553**
Lord Yo 1994 **224/225, 552**
Louis Ghost 2000 **220, 552**
Louis XX 1992 **194/195, 551**
Low Cost Clock 1998 **488, 568**
Low Cost Watch 1998 **420/42 564**
Luciana Fortyfour 1988 **447, 5**
Lundi Ravioli 1995 **276, 556**
Lux Lux 1996 **404, 563**

Magic Slab
Maison de **54/55, 545**
Maletti/L'O ing Furnitt **245, 554**
Mandala 19
Manin Rest **108/109, 5**
Max le Chir **456/457, 5**
Mendini Va **460/461, 5**
Miam Miam **565**
Mikli Glass glasses | B Sonnenbri de vue et soleil 1995 **414/415, 5**
Mikli Shops **178/179, 5**
Mimi Bayou
M.I.S.S. 199 **555**
Miss C.O.C **260/261, 5**
Miss Donn
Miss Sissi ·
Miss Trip 1
Miss Yee 19
Miss Zenze **565**
Mister Bliss
Mister Meu **560**
Moa Moa 1
Mondrian H **101, 547**
Monsieur X longue 19
Monsieur X **278, 556**
Montre dig 1996 **418/**
Montre sou (project) 1
Moondog **52/53, 545**
Moondog r **443, 565**
Moosk 199
Moto 6,5 19
M.T Minim **256-259, 5**

A

Alo 1996 **385, 562**
Aloo 1995 **388, 562**
Alu-X **414/415, 564**
Angle (project) 1991 **67, 546**
Apriti 1991 **465, 567**
Ara III **360-363, 560**
Ara Stool 1985 **247, 554**
Ara Table lamp 1988 **305, 557**
Arango Jr. House 1996 **34/35, 544**
ArchiMoon Classic 1998 **308, 558**
ArchiMoon Eco 1998 **308, 558**
ArchiMoon Soft 1998 **309, 558**
ArchiMoon Tech 1998 **308, 558**
Asahi Beer Hall 1990 **16-19, 543**
Asahi model 1986 **443, 565**
Asahy 1991 **228, 229, 232, 553**
Asia de Cuba Restaurant 1997 **154/155, 549**
Attila 1999 **209, 551**
Axor Faucet, two-handled | Mischbatterie, zweiarmig | Mélangeur à deux robinets 1998 **353, 560**

B   # C   # D   # E   # F   # G   # H   # J   # K   # L   # M

Eau St Georges 1997 **476/477, 567**
Ecole des Beaux-Arts 1991 **58/59, 545**
ECU (project) 1996 **424, 564**
Ego 1996 **406, 563**
El Porteño Apartments and Hotel 172/173, 550
Emeco Chairs 1998 **251, 554**
ENSAD (Ecole Nationale Supérieure des Arts décoratifs) 1998 **60-65, 545**
Ero's 1999 **218/219, 552**
Eurostar Lounges 2001 **156/157, 549**

Gaoua 1999 **329, 559**
Gaultier Shops 2001 **180/181, 550**
Glacier Mineral water bottle | Mineralwasserflasche | Bouteille d'eau minérale 1991 **474, 567**
Good Goods Catalogue – La Redoute 1998 **492-509, 568**
Groningen Museum 1993 **44- 47, 545**

Saba Remote Control Unit | Fernbedienung | Télécommande M 5107 1994 **397, 562**
Saint Esprit 1999 **209**, 551
Salon Coppola 1992 **116/117**, 548
Salton Beard Trimmer 2000 **450**, 566
Salton Curling Iron Set 2000 **450**, 566
Salton Flosser 2000 **450**, 566
Salton Hair Dryer 2000 **451**, 566
Salton Toothbrush 2000 **450**, 566
Sanderson Hotel 1998, **176/177**, 550
Sarapis 1986 **230**, 553
Schuh (prototype) 1996 **332/333**, 559
Scooter Lama (prototype) 1992 **382**, 561
Sesamo 1991 **464**, 567
Seven Eleven Products **482-485**, 568
Shoe (prototype) 1996 **332/333**, 559
Slick Slick 1999 **274/275**, 555
Smoki Christiani 1986 **447**, 566
Snake (prototype) 1999 **436/437**, 565
Soft Egg 1999 **240/241**, 554
Soft Safe 2000 **330**, 559
St. Martins Lane Hotel 1999 **102/103**, 547
Star's Door 1992 **49**, 545
Starck Club 1982 **104/105**, 547
Starck Eyes for Mikli 1995-2002 **410-415**, 564
Starck House (3 Suisses) 1994 **13, 28-33**, 543, 544
Starck House (project) 1991 **67**, 546
Starck House 1991 **40/41**, 544
Starck Watches 1999 **422/423**, 564
StarckNaked 1998 **490**, 568
Strange Thing 1999 **266/267**, 555
Street Master 1996 **403**, 563
Su Mi Tang 1992 **340**, 560
SUMO Table 1998 **254**, 555
SuperArchimoon 1999 **310**, 558

O'Kelvin 1989 **445**, 565
Oa 1996 **444**, 565
Ola 1996 **398**, 563
Olly Tango 1994 **226/227**, 552
Olympic Flame | Olympisches Feuer | Flambeau Olympique 1992 **462**, 565
Onabio **414/415**, 564
Os Library 1998 **278**, 556
Oz TV 1994 **394**, 562

W.W. Stool 1990 **193**, 551
Walla Walla 1994 **305**, 557
Walter Wayle 1989 **425**, 564
Wedge Too 1999 **370/371**, 561

Yeza 1999 **329**, 559
Yoo Apartments 2001 **186/187**, 551

O

lani 1989 **22/23**, 543
lani model 1986 **445**, 545
on 1999 **209**, 551
997-1999 **238/239**, 554
and Day 2000 **290-293**,
57

P

Palais de l'Elysée 1983-1984 **80/81**, 546
PalaPala 1996 **391**, 563
Paramount Armchair 1991 **228, 229, 233**, 553
Paramount Hotel 1990 **92-95**, 547
Paramount II 1990 **445**, 565
Paramount IV 1990 **445**, 565
Pat Conley II 1986 **276**, 556
Patastarck 2000 **432/433**, 565
Peninsula 1995 **276**, 556
Peninsula Hotel 1994 **150-153**, 549
Perso 1996 **407**, 563
Picfeu 1986 **447**, 566
Placide of the Wood 1989 **231**, 553
Placido Arango Jr. House 1996 **34/35**, 544
Plasmaa 1995 **386**, 562
Ploof 1995 **215**, 552
Plywood car (project) 1996 **298/299**, 557
Poaa 1999 **282/283**, 556
Poe 1996 **401**, 563
Pointus 1986 **445**, 565
Popopo 1993 **278**, 556
Pour la vie 1990 **442, 443**, 565
Powerboat 2002 **366/367**, 561
Pratfall 1985 **230**, 553
Président M. 1984 **198/199**, 551
Prince Aha 1996 **205**, 551
PS 1 Door handle | Türgriff | Poignée de porte 1991 **465**, 567
Puzzle 1987 **114/115**, 548

Q

R

Ray Hollis 1986 **435**, 565
Ray Menta (project) 1984 **248**, 554
Restaurant Asia de Cuba 1997 **154/155**, 549
Restaurant Bon 1 2000 **162/163**, 550
Restaurant Bon 2 2001 **164/165**, 550
Restaurant Felix in the Peninsula Hotel 1994 **146-149**, 549
Restaurant Kong 2002 **160/161**, 549
Restaurant Manin 1987 **108/109**, 547
Restaurant Teatriz 1990 **120-127**, 548
Restaurant Theatron 1985 **132-137**, 548
Richard III 1985 **202**, 551
Rock'n'Rock 1996 **408**, 563
Romantica 1987 **231**, 553
Romeo Moon 1995 **304**, 557
Romeo Moon Soft T2 1998 **306**, 558
Romeo Moon T2 1998 **307**, 558
Rosy Angelis 1994 **304**, 557
Royalton Armchair 1991 **232**, 553
Royalton Bar Stool 1988 **276**, 556
Royalton Bed 1992 **233**, 553
Royalton Chair 1988 **233**, 553
Royalton Chair and bench 1991 **229**, 553
Royalton Couch 1991 **232**, 552
Royalton Hotel 1988 **87-91**, 546, 547
Royalton Long Chair 1991 **232**, 553
Rue Starck (project) 1991 **66**, 546

S

T Book 1999 **481**, 567
Target Products 2000 **320-327**, 558/559
TASCHEN Shop Los Angeles 2002 **184/185**, 550
TASCHEN Shop Paris 2000 **182/183**, 550
Teatriz 1988 **445**, 565
Teatriz Restaurant 1990 **120-127**, 548
Techno 1989 **245**, 554
TeddyBearBand 1998 **302**, 557
Telefunken Remote Control Unit | Fernbedienung | Télécommande 1995 **397**, 562
Tessa Nature 1989 **231**, 553
The Club 1999 **289**, 556
The Tooth 2002 **286**, 556
Théâtre du Monde 1984 **276**, 556
Theatron Restaurant 1985 **132-137**, 548
Thomson Radio 1995 **388**, 562
Thomson Remote Control | Fernbedienung | Télécommande 1994 **384**, 562
Thomson Remote Control Unit | Fernbedienung | Télécommande 1995 **397**, 562
Thomson Speaker | Lautsprecher 16.9 1995 **388**, 562
Thomson Speaker | Lautsprecher | Haut-parleur 1994 **388**, 562
Thomson Television | Fernseher | Téléviseur 14'' 1994 **388**, 562
Thomson Television | Fernseher | Téléviseur 1995 **388**, 562
Thomson Videorekorder | Video recorder | Lecteur vidéo 1995 **338**, 562
Ti Tang 1992 **340**, 560
Tippy Jackson 1985 **230**, 553
Tito Lucifer 1986 **447**, 566
Titos Apostos 1985 **230, 231**, 553
To Yoo 1996 **401**, 563
Toccata 1996 **450**, 563
Torche radio 1996 **398**, 563
Toto la toto car (project) 1996 **300/301**, 507
Tour de Contrôle 1993 **51**, 545
Toy 1999 **236/237**, 553
TV Bicolonne 1996 **390**, 562
TV Bicolonne M5116F Screen 1995 **391**, 562
TV Bicolonne T7049SLT 1994 **391**, 562
TV Partoo 1996 **404**, 563

T

Vase Mendini 1990 **460/461**, 566
Vertigo 1996 **402**, 563
Vicieuse 1992 **228**, 553
Virtuelle 1997 **364/365**, 561
Visionnaire 1999 **478**, 567
Vitry 2001 **56/57**, 545
Von Vogelsang 1985 **230**, 553

U

V

X 3 Motorbike | Motorrad | Moto 2000 **381**, 561
X Ray 1996 **380**, 561
X-Acto Knife 1998 **486**, 568

W

X

Y

Zbork 2000 **215**, 552
Zéo TV 1994-1995 **392**, 562

Z